George Nnaemeka Oranekwu

# The Significant Role of Initiation in the Traditional Igbo Culture and Religion

Die Reihe **Ezi Muoma – Afrika verstehen**
wird herausgegeben von

Prof. Dr. Obiora F. Ike;
Prof. Dr. Johannes Hoffmann
Fachbereich Katholische Theologie
Universität Frankfurt am Main

George Nnaemeka Oranekwu

# The Significant Role of Initiation in the Traditional Igbo Culture and Religion

An Inculturation Basis for Pastoral Catechesis of Christian Initiation

Ezi Muoma – Afrika verstehen

IKO – Verlag für Interkulturelle Kommunikation

D 25

Bibliographische Information Der Deutschen Bibliothek
Die Deutsche Bibliothek verzeichnet diese Publikation in der Deutschen Nationalbibliographie; detaillierte bibliographische Daten sind im Internet über http://dnb.ddb.de abrufbar.

© IKO-Verlag für Interkulturelle Kommunikation
Frankfurt am Main • London, 2004

Frankfurt am Main  London
Postfach 90 04 21  70 c, Wrentham Avenue
D - 60444 Frankfurt  London NW10 3HG, UK
e-mail: info@iko-verlag.de • Internet: www.iko-verlag.de

ISBN: 3-88939-710-7

Umschlaggestaltung: Volker Loschek, 61184 Karben
Herstellung: Digital PS Druck AG, 96158 Birkach

# Contents

| | | |
|---|---|---|
| DEDICATION | | 11 |
| ACKNOWLEDGEMENTS | | 13 |
| FOREWORD | | 19 |
| ABREVIATIONS | | 23 |
| GENERAL INTRODUCTION | | 27 |

**CHAPTER ONE**
**IGBO HISTORICITY: ORIGIN AND LOCATION**     39

| | | |
|---|---|---|
| 1.1 | INTRODUCTION | 39 |
| 1.2 | ORIGIN AND LOCATION OF THE IGBO | 39 |
| 1.3 | DEMOGRAPHY | 52 |
| 1.4 | VALUES AND RITUALS IN IGBO CULTURE AND TRADITION | 56 |
| 1.4.1 | IGBO VALUE OF LIFE | 56 |
| 1.4.2 | IGBO VALUE OF MARRIAGE | 58 |
| 1.4.3 | IGBO VALUE OF MAN | 60 |
| 1.4.4 | IGBO VALUE OF COMMUNITY LIFE | 62 |
| 1.4.5 | FAMILY BED-TIME STORIES | 64 |
| | Example 1 The Origin of Day and Night | 65 |
| | Example 2 The Origin of Death | 66 |
| | Example 3 Why the Tortoise Lives in River Swamps | 67 |
| 1.4.6 | IGBO KOLANUT RITUALS | 71 |
| 1.4.6.1 | A MARK OF IGBO SOCIO-CULTURAL AND RELIGIOUS IDENTITY | 71 |
| 1.4.6.2 | THE PRINCIPAL PARTS OF KOLANUT RITUALS | 74 |
| 1.4.6.2.1 | *ICHE OJI* (PRESENTATION OF KOLANUT) | 74 |
| 1.4.6.2.2 | *IGO OJI* (CONSECRATION OF KOLANUT) | 76 |
| 1.4.6.2.3 | *Iwa OJI* (BREAKING OF KOLANUT) | 78 |
| 1.4.6.2.4 | *IKE OJI* (DISTRIBUTION OF KOLANUT) | 78 |

| | | |
|---|---|---|
| 1.5 | IGBO WORLD-VIEW | 80 |
| 1.6 | CONCLUSION | 90 |

## CHAPTER TWO
## INITIATION IN THE TRADITIONAL IGBO CULTURE AND RELIGION  93

| | | |
|---|---|---|
| 2.1 | INTRODUCTION | 93 |
| 2.2 | IGBO IDEA OF INITIATION | 94 |
| 2.3 | TYPOLOGIES OF TRADITIONAL IGBO INITIATION RITES | 97 |
| 2.3.1 | BIRTH INITIATION RITES | 98 |
| 2.3.2 | IGBO NAMING RITUAL AND CEREMONY | 100 |
| 2.3.3 | IGBO PUBERTY RITES | 104 |
| 2.3.3.1 | EXPRESSIVE ASPECTS OF PUBERTY INITIATION RITE | 105 |
| 2.3.3.2 | ACTIVE MEMBER OF THE SOCIETY | 105 |
| 2.3.3.3 | AGE GROUP | 106 |
| 2.3.3.4 | MASQUERADE SOCIETY | 108 |
| 2.3.3.5 | MARRIED LIFE | 109 |
| 2.3.3.6 | TITLE-TAKING | 109 |
| 2.4 | MARRIAGE INITIATION RITES | 111 |
| 2.5 | DEATH AND FUNERAL INITIATION RITES | 114 |
| 2.6 | THE PECULIARITY OF THE IGBO INITIATION RITES | 116 |
| 2.7 | TRIADIC MOMENTS OF INITIATION RITES | 122 |
| 2.7.1 | RITES OF SEPARATION – PRE-LIMINAL RITES | 123 |
| 2.7.2 | RITES OF TRANSITION – LIMINAL OR THRESHOLD RITES | 124 |
| 2.7.3 | RITES OF INCORPORATION –POST-LIMINAL RITES | 126 |
| 2.8 | AGENTS OF INITIATION RITES IN IGBO TRADITIONAL RELIGION | 127 |
| 2.8.1 | THE FATHER OF THE FAMILY | 127 |
| 2.8.2 | THE TRADITIONAL CHIEF-PRIEST | 129 |
| 2.8.3 | 'OZO' OR 'NZE' TITLE-HOLDER | 130 |

| | | |
|---|---|---|
| 2.9 | OBSTACLES TO THE INITIATION RITES AMONG THE TRADITIONAL IGBO | 134 |
| 2.9.1 | CHRISTIAN AND ISLAMIC RELIGIONS | 136 |
| 2.9.2 | SCHOOLING AS A FACTOR AGAINST INITIATION | 137 |
| 2.10 | THE SIGNIFICANT ROLE OF INITIATION IN TRADITIONAL IGBO CULTURE AND RELIGION | 138 |
| 2.11 | CONCLUSION | 144 |

## CHAPTER THREE
## CHRISTIAN INITIATION 147

| | | |
|---|---|---|
| 3.1 | INTRODUCTION | 147 |
| 3.2 | A BRIEF HISTORICAL DEVELOPMENT OF THE CONCEPT 'SACRAMENT' AND OTHER VARIOUS TEACHINGS ON SACRAMENT | 149 |
| 3.2.1 | A BRIEF HISTORICAL DEVELOPMENT OF THE CONCEPT OF THE TERM 'SACRAMENT' | 149 |
| 3.2.2 | OTHER VARIOUS TEACHINGS ON SACRAMENTS | 151 |
| 3.2.2.1 | THE VATICAN COUNCIL II (1962-1965) ON THE SACRAMENTS | 151 |
| 3.2.2.2 | THE CATHOLIC CATECHISMS ON SACRAMENTS | 152 |
| | a) Roman Catechism (1566) | 152 |
| | b) Catholic Catechism (1847) | 152 |
| | c) Catholic Catechism for German Dioceses (1955) | 152 |
| | d) Faith – life – act (1969) | 153 |
| | e) Good-News of Faith: A Catholic Catechism (1978) | 153 |
| | f) Catechism of the Catholic Church (1993) | 153 |
| | g) Katikiizim nke Okwukwe Nzuko Katolik N'asusu Igbo (1996) | 153 |

| | | |
|---|---|---|
| 3.2.2.3 | EXPRESSIONS OF SOME RENOWNED THEOLOGIANS ON THE SACRAMENT | 154 |
| | a) Michael Schmaus | 154 |
| | b) Karl Rahner | 154 |
| | c) Joseph Ratzinger | 154 |
| | d) Edward Schillebeeckx | 155 |
| | e) Hans Urs von Balthasar | 155 |
| | f) Walter Kasper and Karl Lehmann | 155 |
| | g) Herbert Vorgrimler | 156 |
| 3.3 | THE SACRAMENTS OF CHRISTIAN INITIATION | 157 |
| 3.3.1 | THE SACRAMENT OF BAPTISM | 161 |
| 3.3.1.1 | THE ADMINISTRATION OF BAPTISM | 163 |
| 3.3.2 | THE SACRAMENT OF CONFIRMATION | 164 |
| 3.3.3 | THE SACRAMENT OF THE EUCHARIST | 166 |
| 3.4 | THE EFFECTS OF CHRISTIAN INITIATION | 169 |
| 3.5 | MINISTERS OF CHRISTIAN INITIATION | 173 |
| 3.5.1 | PRIMARY-DIVINE MINISTER | 173 |
| 3.5.2 | SECONDARY-HUMAN MINISTER | 174 |
| 3.5.2.1 | THE MINISTER OF BAPTISM | 175 |
| 3.5.2.2 | THE MINISTER OF CONFIRMATION | 176 |
| 3.5.2.3 | THE MINISTER OF THE EUCHARIST | 178 |
| 3.6 | THE SIGNIFICANT ROLES OF THE SACRAMENTS OF CHRISTIAN INITIATION | 178 |
| 3.6.1 | THE BAPTISM | 178 |
| 3.6.2 | THE CONFIRMATION | 180 |
| 3.6.3 | THE EUCHARIST | 181 |
| 3.7 | CONCLUSION | 183 |

CHAPTER FOUR
TRADITIONAL IGBO INITIATION VIS-À-VIS
CHRISTIAN INITIATION                                              187

| | | |
|---|---|---|
| 4.1 | INTRODUCTION | 187 |

| | | |
|---|---|---|
| 4.2 | COMMON CHARACTERISTICS OF TRADITIONAL IGBO AND CHRISTIAN INITIATIONS | 187 |
| 4.3 | DISSIMILARITIES IN TRADITIONAL IGBO AND CHRISTIAN INITIATIONS | 191 |
| 4.4 | CONCLUSION | 194 |

## CHAPTER FIVE
## AN INCULTURATION BASIS FOR PASTORAL CATECHESIS OF CHRISTIAN INITIATION     197

| | | |
|---|---|---|
| 5.1 | INTRODUCTION | 197 |
| 5.2 | WHAT IS INCULTURATION? | 198 |
| 5.2.1 | A BRIEF HISTORICAL ORIGIN OF INCULTURATION | 198 |
| 5.2.1.1 | PREVIOUS TERMINOLOGIES FOR INCULTURATION | 200 |
| 5.2.2 | EXAMINING THE PREVIOUS TERMS FOR INCULTURATION | 203 |
| 5.3 | DEFINITION OF INCULTURATION | 206 |
| 5.4 | THE SCOPE OF INCULTURATION | 209 |
| 5.5 | THE IMPORTANCE OF INCULTURATION | 212 |
| 5.6 | THE PRINCIPLE FOR INCULTURATION | 217 |
| 5.7 | CONCLUSION | 222 |

## CHAPTER SIX
## PASTORAL CATECHESIS FOR INCULTURATION OF TRADITIONAL IGBO INITIATION RITES: PROPOSED MODELS     225

| | | |
|---|---|---|
| 6.1 | INTRODUCTION | 225 |
| 6.2 | INTEGRATION OF MYTH, STORIES AND PROVERBS AS EFFECTIVE AID OF TEACHING-LEARNING METHOD IN PASTORAL CATECHESIS | 225 |

| 6.3 | TRADITIONAL IGBO NAMING CEREMONY AND CHRISTIAN BAPTISM | 228 |
| --- | --- | --- |
| 6.4 | OTHER IGBO CULTURAL BASIS FOR INCULTURATION OF PASTORAL CATECHESIS OF CHRISTIAN INITIATION | 238 |
| 6.5 | CONCLUSION | 240 |

GENERAL CONCLUSION — 243

BIBLIOGRAPHY — 253

# Dedication

In appreciation to the 'Institut für Praktische Theologie Arbeitsbereich Religionspädagogik und Katechetik, Albert-Ludwigs-Universität Freiburg im Breisgau', especially to Prof. Dr. Werner Tzscheetzsch, who in the spirit of Vatican Council II, encouraged this project and gave it a maximum support, all for the good of the Church in Africa, especially in Igboland. Also to all those who dedicate themselves for the work of inculturating the Good News especially in the so-called mission lands.

# Acknowledgements

My deepest gratitude goes first and foremost to the Almighty, All-knowing, Ever-living and Triune God, who not only created man in His own image and likeness, but has revealed Himself to man through man. And ever since then has remained with man, and has promised to remain with him till the end of time. To Him be glory and honour and thanksgiving forever and ever.

To all others who in one way or the other have given help and encouragement either in cash or in kind in the course of producing this work, I say, 'thank you so much!'

The following, however, deserve my special thanks for their generous, substantial and prayerful support to me: My former Archbishop (of Onitsha, Most. Rev. A. K. Obiefuna) who allowed my travel to Europe just a few months after my ordination, for further studies; in the same vein is my new Bishop of Nnewi Diocese, Most. Rev. Dr. H-P. O. Okeke. Others include: the Bishop of Osnabrück diocese in Germany, Dr. theol. Franz-Josef Bode, his assistant Bishop Dr. Theo Kettmann, the Vicar General, Dr. Theo Paul, Domkapitular and Personalreferent Heinrich Silies, Frau Renate Heuer, Domkapitular Rector Norbert Friebe, Herr Richard Schweer, and the loving, welcoming brother-priests and the entire faithful of Osnabrück diocese, Germany. Mutter M. Laetare, Srs. M. Magdalis and M. Aquinas are specially remembered for their kindness to me. Here also special thanks are due to Msgr. Frank, the Catholic Archbishop of Luxembourg and to Prof. Dr. Ernst Leuninger (Priest of Limburg diocese in Germany) for extending their friendship to me.

Many thanks also to the following family-friends: Mr. & Mrs. Drangan Lovrincevic, the family members of Mrs. Hazel Cornelius and Peter, Mr. & Mrs. Otto Borgmann, Mrs. Berter Riedl, Mr. & Mrs. Walter Bohn,

Mr. & Mrs. Erich Passau, Mrs. Gertrud Henn, Mrs. Hildegard Noe, Mr. Erwin Breinneis, Mr. and Mrs. Heinz Breinneis, and my benefactress in Malter, Miss Carmen Borg and the entire members of Borg family, Malta.

Naturally my thanks extend also to the many libraries in Europe and America, and of course in Nigeria, where I visited in search of one information or the other during the course of this work. Some of them include: Library of the Institute of Religious Education and Catechesis, Catholic theology Faculty, University of Freiburg im Breisgau, Germany, University of Bonn Library, University of Münster, University of Tübingen, St. Augustin Styler Mission by Bonn, Missio Wissenschaftliches Institute in Aachen, Priesterseminar Library in Osnabrück (all in Germany), Bisschppelijk Centrum (Seminary Libry) Rolduc, Holland, Catholic University of Leuven, Belgium, Archdiocese of Chicago Catechetical Center, USA., Catholic Theological Union (CTU) Chicago, USA., Catholic University, Washington DC, USA., University of St. Thomas School of Theology at St. Mary's Seminary, Faculty of Catholic Theology Library, Houston-Texas, USA., Marquette University Library, Milwaukee, Wisconsin, USA., School of Oriental Studies in London, Catholic Institute of West Africa (CIWA), Port Harcourt-Nigeria.

I remain ever grateful to Prof. Dr. Werner Tzschteezsch for his constructive criticisms, his availability and readiness for consultation, and for his useful pieces of advice and suggestions, and above all for his friendliness and understanding that gave me great encouragement throughout the course of this work. May God continue blessing him for his openness, warm reception and friendliness. In the same vane I remain ever grateful to Prof. Dr. Peter Walter (my second moderator) and Prof. Dr. Hubert Irsigler (The Dean, faculty of Theology, University of Freiburg) for their kindness, friendliness and love extended to me. And of course other Professors and the students of the University of Freiburg have been very good to all. I will not forget Mrs. A. Ramson, the secretary of the Institute for Religious Education and Catechetics, University of Freiburg for all her help to me. Mrs Ramson, God bless you! I thank also Mrs. Angela Kaupp and the members of our colloqium. Their friendliness was a source of inspiration to me. I thank also Prof. Dr. Johannes Hoffman for his interest in this work and for his involvement in the publication.

Very many thanks to Prof. Dr. Dr. Msgr. Obiora Ike (the Vicar General of the Catholic Diocese of Enugu, and the Director Catholic Institute for Development, Caritas, Justice and Peace (CIDJAP), Enugu, Nigeria) for writing the foreword to this work, not minding his tight schedule. God love you Msgr. Obiora Ike! Thanks also to Prof. Dr. Ukachukwu Chris Manus (of OAU, Ife-Nigeria) for reading through the work and for the wonderful remark. Thanks also to Rev. Fr. Robert Okongwu for his disposition and useful suggestions.

I will not forget my Parents Mr. and Mrs. P. N. Oranekwu, my dear sisters and brothers, my previous teachers in various levels of my academic life, my colleagues, friends in Nigeria, Europe and America, especially in various parishes and communities where I stayed either for holiday or for some research during my study period in Germany. God love you all!

To those whose name could not appear here, my deepest appreciation.

Bonn, Germany, 29 July, 2003

George Emeka Oranekwu, Ph.D

## About the Author

Rev. Fr. George Oranekwu, formerly a priest of the Catholic Archdiocese of Onitsha, (now Catholic Diocese of Nnewi) hails from Akamili Umudim Nnewi, Anambra State. He had his junior seminary formation at St. Paul's Seminary, Ukpor and All Hallows' Seminary, Onitsha respectively. He obtained a Bachelor's degree in Philosophy (B.Phil) at Bigard Memorial Seminary (now St. Joseph's Major Seminary), Ikot-Ekpene and another Bachelor's degree in Theology (B.Th) at Bigard Memorial Seminary, Enugu both affiliate of Urban University, Rome. He has also Diploma in Latin, MBA (Luxembourg), Licentiate in Theology (Lic. theol). Fr. George has great interest in religions, peoples, cultures and traditions, and has specialised in Intercultural Theology. He is looking foreword to producing another book in the same field.

# Foreword

I consider it an honour to be asked by the author introduce this thoroughly researched book on the significant role of initiation in an African cultural milieu as basis fort he inculturation and sustainability of Christianity in a modern society. Whichever way one might like to wish it away, even ignore it as out modish and primitive, sulture, has remained and continues to be he social air we breathe and a critical actor in the consideration of a people's entire identity and way of life. It is all over the place and there is no way of escaping it. Our language, dressing, homes, architecture, rites, religion, signs and symbols, thought patterns and organisational systems, the food we eat and the way they are prepared, in fact, our overall idiosyncracies are products of culture. The great masterpieces of art and literature in which people of every age habe expressed themselves form what we call today „*our cultural heritage*". The past lives on among us in architecture, institutions, works of art and literature, and the culture of the future must refer to this heritage. It can reject it, adapt it, go beyond it, react against it, but it cannot ignore the cultural past.

Since culture is not static but continuously dynamic, studies of anthropologists and the growing discipline of sociology, religion and cultural studies indicate a trend which confirm what the Second Vatican Council in the Pastoral Constitution of the Church in the Modeern World of Today says, namely, that „*it is only through culture that humankind can achieve true and full humanity*" (nr. 53). In a general sense, culture stands for everything by which humankind develops and refines their various gifts of mind and body. In subduing the world by knowledge and labour, culture develops in manifold forms. This is seen when peple „humanise social life on the family scale and on the civic by the progress of manners, institutions and technologies". Thus in the history of cultures, humankind who ware not isolated individuals but communal beings impact on history and ideas, transformin it in such a way that a human culture rvolves. Culture necessarily therefore has a historical and social aspect. It lives only in the people who make it and are made by it. In the cours of time, the achievements of peoples, their great spiritual experiences and aspirations are communicated and preserved so that they may profit generations yet to come, even, the whole human race.

The Fathers and Mothers of the Vatican Council noted quite rightly that the phenomenon and mystery of the Incarnation, Christ as the Second Adam has restored humankind to their full dignity in the mind of the Creator, for He, Christ, is the pattern of human behaviour and human perfection. *„Whoever follows Christ, the perfect man, becomes more human"*. Culture, therefore represents the efforts from below to move towards full humanity: it is therefore a movement towards Christ, whether conscious or not. In the light of the Gospel, the Good News, culture is the fruit of human experience, written or oral, formal or informal and it continues to be an attempt to remain faithful both to God an to humankind (GS, Nr. 46). Through education, generations are initiated into this tradition and ist handing on. It is more than the doling out of facts: it imparts values too which guide our outlook to the universe and our actions. To sum up, Culture in the language of the Church refers to humankind at *„work, in society and in learning"*.

In this book, te author, Nnaemeka Oranekwu, a Nigerian priest an scholar, a theologian and pastor has used the skills of modern science, research and communication to analyse the wealth and profound traditional heritage of Igbo Culture and People who live in modern Nigeria as basis for pastoral catechesis and understanding of rites of Christian initiation. Due to the probemes posed by colonial and missionary history with ist incursion into African societies in the last 150 years (1850 – 2000), this intrusion has led to crisis of identity for the African Personality, leading to a *„schizophrenia of either African or Christian"*, and such other manifold problems. This work delves into the historical sources, the origin, location and values embedded in the way of life of ancient Igbo traditions. This background enables a proper foundation fort he study of initiation rites in Igbo culture and relgion. He offers interesting insight into typologies of traditional Igbo rites of initiation and birth, naming ceremonies, puberty rites, age grade memberships, the masquerade and adulthood, married life, title taking, death and funeral rites. In all, he summarises in a very clear manner, the significant role of initiation in traditional Igbo culture and religion und translates this in a new society where the modern Christian Culture has come to stay. His expertise of theology helps him to offer a historical development of the concept of „Sacrament" and the teaching of the Church in the available magisterial documents. This is a great achievement and the product of profound research and enterprise. People who do not look back to posterity cannot look forward to prosperity. Father Oranekwu in this research, studies very generally, the poistions of individual theologians, mostly western thinkers to make his point thereby presenting the „cultural antinomy" based on „cultural bias" which characterised the historical mode of thought of the western world in the 19$^{th}$ century carried over into Africa during the missionary era. This era depicts African cultural values as „pagan" and „not Christian", provoking an unnecessary „clash of cultures" by „innocent but uniformed evangelisers" steeped in western anthropological bias of the time which outlook was a „racial religious and cultural superiority". The cliché: either „African or Christian" was part of this antinomy.

In discussing Initiation Rites and Inculturation of Christianity in Africa today, the great works of our revered African original thinkers and theologians of the first 400 years of the Church, such as Tertullian, Origen, Ignatius, Clement, St. Augustine among many other sons and daughters of the African continent need to be revisited. In chapter four of this book, the author creates a „direct front of apparent opposition" in the fomulation: „Traditional Igbo Initiation Bis a Vis Christian Initiation". From available research, these are not contradictory. The New Testament history of the early Church and further study of the development and spread oft Christianity in apostolic Greece, Rome,. Asia and Africa, and later to other cultures is an attempt to set the possibilities and limitations in the reception and inculturation of the Good News of Christ in these cultures.

Igbo traditional initiation forms are truly human and therefore suitable soil for Christian witness, because they promote life, enhance life, protect life and enhance human dignity. The values they offer are indeed universally appreciated and replicable values, with solid biblical foundations. They are sustainable and emphasise the Christian virtues of faith, hope and charity. They recognise the principles of individuality, solidarity and personality. They promote the dignity of labour, the family as the foundation of every social institution and have high regard for such practices that erich communality, ethics, religiosity, piety, worship, a sense of the sacred, respect for elders, the divine and reverence fort he ancestors. These values alse encourage environmental protection, sing myth to recreate meaning in a seemingly meaningless world. Here, the beauty and essence of music, dance, celebration, joy, sharing, peace, jsutice and courage have their „sitz im Leben" in need of renewal (Aggiornamento). The essence ist hat. A pastoral catechesis fort he Inculturation of Traditional Igbo Initiation Rites as the author has tried to propose shall be really Salvific and Christic if such catechesis lead to inculturation modelst hat help the rediscovery of human values which Igbo Culture, standing as a pradigm for many other African societies offers as a culutrual a contribution to a growing universal and globalising culture.

Obiora F. Ike<br>
Director, Catholic Institute for Development<br>
Justice and Peace, Enugu

## Abreviations

| | |
|---|---|
| AAS | Acta Apostolicae Sedis |
| Acts | Acts of the Apostle |
| ADK | Allgemeines Direktorium für Katechese |
| AFER | African Ecclesial Review |
| AGD | Ad Gentes Divinitus |
| AL | Ad Limina |
| AMECEA | Association of Members of Episcopal Conferences of East Africa |
| Bd | Band (volume) |
| BMS | Bigard Memoral Seminary |
| BTS | Bigard Theological Studies |
| CBCN | Catholic Bishops' Conference of Nigeria |
| CCC | Catechism of the Catholic Church |
| CIC | Codex Juris Canonici |
| CCEO | Corpus Canonum Ecclesiarum Orienatalium |
| Cf. | Confer |
| CIDJAP | Catholic Institute for Development, Justice and Peace |
| CHIEA | Catholic Institute of East Africa |
| Col | Colossians |
| Cor | Corinthians |
| CT | Catechesi Tradendae |
| CUA | Catholic University of America |
| DC | Dominae Cenae |
| Dt | Deuteronomy |
| DZ | Denzinger |
| Eccl. | Ecclesiasticus |
| ed. | Editor/ Edition |
| EN | Evangelii Nuntiandi |

| | |
|---|---|
| Eph | Ephesians |
| et al. | And others |
| Ezek | Ezekiel |
| FDP | Fourth Dimension Publishers |
| Gal | Galatians |
| Gen. | Genesis |
| GS | Gaudium et Spes |
| Hrsg. | Herausgegeben or Herausgeber (edited or editor) |
| Heb | Hebrews |
| IL | Instrumentum Laboris |
| IZT | International Zeitschrift für Theologie |
| Jn. | John |
| KKK | Katechismus der Katholische Kirche |
| KOKI | Katikiizim nke Okwukwe nzuko Katolik n'asusu Igbo |
| LG | Lumen Gentium |
| Lk. | Luke |
| Mal | Malachy |
| Mk. | Mark |
| Mtt. | Matthew |
| NA | Nostra Aetate |
| nd | No Date (of publication) |
| npl | No place of publication |
| OJT | Ogbomoso Journal of Theology |
| OR.EE. | L'Osservatore Romano, English Edtion |
| Pet | Peter |
| PO | Presbyterorum Ordinis |
| Ps | Psalm |
| PTHV | Philosophisch-Theologische Hochschule Vallendar |
| RCIA | Rite of Christian Initiation of Adult |

| | |
|---|---|
| Rev | Revelation |
| RM | Redemptoris Missio |
| Rom | Romans |
| SC | Sacrosanctum Concilium |
| SECAM | Symposium of Episcopal Conferences of Africa and Magadascar |
| SIMSVD | Studia Institute Missiologici Soceitas Verbi Divini |
| UR | Unitatis Redintegratio |
| Vol | Volume |
| Wis | Wisdom |

# General Introduction

The term Initiation, in the most general sense denotes a body of rites and oral teachings whose purpose is to produce a radical modification of religious and social status of the person to be initiated. In philosophical terms, initiation is equivalent to an ontological mutation of the existential condition. The novice emerges from his ordeal,[1] a totally different being: he has become „another",[2] in the ascending order of quality and responsibility in both religious and social life.

Generally, in most African societies initiation *per se* is considered a common phenomenon. All African peoples in one form or another know it.[3] But in the traditional Igbo world, it plays a very significant role in family, social, political and religious life of the people. Most cherished are its practical and effective teaching-learning methods. This is the quintessential and fundamental basis of our study of Initiation in the traditional Igbo culture and religion, as an inculturation basis for the pastoral catechesis of Christian initiation. Catechesis understood from its Greek meaning, as 'to resound'. More details on this point will be seen in the main body of our work.

Among the traditional Igbo, the uninitiated is not only anonymous, he is

---

[1] 'Ordeal' here refers to the 'dehumanising', stringent and rigorous trainings one must undergo in the process of Initiation (Entpersonalisierung durch extreme körperliche Behandlung). For a detailed meaning of 'Ordeal' in relation to Initiation, see Eliade, M; Initiation: An Overview, in: Eliade, M; (ed.), The Encyclopedia of Religion, Vol. 7, New York 1987, 226ff.

[2] Cf. Eliade, M; 225.

[3] Cf. A Study Document on Inculturation (nn. 81-89) for IMBISA, 3rd Plenary Assembly in Maputa (February 1992); Cf. Also AMECEA Documentation Service, June 15, 1993. Uzukwu, E., notes in one of his works that Initiation rite is found in the majority of the world's religions. For this see Uzukwu, E., Traditional Initiation Rites: Anthropological and Religious Viewpoints, in: Lucerna, Vol. 7, nr. 1 (Dec.1986-June1987), 31.

equally ignonymous. He is 'no body' and belongs to 'no where'. To put it mildly enough, such a person is regarded as a 'good for nothing human being'. The traditional Igbo describe such a person (in derogatory and repulsive terms) with such words: '*Ntufuluku*', '*Onye iberibe*', '*Efulefu lere mma tulu obo*', '*mmadu di ma mmadu ako*',[4] all of which means something worse than a fool. How could he appear in the traditional gathering of his kinsmen or raise his voice in the gathering of the initiated? Since he is not recognised as yet a complete human being, how could he be entrusted with any responsibility irrespective of his academic status, wealth or other worldly influence? This is to demonstrate the importance and the significant role of initiation among the traditional Igbo of Africa. Through the process of initiation one is prepared adequately for life and is made strong to face the challenges of life. He is made to discover the deep springs of humanity and to hold up to society a mirror in which are reflected its most cherished values.[5]

What then is initiation? What are the categories or types of initiation? Who initiates who? Why? When? How? And where? Have Initiation rites any pedagogical influence in teaching and learning processes among the traditional Igbo? Which aspect of Initiation rites gives the *forum* for practical and effective teaching-learning and how? What is the essential religious significance of initiation? What are the processes involved and why the initiation ordeal? From where is the traditional Igbo idea of initiation drawn? Or what influences the traditional Igbo idea of initiation that it plays such an essential, significant role among the traditional Igbo? What effect does initiation produce on the

---

[4] These abusive and derogatory terms are such words used to describe the worthlessness of the uninitiated among the traditional Igbo. The phrase: '*Mmadu di ma mmadu ako*' (literally translated: There are people but human beings are lacking), expresses the point clearly.

[5] Cf. Shorter, A., African Christian Theology- Adaptation Or Incarnation, N.Y. 1975, 35. See also Ebo, S.O., *Ozo* Title Institution in Igboland, Germany 1993, 108.

traditional Igbo, his social and religious life? How can the traditional Igbo idea of initiation help the Igbo Christian especially on the basis for the proper understanding of Pastoral Catechesis of Christian initiation? In other words, how can the traditional Igbo understanding of initiation contribute to the right ordering of (the Igbo) Christian life?[6]
Attempt to answering the above fundamental questions form the '*kern*' of this work and makes it fundamentally unique from other pieces of works and articles from various writers on one aspect of initiation or the other. What then motivates this study?

## Motivation

Scholars have done a number of advanced studies on the social aspects of initiation in African societies[7] but comparable attention has not been given to the religious dimensions.[8] Moreover, the universal Church has challenged, empowered and encouraged the Church in Africa to find ways and means of being deep-rooted and make the Gospel message of Jesus Christ original in Africa and in Africans.

In a symposium of Episcopal Conference of Africa and Madagascar, Pope Paul VI solemnly commanded the Bishops of Africa and Madagascar thus: „... you must have an African Christianity."[9] John Paul

---

[6] Cf. *AGD* 11; *LG* 13.
[7] Cf. Turner, V., The Forest of Symbols: Aspects of Ndembu Rituals, 1970; Nadel, S.F., Nupe Religion, London 1954; Wilson, M., Ritual of Kinship Among the Nyakusa, Oxford University Press 1957; Cazeneuve, J., Sociologie du Rite, Paris, 1971; Van Gennep, A., The Rites of Passage, London 1960; Grainger, R., The Language of the Rite, London 1974; Thomas, L. V., „*Mort Symbolique et Naissance Initiatique*", in: *Cahiers des Religion Africaines* 7(1970).
[8] Cf. Metuh, E.I., African Religions in Western Conceptual Schemes, Imico Press, Nigeria 1991, 123.
[9] Paul VI, To The Symposium of Episcopal Conferences of Africa and Madagascar (SECAM), Kampala, 31 July,1969. *A.A.S. LXI*, 1969, 576-578.

II addressing the Bishops of Mozambique during their „ad Limina" in Rome says: „As long as the peoples of Africa do not feel Christianity as part of their own flesh and blood, their own soul, they will not be disposed to defend it ..."[10]

From the deep Anthropological, Missiological Studies and from Church History so far made, it shows that the effective response to this challenge could be inculturation.[11] Inculturation seen as „the process through which the gospel is incarnated in a particular human culture,"[12] and „as a corollary of evangelisation"[13] which is „carrying out the mandate of Christ: Go, therefore, make disciples of all nations."[14] It is also observed that if the gospel itself must encounter all nations and christianise them, it must also encounter and transform their cultures. This is because „evangelization properly defined implies bringing the Good News into all strata of humanity."[15] Hence, the announcing of the gospel to all peoples of the earth is inconceivable without inculturation. One of the ways to effect this inculturation is through an in-depth study of African Traditional Religions in which are documented as it were, the Africans' experiences of encounter with the sacred.[16] It is no doubt, the above mentioned and especially the spirit of Inculturation that motivates this study. What is the expectation of this study, its goal, in other words, its aim?

---

[10] John Paul II, To the Bishops of Mozambique on „*ad Limina*" visit, Rome 23 September, 1982. *OR.EE.*, 22 November, 1982, 10.
[11] Cf. Metuh, E.I.,(ed.), African Inculturation Theology: Africanizing Christianity, Onitsha 1996, VII.
[12] Metuh, E.I., (ed.), African Inculturation, VII.
[13] Metuh, E.I., (ed.), African Inculturation, VII.
[14] Metuh, E.I., (ed.), African Inculturation, VII.
[15] Metuh, E.I., (ed.), African Inculturation, VII.
[16] Cf. Metuh, E.I., (ed.), African Inculturation, VII.

## Aim

In the '*Relatio ante disceptationem, Synodus Episcoporum* Bulletin', Cardinal Hyacinth Thiandoum of Dakar, Senegal, observes and unmistakably states: „Initiation rites common in many African cultures can enrich and offer powerful symbolism for the Christian rites of initiation..."[17] Pope John Paul II, addressing the faithful gathered for the *„Angelus Domini"* in Rome says of the Church in Africa: „The great challenge before her (the Church in Africa) is to incarnate the faith in this continent's culture, so that no genuine value of the African tradition is lost and that it is all transfigured by the Gospel."[18] In a very authoritative and commanding but fatherly manner, John Paul II empowers the Church in Africa thus: „Church in Africa, go ahead! Assume your responsibilities courageously! Justify the hope that is in you."[19]

Initiation, one of those genuine values of the African tradition[20], involves a progressive movement, from a lower to a higher status. From 'no body' to 'somebody'. In this direction, each movement is enveloped in sacred rites designed not only to provide meaning to the individual in transition but also to re-orientate him or her in the morals and ideals of the new

---

[17] Thiandoum, H., *Relatio ante disceptationem*, 18., *Synodus Episcoporum* Bulletin, 5, 11 April, 1994.

[18] John Paul II, To the Faithful gathered for the *"Angelus Domini"*, Rome 24 September, 1995., *OR.EE.*, 27 September, 1995, 1.

[19] John Paul II, *"Angelus Domini"*, Rome 24 September, 1995.

[20] In one of the documents of the Pontifical Magisterium, *Africae Terrarum*, 29 October 1967, nr.14, Paul VI states: "The Catholic Church has great respect for the moral and religious values of African tradition. Not only do they have deep significance in themselves, but they also ... provide a valuable foundation for the preaching of the Gospel, and for the erection of a new society in Christ." See also His address to President Milton Obote of Uganda, Kampala 31 July, 1969, *Insegnamenti* 1969, VII, 537.

state, and at the same time creating a proper forum for integration.[21] This shall be discussed in detail later but suffice it to say that at the end of this ritual-laden progressive movement, the initiated discover the deep springs of their humanity and hold up to society a mirror in which are reflected its most cherished values.[22] Here the observation of Uzukwu merits a proper consideration. According to him, „... in traditional societies the sacred is more often than not implicated in profane activities."[23] He, therefore, suggests that, „one should go beyond the social significance of initiation and life-crises rituals to appreciate their density of meaning."[24]

Our major prospect among other things, therefore, is to study properly the significant role of initiation in the Traditional Igbo culture and Religion, not only to appreciate the density of meaning but more to see how it can form a valuable foundation, an inculturation basis for a fruitful, meaningful and enduring pastoral catechesis of Christian Initiation. In other words, how can the idea of initiation in traditional Igbo culture and religion be used to make „*Christus pro nobis*" become „*Christus in nobis*".[25]

If every work or study must have a method of approach, ours then will not and cannot be an exception. Which system of approach is adopted here for this study?

---

[21] Cf. Eboh, S.O., *Ozo* Title Institution in Igboland, 107. (Hence, Eboh).
[22] Cf. Shorter, A., African Christian Theology – Adaptation or Incanation? New York 1975, 35.
[23] Uzukwu, E. E., Traditional Initiation Rites, 31.
[24] Uzukwu, E. E., Traditional Initiation Rites, 31.
[25] Cf. Wainwright, G., Christian Initiation: Ecumenical Studies in History, London 1969, 51.

## Approach

The system of approach majorly adopted in this study is historico-analytical. It is nonetheless also descriptive, expository and synthetical. The nature of this study and the aim it is set to achieve demand that the above approach be adopted for the purpose of coherence and clarity.

The approach having been taken care of, what then is the scope of this study?

## Scope

„Culture", it is said, „provides society with inherited transmissible code of conduct as both part and junction of the total system of ideas, values, knowledge, philosophy, law, moral, and belief systems which constitute the content of life of a society."[26] Even centuries before the science of culture was born, the most effective missionaries were those blessed with a deep appreciation of the diversity of cultures and of the important role which cultures play in human behaviour. The most successful apostolic approaches have always been the ones geared most closely to the character and needs of the particular life-way. Effective mission has always gone hand in hand with immersion in local cultures.[27] Hence the Church of Vatican II, however, became increasingly aware of its catholicity in the most authentic sense; the council fathers realised anew that the Christian faith is too rich to be portrayed adequately through a single cultural expression.

God did not wait for missionaries to arrive to show Himself. Through the ages God has been revealing Himself in the customs, history and traditions of all peoples. He is present everywhere and missionaries help make explicit what is already implicit. What the missionaries introduced

---

[26] Luzbetak, L., The Church and Cultures, Illinois 1970, 4.
[27] Costa, R., (ed.), One Faith, Many Cultures, (The Boston Theological Institute Annual, Vol. 2), New York 1988, Introduction.

to Africans was not God but Christianity. The second Vatican Council brought out this theme very strongly. Some key texts of the Council serve as background for a return to an understanding of religious symbols of the people. For the Spanish-speaking apostolate in Latin America, that is the beginning of any effective catechesis today. Some of these key texts of the second Vatican Council are quoted extensively thus: „It follows that among all the nations of the earth there is but one people of God which takes its citizens from every race .... The Church, or People of God, takes nothing away from the temporal welfare of any people by establishing that kingdom. Rather does she foster and take to herself, insofar as they are good, the ability, resources, and customs of each people. Taking them to herself she purifies, strengthens and ennobles them."[28] In another number it continues: „The effect of her work is that whatever good is found sown in the minds and hearts of men or in the rites and customs of peoples, these not only are preserved from destruction, but are purified, raised up, and perfected for the glory of God, the confusion of the devil, and the happiness of men."[29] In these and in other numerous decrees, especially '*Ad Gentes*' (On the Mission of the Church), and the decree '*Nostra Aetate*' (On the Relationship of the Church to non-Christians), the Church sees clearly that the task is not to destroy but to ennoble and to perfect.

The decree '*Ad Gentes*' understood mission not in the sense of the 'the pagan countries out there', but in the sense that all men are in the process of conversion and all have God's grace already working in them. Mission means going out of ourselves to give witness to the presence of the risen Lord. „That they (The Missionaries) may be able", the document advises; „to give this witness to Christ fruitfully, let them be joined to those men by esteem and love and acknowledge themselves to be members of the group of men among whom they live. Let them share

---

[28] *LG* 13.
[29] *LG* 17.

in the cultural and social life by the various exchanges and enterprises of human living. Let them be familiar with their national and religious traditions and gladly and reverently laying bare the seeds of the word which lie hidden in them ...."[30] Going further, it says: „From the customs and traditions of their people, from their wisdom and learning, from their arts and sciences these churches borrow all those things which contribute to the glory of their creator, the revelation of the Saviour's grace or the proper arrangement of Christian life .... Thus, it will be more clearly seen in what ways faith can seek for understanding in the philosophy and wisdom of these peoples .... Thanks to such a procedure every appearance of syncretism and false particularism can be excluded, and Christian life can be accommodated to the genius and the dispositions of each culture."[31]

Other decree of Vatican II, which reflects on the cultural expression of religion is *'Nostra Aetate'*. If the Church can speak favourably about those who have not even begun the process of Christianity, how much more can she affirm those who are already in the process of Christianity. The Catholic Church rejects nothing which is true and holy in these religions. She, therefore, has this exhortation for her sons and daughters: „Prudently and lovingly, through dialogue and collaboration with the followers of other religions, and in witness of Christian faith and life acknowledge, preserve and promote the spiritual and moral goods found among these men, as well as the values in their society and culture."[32]

Adhering to the instructions and guidelines of the Church, as we have seen above, the scope of this study is limited to the Igboland and its people. This gives better chance for a thorough and in-dept study of the subject matter. However, cogent examples outside our scope, that help for better illustrations and understanding of certain important points are

---

[30] *AGD* 11.
[31] *AGD* 22. For the first part see also *LG* 13.
[32] *NA* 2.

not neglected.

From where is the information contained in this study obtained? What is the source or are the sources, as the case may be?

## Source

The experience of the writer of this work as an Igbo, born, trained and brought up in Igboland and moreso as a Catholic priest, trained, ordained and worked in Igboland, form the primary source. No doubt valuable and important literatures written by indigenous and non indigenous writers on Igbo people, their life, environment, culture, religion, custom and tradition also form a major material for this study.

The Holy Bible, other Church's documents, some theological books, dictionaries, encyclopaedias, very important articles relevant for our work and other useful scientific works from various Libraries (private as well as public) form important part of the sources also.

However, inspite of the availability of all the necessary materials for this work, the task has not been an easy one. Below are considered the 'necessary' obstacle, limitation and problem.

## Obstacle, Limitation and Problem

As already mentioned above, it must be acknowledged that the task of writing generally on initiation rites in Africa is a very difficult one. This is given to the fact that at one time or the other in the process of initiation rites, absolute secrecy is maintained the breaking of which is considered a taboo.

Among the Igbo of Nigeria, tampering with the absolute secrecy of initiation rites is sometimes punishable by confiscation, destroying and burning of the property or even death of whoever reveals the secret.

Nevertheless, the maintenance of the absolute secrecy is essentially very important because in it lies the 'life-force' and the success of all Igbo-African initiation rites. Hence the necessity.

Having seen the 'necessary' obstacle, limitation and problem in our study, how then are we going to study the subject matter? In other words, what is the sequence of our study?

## Sequence of Study

General introduction having been taken care of, the major focus of this study that is divided into six chapters is based on the Igbo[33] of southeastern Nigeria. As a result of that, the study of the people constitutes the first chapter of this work. This is also considered very important because Igbo religious beliefs are strongly influenced by their historical, geographical, social and cultural background. A.C. Haddon is proved correct here as he says: „... no phase of religious development can be understood apart from the history of the people."[34]

Chapter two is concerned with the title 'Initiation in the Traditional Igbo Culture and Religion'. What is the traditional Igbo idea of initiation? What are the major types of initiation, the perculiarity of the Igbo initiation rites, the three distinctive and characteristic moments in the traditional Igbo initiation rites? Who are the agents of traditional Igbo initiation rites and what do they do? What are the obstacles to the initiation rites among the traditional Igbo?

The significant role of initiation in the traditional Igbo culture and religion is also treated. At this juncture, it is good to observe that every other chapter has a short introduction, which gives an overview (*Überblick*) of the content of that particular chapter, and then a short conclusion, which gives a brief summary of what has been discussed in the particular chapter. The observation having been taken note of,

---

[33] The word 'Igbo' refer to the people as well as their language. It can be used as a noun or as an adjective, depending on which context it is used. It can also be used in a singular sense (when one talk of the Igbo language or for emphatic purpose, for example: the Igbo man) or in plural (as a collective noun). It is mostly used here in the plural sense, as a collective noun.

[34] Haddon, A. C., The Lower Niger and Its Tribes, London 1906, 8.

chapter three treats 'Christian initiation'. It sets off with a brief historical development of the concept of sacrament and other various teachings of the church on the same subject (sacrament). Before the study of the sacraments of Christian initiation, their effects and the ministers, some expressions of some renowned theologians on the sacrament in general, were presented. Also treated is the significant roles of the sacraments of Christian initiation.

A comparative study of traditional Igbo and Christian initiations formed the centre of attention in chapter four. Initiation on both sides were placed side by side, bringing out the common characteristics and dissimilarities in other to present a point of connection for a formidable and fundamental inculturation basis for pastoral catechesis of Christian initiation.

What then is inculturation and how do we go about it? Chapter five handles this question and even goes further to give the scope, the importance and the principle for it, after presenting a brief historical origin of inculturation, its previous terminologies and the examination of those previous terms (of inculturation).

'Pastoral Catechesis for Inculturation of Traditional Igbo Initiation' constitutes chapter six, which is the last chapter before the general conclusion. The highlight here is proposing models of traditional Igbo initiation that can form solid and fruitful basis for pastoral catechesis of Christian initiation for the Igbo Christians.

A comprehensive List of works consulted for this study (Bibliography) marks its *terminus ad quem*.

# Chapter One

# Igbo Historicity: Origin and Location

## 1.1 Introduction

It has been already indicated in the earlier part of this work, the need for, and the importance of the knowledge of the Igbo people who form the centre around which this work revolves. For A. Afigbo, „The Igbos are among the few African people who probably require little introduction to the outside world."[35] However, our aim is not just to introduce the Igbo to the outside world. It is rather to present an idea of the knowledge of whom these people are, their environment and what influences their thought pattern and make them behave in a way that is particular and peculiar. Hence the importance and relevance of the question: From where did the Igbo come and where can they be located in the globe? Perhaps, the attempt at answering the above fundamental questions could give a clue of whom the Igbo are. Let us then consider the origin and the location of the Igbo.

## 1.2 Origin and Location of the Igbo

Considering the science of Anthropology as dealing with human beings and especially with their physical characteristics, origin and distribution into races, environmental and social relations and culture[36], one sees that our consideration of the origin of the Igbo is not out of place.

F.C. Ogbalu makes an important observation that not only evokes the question but also heightens the desire for the quest about the origin of

---

[35] Afigbo, A.E., Ropes of Sand, Ibadan 1981, X.
[36] Cf. Webster's New Encyclopedic Dictionary, Germany 1996, 41.

the Igbo. He says: „Today, there are more than 15 million Igbos who are divided into, at least, two thousand separate units; they are ... a pragmatic and forceful race ... one of the most distinctive and all-important Nigerian-African tribes. They live in multitudinous villages, fragmented into small family groups. They have a comprehensive language of their own, the same customs, traditions, religious belief, socio-political and economic systems."[37] Forde and Jones describe the Igbo as „a single people in the sense that they speak a number of related dialects, occupy a continuous track of territory and have many features of social structure and culture in common, but they were not formerly politically unified."[38]

It has to be noted, however, that the task of the origin of the Igbo has not been an easy one.[39] Early writers on Igbo history and culture never found it easy either.[40] What could be then accountable for this fundamental and perennial difficulty?

The above difficulty is attributed to the lack of written chronological records. What obtains is from oral tradition, usually from the elders and

---

[37] Ogbalu, F.C., Igbo Institutions and Customs, Onitsha (n.d), 21.

[38] Forde, D./Jones, G.I., The Ibo and Ibibio-speaking peoples of South-Eastern Nigeria, London 1962, 25. The conclusion of Forde and Jones that 'they (the Igbo) were not formerly politically unified', is very correct. This lack of political unification is also to a large extent, a contributive factor to the marginalisation of the Igbo, that is as clear as noon-day in the history of Nigerian politics. To say more on this will take us away from our major concern, which is not Nigeria politics. But from the same conclusion of Forde and Jones, one sees already that efforts are being made for the political unification of the Igbo as a people.

[39] Cf. Afigbo, A.E., Towards a History of the Igbo Speaking People of Nigeria, in: Ogbalu, F.C./Emenanjo, E.N., (eds.), Igbo Language and Culture, Vol. 1, Ibadan 1975, 11-27; 28-50 (henceforth "History"); See also Isichei, E., A History of the Igbo People, London 1976, 1-16; Ilogu, E., Christianity and Igbo Culture, Onitsha 1985,1-9.

[40] Cf. Talbot, P.A., The People of Southern Nigeria, Vol. 1, London 1926, 19.

their historical accounts vary from person to person and from place to place. Due to this 'handicap', several efforts by various Scholars on the attempt to trace the exact historical origin of the Igbo have proved elusive. Historians and even research Scholars have not arrived at a consensus regarding the origin of the Igbo. Consequently we have bits and pieces of information, disjointed, sometimes fabulous, and yet, for all that, valuable. Madubuko critically describes the situation thus: „The history of the Igbo people is still a problem area in the field of African studies and even in the context of Nigerian history. What we have so far are mainly bits of information covering this or that area, this or that event of Igboland– a situation which ... refer to the present state of history of the Igbo as 'Ropes of Sand'."[41]

The above critical view of Madubuko surely contains some air of over exaggeration, to say the least. Using the expression 'Ropes of Sand' (which he borrowed from Afigbo[42]) to describe the situation of the present state of history of the Igbo is all together misleading. No history of a people could be described and referred to as ropes of sand, no matter how difficult and complex it may seem to be. What constitutes the problem area in the history of the Igbo of Nigeria? Where lies the problem then? Have the so called scholars and historians (both past and present) adequate and proper knowledge of the Igbo; their culture, thought patterns, beliefs, traditions, philosophy of life, even the language which has been described as „the carrier of culture and the mother tongue (which) constitutes the warp and woof of the mental life of a given people"[43]? Or have they been unable to interpret the facts they

---

[41] Madubuko, L., Igbo World-View, in: BTS, Vol. 14, Nr. 2, Enugu 1994, 11.
[42] Afigbo, A.E., published one of his works in 1981, which he titled 'Ropes of Sand (Studies in Igbo History and Culture)'. It was published in Ibadan by the University Press Limited. This is where Madubuko borrowed his idea from.
[43] Esomonu, L., Respect for Human Life in Igbo Religion and Morality, Rome 1981, 131.

gathered during the course of their researches? Or could it altogether mean that the Igbo have no history of origin? What then are the contents of the Igbo legends and folklores, proverbs, metaphors, myths and narratives, imageries and elegies? We shall make a brief study of some of these in the subsequent part of this section of our work.

Isichei observes that no historical question arouses more interest among the present-day Igbos than the enquiry, 'Where did the Igbos come from?'[44] From the observation of Isichei, one sees that the historical question arouses interest not only among the present-day Igbo but far beyond. According to her. „It is sometimes discussed in the press, and often put to the author (that is, Isichei herself) in conversation. It is as if the question of origins contained, somewhere a key to the elusive problem of the Igbo identity."[45] She then concluded: „In a sense, this whole book is an attempt to answer the question."[46]

Isichei on her own honest attempt on investigating into the origin of the Igbo seems to throw in the towel and agree with an elder of Mbaise[47] in 1972, who on her inquiry about the origin of the Igbo people told her: „We did not come from anywhere and if anyone tells you we came from anywhere he is a liar."[48] He convinced Isichei and told her: „write it

---

[44] Cf. Isichei, E., A History of the Igbo People, London 1976, 3. Language is also described as 'the central mechanism of culture. It is an opening on to another mental world.' –Shorter, A., Christianity and African Imagination (After the African Synod- Resources for Inculturation), Kenya 1996, 26. For further explanations, see the same, 43.

[45] Isichei, 3.

[46] Isichei, 3.

[47] Mbaise is one of the towns in Igbo territories, in the Southern part of Nigeria. Isichei, during her research on 'The History of the Igbo People', was in this town for some interviews and inquiries. One of her encounters was with an elder from this town who is referred to in her work as 'an elder of Mbaise'.

[48] Isichei, 3.

down."[49] Later Isichei concluded a part of that section of her work thus: „The words of the elder of Mbaise, quoted as epigraph to this chapter, embody an essential historical truth."[50] Is the embodiment of an essential historical truth in the words of the said elder of Mbaise, in 1972, truly that the Igbos did not come from anywhere? Isichei, however, did not make this explicitly clear. Or could it be that the said elder of Mbaise spoke figuratively (as is normal with most Igbo-African elders) and Isichei did not understand him and consequently misinterpreted him? This is, of course, a possibility. However, the words of the elder of Mbaise, in 1972, as recorded by Isichei, must be seen as 'historical cypher awaiting decoding'[51].

Interestingly, Obiagwu reports that the informant of Isichei (the said elder of Mbaise) is not a lone voice in saying that the Igbo did not come from anywhere.[52] He says: „One traditional Chief from Alor in Anambra State of Nigeria, Chief Ezeoke Nwangwu re-confirmed that the Igbos did not migrate from anywhere."[53] Chief Nwangwu is reported to have said: „This land where you see the Igbos living is where they originated. All their migration ended within the confines of the land:"[54] For Obiagwu then: „It should therefore be recognised that there are some elements of internal migration among the Igbo people."[55] A little further he says:

---

[49] Isichei, 3.
[50] Isichei, 3.
[51] Cf. Ki-Zerbo, (ed.), General History of Africa, Vol. 1, London 1981, 157.
[52] Cf. Obiagwu, M., Healthcare of the sick among the Igbos of Nigeria vis a vis the Healing Ministry of the Church and the Pastoral challenges of Today, Rome 2000, 14.
[53] Obiagwu, 14.
[54] See Obiagwu, 14. He orally interviewed Chief Nwangwu in Alor in 1980, as he claims. Chief Nwangwu was also claimed to be the oldest man in Alor as at the time of the interview and Obiagwu is said to be from this Alor town.
[55] Obiagwu, 14.

„Those settling at the fringes like the Onitsha people were traced to have migrated from Benin."[56]

S. Eboh in his own search and study for the origin of the Igbo takes to character traits. He argues: „Some character traits of the Igbos resemble those of the Jews to such an extent that some historians postulate that the Igbos descended from the Jews. According to them (the Historians), the Igbos is the split group of the Israelites who, instead of going with Moses to the Northeast during the Exodus from Egypt, preferred to migrate to the South. Finally, they arrived at their present place."[57] He goes further to demonstrate that such words as „Igbo", „Hebrew" and „Ibru" sound alike, and that in Afikpo in Imo State (of Nigeria), there is a town called „Ibru".[58] C.N. Niven is also cited to have maintained that the Igbo came from the East from Mecca, from Egypt and from elsewhere but always from East.[59]

A few Scholars, however, hold onto the above view on the conviction that Igbo culture manifests striking similarities with that of the Ancient Hebrews. They mention such similarities as: „Circumcision and bloody sacrifice, the rites for the presentation and redemption of the first born son, inhibitions and taboos with respect to food and drink imposed on individual, respect for old age, the observance of the new moon and harvest festivals, mourning the dead, purification, marriage customs,

---

[56] Obiagwu, 14. Benin is not an Igbo town. It is located in the Western part of Nigeria. One could however argue that there are also Benin-Igbo. But here the name (Benin-Igbo) suggests that perhaps these people must have had more contact with the real Igbo. They have a lot of influence from the Igbo that they now have dual identity (i.e. Benin by birth but they speak Igbo language). As a result, they are described as Benin-Igbo. This is a possibility. On the other side, it could be that they are some Igbo that migrated into that part of Benin as there is such case in Siera Leon, a neighbouring country from Nigeria.

[57] Eboh, 43.
[58] Eboh, 43.
[59] Eboh, 43.

menstrual seclusion and sterility."[60] The others include: Some features in language, land ownership, law of retaliation, law of sanctuary, women not allowed to wear men's attire[61], laws stipulating penalties for adulterers, abhorrence of witches[62], regulation for inheritance in reference to women going in for marriage.[63]

In the Jewish customary marriage, there is what is called 'Mohar'. *Mohar* is ordinarily, a sum of money which the fiance` had to pay to the father of the girl he is to marry.[64] The amount varied according to the demands of the father[65] or the social position of the family.[66] The payment of the *Mohar* could be substituted by a term of work, as for the marriages of Jacob[67] or by a service rendered, as for the marriage of David with Michal.[68] This practice existed among the traditional Igbo till the recent time.

However, there are no doubts that some aspects of Igbo culture, as mentioned above, manifest striking similarities with that of the Ancient Hebrews or the Jews. But at the same time, it is not enough ground to conclusively say that the Igbo, consequently, came from elsewhere but

---

[60] Basden, G.T:, Niger Ibos, London 1966, 415.
[61] Cf. Basden, 1966, 416.
[62] Cf. Basden, 1966, 418.
[63] Cf. Basden, 1966, 422.
[64] Cf. Gen 34: 12., Ex 22: 16., 1Sam 18: 25. The sum of money paid for the marriage does not mean that the man now buys the woman. As R. de Vaux explains: "The *Mohar* seems to be not mush the price paid for the woman as a compensation given to the family, and, inspite of the apparent resemblance, in law this is a different consideration. The future husband thereby acquires a right over the woman, but the woman herself is not bought or sold." See de Vaux, Ancient Israel, London 1961, 21.
[65] Cf. Gen 34: 12.
[66] Cf. Harrington, W., "Marriage in Scripture", in: Mc Donagh, E., (ed.) The Meaning of Christian Marriage, Dublin 1963 (14-35), 16.
[67] Cf. Gen 29: 15-30.
[68] Cf. 1Sam 18: 25-27.

always from the East or that they descended from the Jews, as some of the Scholars would argue. The Igbo alone do not only share the so-called cultural similarities of the Igbos and the Jews mentioned above to demonstrate the former's origin from the later, but also by some other Africans. P.K. Sarpong, writing on African Values makes it clear that „ownership of property is corporate. Succession, inheritance, status and ranks are determined by one's lineage."[69] Besides, it is a known fact that the Jews consider themselves as a chosen people. They see themselves as a pure race. They live together wherever they found themselves. A fact Quaknin in no uncertain terms put foreword: „*Die Juden der ganzen Welt haben trotz der kulturellen Vielfalt der Länder, in denen sie leben, etwas gemeinsam: das Judentum.*"[70] The Igbo also live together wherever they found themselves. But they neither consider themselves as a pure race nor see themselves as a special or chosen people. Similarity or resemblance does not mean the same. Two people can resemble one another but they are not of the same parents or even of the same nationality. On the other hand the Igbo culture could even be the same with that of the Ancient Hebrews or the Jews without the Igbo having any connection as such with neither the Hebrews nor the Jews.

Further, V.C. Uchendu in his own search for the origin of the Igbo, on the contrary from other Scholars argues from a non-migration theory. For him: „The belt formed by Owerri, Awka, Orlu and Okigwe divisions constitute this nuclear area. Its people have no tradition of coming from any other place."[71] He explains further: „We assume an early migration from this area into Nsukka-Udi highlands in the north and into Ikwerri, Asa and Ndoki in the south. The eastern Isuama claim to have come

---

[69] Sarpong, P.K., The Gospel as Good News for Africa Today, in: *Cultures et foi Potificium Consilium de Cultura*, Citta del Vaticano, Vol. Vi, no. 2, 1998, 126.
[70] Quaknin, Marc-Alain, *Symbole Des Judentums*, Augsburg 1999, 7.
[71] Uchendu, V.C., The Igbos Of South-Eastern Nigeria, New York 1965, 3.

from this centre. Ngwa traditions point to their secondary migration from Mbaise."⁷²

Isichei reacts differently from the above opinion of Uchendu. She explains that as time progressed, Igbo populations dispersed more widely in the forests of Igboland. They came to concentrate especially in what much later became Owerri, Okigwe, Orlu and Awka divisions.⁷³ Sequel to this explanation she comments: „Most Scholars follow G.I. Jones in regarding this (the above named places) as an Igbo heartland, basing their views on linguistic and cultural evidence. It is also strikingly confirmed by demography, for a glance at the modern population map ... shows that it is also the area of densest population. As one moves further from the heartland, the population density falls in a series of steady diminishing rings."⁷⁴

Oguejiofor sees the cause of this conflicting and opposing ideas as a result that „each Igbo clan or village seems to possess a tradition that is specific to it."⁷⁵ He points out that Onitsha people claim Bini Origin. The same goes for most of the Western Igbo Communities.⁷⁶ According to him: „The Nri clan has a tradition which is neatly fitted to the religious hegemony of their people over a large section of Igboland. According to this tradition, Eri, the father of all Nri, is said to have come from Chukwu (God), sent specifically to rule the people of Anambra who had no king at the time. The people occupying the north-east of Igboland claim Ogoja and Ekoi origins, and some of the Aro have a fanciful tale of how their ancestors were part of the Jewish community who were expelled from Spain by Ferdinand and Isabella."⁷⁷ Oguejiofor may be

---

⁷² Uchendu, !965, 3.
⁷³ Cf. Isichei, 4.
⁷⁴ Isichei, 4.
⁷⁵ Oguejiofor, J., The Influence of Igbo Traditional Religion on the Socio-Political Character of the Igbo, Nsukka 1996, 7-8.
⁷⁶ Cf. Oguejiofor, 8.
⁷⁷ Oguejiofor, 8.

claiming to have said it all but he never gave any clue to neither the way of tracing the origin of the problem nor to a way of finding a solution to it. How could these conflicting and opposing ideas be resolved and a proper and true history of the Igbo be shown?

It is of great interest to discover in the course of our study, that in Old Testament, Gad, one of the sons of Israel, had sons among whom were: „Eri, Arodi and Areli."[78]

In some parts of Igboland, there are people up till today whose names very much suggest that they are likely descendants of a person whose name was *Eri*. For example: *Umu-Eri* or *Umuleri*. This means descendants or children of *Eri*. This is a name of a town near the Riverrine part of the Igboland.[79] Other towns in Igboland that have such similar biblico-historical connection with the Jewish race are *Aguleri* and *Oraeri*. Perhaps *Oraeri* could be a distortion or corruption of *Areli*. The people of Arondizuogu, Arochukwu and some parts of the old Cross-River State (probably, the Efik in Nigeria) could also trace their origin to Arodi, one of the sons of Gad, the son of Israel.[80]

Further, for the Igbo people, as for the Hebrews, a name is not just a personal label for the sake of identity. It means much more. In ancient Hebrew tradition in general, to give a name was the special privilege of a superior as when Adam exercised his dominion over the animals by giving them their names (Cf. Gen. 2: 18ff).

---

[78] Gen 46: 16-17.

[79] It is customary that in most part of Igboland, children are mostly identified with their father. This is so because men are more prominent and more recognised in their tradition. This is, of course, one of the points against the men that in Igbo tradition and culture, the women are being suppressed so much. An Igbo proverb: *Nwa malu eme, oyie Nna ya; ma omaghi eme, oyie Nne ya* (a well behaved child resembles the father but the bad resembles the mother) demonstrates the position of women in Igbo culture clearly and eloquently.

[80] Cf. Gen 46, 16.

According to Hebrew usage, a person received a new name to indicate a change in his rank or appointment to a new post (Gen. 17: 5; 32: 28). But by far the most frequent source of the name which was given, was some circumstance at the time of the birth of a child. It might concern the mother who bore the child (Gen. 4: 1). Eve called her first born Cain because she had 'acquired' a man. Rachel dying in child-birth called her son Ben-oni, 'son of my sorrow' (Gen. 35: 18).

Less often, the name concerns the father (Ex. 2: 22). In some cases, this circumstance was prophetic as in the naming of Jacob (Gen. 25: 26). However, the most important category of names is that which contains some divine name or title. This is the most impressive characteristic of Hebrew names because it shows the people's close relationship with, and trust in God.

These names express the power or the mercy of God, the help expected from Him, the feeling of kingship with Him. Sometimes these names relating to their national God are abridged, the divine elements being understood.

The similarities mentioned above of the Hebrew custom are still much alive today in the custom and tradition of the Igbo people of Nigeria. Further explanations and examples in the later part of our work will elucidate the point more.

Faced with the above contradicting, conflicting and opposing opinions and ideas about the origin of the Igbo, an outsider may ask: What is actually the fundamental problem about tracing the origin of the Igbo? Could one believe with Isichei and her informant (the said elder of Mbaise, in 1972) that the Igbo did not come from anywhere, and that anyone who says that the Igbo came from anywhere is a liar[81]? Or do we believe with Obiagwu whose informant (the said Chief Ezeoke Nwangwu) told him that the land where the Igbo are living is where they originated and that their migration ended within the confines of the

---

[81] Cf. Isichei, 3.

land[82]? Or is the problem really (and not imaginary) that the Igbo have no common tradition of origin as Oguejiofor claims[83]?

It is an obvious and clear fact that history itself is one and objective. But unfortunately, historians are many and often subjective[84]. Each tells the same story but in a different way and according to his understanding. This is where and why the objectivity of history is turned to subjectivity. A clear fact Quaknin candidly and frankly agrees with. In his words: *„Alle Versionen des gleichen Mythos sind verschiedene Seiten, unterschiedliche Wahrnehmungen des gleichen Ereignisses. Die einen erleben es in emotionaler Weise, die anderen auf einer aesthetischen Ebene, wieder andere behalten den ethischen, philosophischen oder poetischen Aspekt."*[85] But the question is: What is the problem with the history of the origin of the Igbo? Is it that historians and anthropologists have not been able to trace the correct origin of the Igbo? Or that they are not able to interpret the facts they discovered during the course of their researches and investigations? This is an open question but it demands an urgent and proper attention from the concerned scholars.

However, we can at this point summarily conclude that the origin of the Igbo, like that of every other people, be it the Bantu, the Hutuh or the Tutsi, Jewish or Gentile, can only be properly traced back to God who created man[86], and through whom all things were made and „in whom all things hold together."[87] From one stock he made every nation of mankind to dwell on the face of the earth. It is he who set limits to their

---

[82] Cf. Obiagwu, 14.
[83] See Oguejiofor, 7.
[84] Cf. Oranekwu, G.N., Sacrifice in Igbo Traditional and Christian Religions and its Significance for Everyday life: A Comparative Study (Unpub. Licentiate Thesis in Theology) *PTHV*, Germany 1999, 18.
[85] Quaknin, 9.
[86] Cf. Gen 1: 27.
[87] Col 1: 16f.

epochs and fixed the boundaries of their regions.[88]

J. B. Taylor in a simple but reflective, deep and condensed manner sums up the point thus: „Man is mono-genesis not poly-genesis. We would have to admit that the whole human race has a single origin ... whether we are talking about the pigmies of Central Africa, the Aborigines of Australia or the so-called super races of the Germanic stock."[89]

The Igboland is geographically located within the tropical rain forest zone of Africa, roughly within the imaginary quadrangle traceable by the parallels of 6 degrees and 82 degrees East Longitude, and 42 degrees and 7 degrees North Latitude. This is the area commonly referred to as the tropical forest zone of Africa.[90] But the Igbo, because of their belief in progress, prosperity and all that go with them, they could be found in any part of Africa, indeed, in any part of the Globe. It is almost a fact and a belief that „any part of the World you go and you do not find an Igboman, leave that area because it is uninhabitable."[91] H. Lord fondly refers to the Igbo people as „the Jews of Africa."[92]

In Nigeria's political administration, the Igbo people occupy what are known today as Abia, Anambra, Enugu, Imo, some part of Ebony, Delta and Rivers States. These are known as Igboland.[93] They are neighboured westward by Bini and Isoko; eastward by Ekoi and Yako; northward by Igala, Idoma and Tiv, and southward by Ibibio, Ijaw and Ogoni towns.

Our next preoccupation will be concerned with demography, that is the statistical study of the Igbo.

---

[88] Acts 17: 26.
[89] Taylor, J. B., Primal World Views, Nigeria 1976, 31.
[90] Cf. Uchendu, 1.
[91] Eboh, 45.
[92] Lord, H., An African Survey, London 1945, 21.
[93] Cf. Falola, T., (ed.), History of Nigeria 2, Ibadan 1991, 128.

## 1.3 Demography

The science of demography deals with the statistical study of human populations and especially their size and distribution and the number of births and deaths.[94] Given to the fact that the role of the family in any society is basic and fundamental[95], and because the mission of being the primary, vital cell of society has been given to the family by God Himself[96], and morestill, for the love the Igbo people have for family, a cursory study of the Igbo family becomes necessary here. Of course, a complete study of human populations especially with regard to the number of birth and death has to begin with, or at least include the family, which is regarded as the foundation, the source of life of every society anthropologically.

The Igbo people have and love large families. For them, the family does not mean only father, mother and children.[97] It goes further beyond that. This is made manifest in their extended family system. P. Schineller's description of African family aptly fits in here. He says: „The isolated self is an abstraction, it is unreal. One's family identifies one, which is the extended family, often including Aunts and Uncles, Cousins, In-

---

[94] Cf. Webster's New Encyclopedic Dictionary, Germany 1996, 266.
[95] Cf. Ezeanya, S. N., The Traditional Igbo Family and the Christian Family, in: B.C. Okolo, (ed.), The Igbo Church and Quest for God, Nigeria 1985, 53.
[96] Cf. *LG* 11.
[97] What Shorter describes as a nuclear family:- the household unit of two parents and their own children. It tries to be autonomous and to operate effectively without reference to other relatives. According to Shorter, "Ideally, the nuclear household is neolocal or separate from the residences of relatives in the paternal and maternal lines. Wedding symbolism centres on the creation of the new household and its climax is the 'going away' ceremony. The mental image of the nuclear system is that of 'cell division'. Families continually split and unite to create new nuclei." See Shorter, A., African Culture, An Overview, Kenya 1998, 83-84.

laws, Nieces and Nephews. Extended also over time, the family is continually linked with those who have gone before. Here one notes the respect and reverence shown to ancestors, particularly to parents, grand-parents and great grand-parents who have died. These ancestors remain present in memory and imagination; they watch over and serve as example to the present generation. There is deep union between the living and the dead."[98]

Great love for children, especially those to maintain the ancestral lineage, take good care of the parents at their old age and give them befitting burial rites after death, make the Igbo to love and have large families. Writing on 'The Child and Melanesian Values', Ennio Mantovani maintains that „the child, above everything else, is a key value of representing identity, meaning, and especially security for people involved."[99] This idea is also found deep-rooted among the traditional Igbo. Also his view that the less identity, meaning, and security in life, the greater the psychological need for more children; the more identity, meaning and security, the less urge to have many children, is transparently evident among the Igbo.[100]

P. Schineller is also right in saying that: „Children too are precious; not to have children is exception and is often seen as a disgrace. For it is the children who care for the parents in their old age, who pass on the family name to the future generations."[101] The traditional number, which will make the Igbo couples contented is nine children.[102] This is consequent upon the belief that through one's children, the ancestral lineage is transmitted. Hence, the Igbo name- „*Amaefuna*" (may my lineage never get lost) or „*Amaechina*" (may my lineage never close or extinct). No

---

[98] Schineller, P., A Handbook on Inculturation, New Jersey 1990, 76.
[99] Mantovani, E., The Child and Melanesian Values: in Piskaty, K., and Rzepkowski, H. (eds.), Studia Instituti Missiologici, Germany 1993, 309.
[100] Cf. Mantovani, 309.
[101] Schineller, 76.
[102] Cf. Arinze, F., Sacrifice in Ibo Religion, Ibadan 1970, 3.

wonder it is a great curse to tell an Igbo: „*Ama gi chikwaa*" (may your lineage be extinct). J. S. Mbiti lucidly clarifies it thus: „You become immortal in and through your children, even if you die eventually. Your name is carried on and not lost, the torch of life is handed down and begins to burn anew –you are rekindled in your children. Through procreation you beat death, you bring together the three dimensions of time: Past, Present and Future."[103]

In another part of one of his great works Mbiti elaborately explains: „If the philosophical or theological attitude towards marriage and procreation is that these are an aid towards the partial recapture or attainment of the lost immortality, the more wives a man has the more children he is likely to have and the more children, the stronger the power of immortality in the family. He who has many descendants has strongest possible manifestation of immortality. He is 'reborn' in the multitude of his descendants, and there are many that remember him after he has died physically and entered his personal immortality. Such a man has the attitude that, the more we are, the bigger I am."[104] „The child is the symbol, the visible guarantee of security and the best hope for the future well-being of both the community and the individual."[105]

For the Igbo therefore, „children are the glory of marriage, and the more there are of them, the greater the glory."[106] Could it then be any wonder that the Igbo could say like the Biblical Rachel: „Give me children or I shall die!"[107] The Igbo believe strongly in the proverbial Biblical saying: „Large population, monarch's glory, dwindling population, ruler's ruin."[108]

---

[103] Mbiti, J. S., Love and Marriage in Africa, London 1973, 43.
[104] Mbiti, J. S., African Religions and Philosophy, London 1975, 142. (Hereafter referred to as African Religions)
[105] Mantovani, 317.
[106] Mbiti, African Religions, 142.
[107] Gen 30: 1.
[108] Pr 14: 28.

Regarding the number of death, there is no accurate official records but the birth rate is quite higher than that of death rate. However, the question of population of the Igbo, who are by size of average height, and mostly dark in complexion, thickly built with broad nose, curly black hair and moderately thick lips[109], has often been a matter of estimation, as there is no accurate official figure, -a phenomenon found also among other peoples of Nigeria. J. Baur is therefore, right (though he over exaggerated) in his observation that: „Nothing is more disputed in Nigeria than the various public population counts so often falsified for religious and political purposes as well as for getting higher quotas of the federal budget."[110]

The 1921 Nigerian census put the Igbo population at nearly four million. In 1953, they numbered between five and six million.[111] E. Ilogu in 1974 put the rough estimate of the Igbo population to be about nine million.[112] If the census figures in Nigeria, because of their association in the popular mind with the so-called 'sharing of national cake'[113], are endemically suspect and controversial[114], one may take for his confirmation of the numerical remarkableness of the Igbo, a remark by a non-involved observer at a time when ethnic numerical strength had no connection with national cake as there was then neither the nation (Nigeria) nor the cake to share. However, before the down of 18th Century, the Igbo were already noted as a numerous 'nation'.

To know a people is to know their culture. To know a people's culture is to understand, accept and appreciate them the way they are, to

---

[109] Cf. Ogbalu, 5.
[110] Baur, J., 2000 Years of Christianity in Africa, Nairobi 1994, 381.
[111] Cf. Arinze, 1.
[112] Cf. Ilogu, 2.
[113] Cf. Arinze, 1. He uses the above expression in explaining the reason for non-accuracy of Nigerian population count/census.
[114] Cf. History of Population Census in Nigeria, in: National Commission Diary, (npl), 1991, 12.

understand the way they think and what makes them think that way and what influences their pattern of belief and behaviour. This brings us into the study of values and rituals in Igbo culture and tradition.

## 1.4 Values and Rituals in Igbo Culture and Tradition

Bringing in the study of Igbo Values and Rituals in this work is very necessary because of the role it will play in the future part of this endeavour. Values and Rituals are the centre of the traditional Igbo life and culture. Remove them, then the traditional Igbo life and culture will be completely annihilated, and the Igbo will be 'no people' any more. E. Uzukwu discovers the root of African problem as a whole, to be cultural. He succinctly declares: „The root of our (African) problem is cultural."[115] He continues: „Consequently, to effect an enduring change, a radical action becomes imperative. Christians in Africa need the African base to construct a church, which bears credible witness to the risen Jesus. This base must be founded on the retrieval of our fundamental cultural values."[116]

However, to treat all Igbo Values and Rituals in this work, will certainly make it heavier than necessary. Consequently, we select and summarise the cogent ones that have much to do with our case study. We begin with Igbo value of life.

### 1.4.1 Igbo Value of Life

*'Ndu'* is the Igbo word for Life. In Igbo tradition and culture, *Ndu* (life) is seen as sacred. Human life (*Ndu mmadu*) is of absolute value. It is

---

[115] Uzukwu, E., A Listening Church: Autonomy and Communion in African Churches, New York 1996, 6.
[116] Uzukwu, A Listening Church, 6. Not only that the Vatican Council II has already made powerful statements on the above point, the guidelines, rules and principles are also given. For details see *Gaudium et Spes*, 57-62.

priceless. For the traditional Igbo, any attempt on human life, even accidentally, is considered an abomination and must be purified.
In some Igbo village-groups, the penalty for accidental killing of human person is seven years of exile (and the property of the 'culprit' is completely annihilated, often times consumed by fire). The Igbo call it „*Igba oso ochu*" (running into exile for having committed murder). F. C. Ogbalu describes it better: „Therefore to kill a person in an encounter or war on family, village or town level is murder '*per se*' and the punishment is so prodigious that it is dreaded by all."[117] He goes further: „'Murder' is not punished simply by the reciprocal death of the person who committed it. According to the customary law of the land, the whole village (and in some places only the *Umu-nna*) is involved, the villagers must run away carrying whatever they could of their possession if they are lucky to have time to do so before the burning of houses and looting of their property would ensue. The village or *umu-nna* is ravished, laid desolate and occupied as a lawful possession by the *umu-nna* or villagers of the 'murdered' person."[118]
E. Uzukwu narrates a story of how the *Nri* people of the Igbo consider any war as evil because it endangers human life by shedding of human blood. He says: „The *Nri* people of the Igbos consider any war an evil because it involves the shedding of human blood. According to *Nri* sacred narrative, such bloodletting would pollute the earth and violate the covenant between God and human. Thus, there was a covenant between earth and man .... No person should defile the earth by spilling human blood in violence on it. This is the covenant. It must be kept. We *Nri* keep it. We told other Igbo to whom we gave yam to keep it."[119] He did not hesitate to narrate further the *Nri* peoples' attitude towards violent activities. For the *Nri* people of the Igbo: „Rather than be

---

[117] Ogbalu, F. C., Igbo Institutions and Customs, 43.
[118] Ogbalu, F. C., Igbo Institutions and Customs, 43-44.
[119] Uzukwu, 25.

involved in violent activities, the priest-king of *Nri*, who presides over the priestly village-group, sent priests all over Igboland to persuade people to live in peace and to purify the earth polluted by violence."[120]

Uzukwu then clearly and smartly puts across the message of his '*Nri* people' historical narrative in these words: „*Nri* civilisation does not tolerate holy wars, crusades or jihad. This is a society where religion is at the service of humane living. Today more than ever such humane living eludes Nigeria, Africa and the World. Our societies need to be reconstructed on the sound ethical principle that an attack on human life sends out shock waves of disorder on the earth. It is an offence against the earth, against the owner of the earth, and against the inhabitants of the earth."[121]

The value and importance the Igbo people attach to life is eloquently testified in the name they give to their children such as: *Ndu ka* (Life is greatest of all) for they say: *Onye di ndu, odikwude ife* (he who is alive has all hope), *Ndu bu ilo* (Life is the only way), *Ndu bu isi* (Life comes first or simply, Life first).

Let us next, turn attention to marriage, through which as a result of the union of man and woman life comes into existence.

### 1.4.2 Igbo Value of Marriage

Marriage is another thing not only the traditional Igbo value so much but the entire traditional Africans. In the whole continent of Africa, marriage is seen and considered, as the centre of existence. Its importance and pivotal role, especially for the Igbo, cannot be over emphasised. J. Mbiti's apt description of marriage for the African is also *ad rem* for the Igbo. He says: „For the African (Igbo) People, marriage is the focus of existence. It is the point where all the members of a given community meet: The departed, the living and those yet to be born. All the

---

[120] Uzukwu, 25.
[121] Uzukwu, 26.

dimensions of time meet here, and the whole drama of history is repeated, renewed and revitalised. Marriage is a drama in which everyone becomes an actor or actress and not just a spectator. Therefore, marriage is a duty, a requirement from the corporate society, and a rhythm of life in which everyone must participate. Otherwise, he who does not participate in it is a curse to the community, he is a rebel and a law-breaker, he is not only abnormal but 'under-human'."[122] Mbiti's conclusion is worthy of note. He says: „Failure to get married under normal circumstances means that the person concerned has rejected society and society rejects him in turn."[123]

Marriage then has a foremost place in the life of the Igbo. It looms upon the horizon of every maid and youth as an indispensable function to be fulfilled with as little delay as possible after reaching the age of puberty.[124]

It has to be noted with particular emphasis that for the traditional Igbo community, marriage must be fruitful. Its fruits are children. Therefore, marriage and procreation in Igbo community are a unity. Without children, for the Igbo, marriage is incomplete.

What Mbiti says of marriage in Africa is *ipso facto* typical of the traditional Igbo. Mbiti sees marriage as „a religious obligation by means of which the individual contributes the seed of life towards man's struggle against the loss of original immortality. Biologically both husband and wife are reproduced in their children, thus perpetuating the chain of humanity .... A person who, therefore, has no descendants in effect quenches the fire of life, and becomes forever dead since his line of physical continuation is blocked if he does not marry and get children. This is a sacred understanding and obligation which must neither be abused nor despised."[125] Mbiti did not want to say 'half truth' or to cover

---

[122] Mbiti, African Religions, 133.
[123] Mbiti, African Religions, 133.
[124] Cf. Basden, Niger Ibos, 213.
[125] Mbiti, African Religions, 133.

anything, thus he goes on to say the facts the way they are. He powerfully and eloquently emphasises that: „To lack someone close who keeps the departed in their personal immortality is the worst misfortune and punishment that any person could suffer. To die without getting married and without children is to be completely cut off from the human society, to be disconnected, to become an outcast and to lose all link with mankind."[126]

The above points of Mbiti are self explanatory. They need no other comment as they are put in clear and very simple unambiguous terms. Shall we then, not move from here to discuss the Igbo value of man?

### 1.4.3 Igbo Value of Man

*Mmadu* is the Igbo word for man[127] in the general sense of the term as creature of God. It means, „let goodness be" or „let there be goodness". The term is derived from two Igbo words, namely: „mma" (which means goodness or beauty) and „du" or „di" (meaning, come into existence or exist or simply, is).

In the Bible, the creation account has it that God created all things and created them beautifully. He saw that all He made was good.[128] It was and still is His will that all He created remain good. Then at last He created man as a synthesis of all that is good in creation. This is the view of the traditional Igbo, about God and creation. Hence the etymology of the name „*mmadu*" or „*mmadi*" (let goodness or beauty remain).

For the Igbo, therefore, „*mmadu*" is a special creature and he occupies a special place in creation. The Holy Father, Pope John Paul II's summary of man (*vivens homo*) as 'the epiphany of God's glory'[129] is most fitted

---

[126] Mbiti, African Religions, 134.
[127] Igbo language has only one word „*mmadu*" for the followings: man, mankind, human being. Gender has no role to play in this sense.
[128] Cf. Gen 1: 25.
[129] John Paul II, *Tertio Millennio Adveniente*, 2000, 6.

in the Igbo idea of man. He is the embodiment of the sum total of all the beauties in creation and every other thing in the visible world is placed under his care. The Igbo idea of man is then in perfect agreement with the Psalmist who extols man as being greater than ordinary things and above everything created in the visible universe. In an amazing wonder the Psalmist asks: „... what is man that you should keep him in mind, mortal man that you care for him? Put all things under his feet."[130]

The Igbo value of man (as the sum total of beauty of God's creation) reflects also in the way the dead are treated and buried in Igboland and custom. They believe that man is a component of body, soul (spirit) and mind. When the soul (spirit) and mind separate from the body, then death occurs and the body is called *Ozu* (corps). But even at that, the *Ozu* (corps) is still treated with maximum last respect.[131] In most places, the *Ozu* (corps) is buried within the family compound because it is strongly believed that he or she is still part of the family as we have seen somewhere. The burial is celebrated with a big feast though with mixed feeling that the person will no longer be seen physically as a human being, but at the same time happy that he or she has gone to join the ancestors in the spiritual world. From the spiritual world, they help to fight for the living members of their family against the malignant evil spirits. In this way they help in protecting the living members of their family. We shall explain more on death at the appropriate time. It has its proper place in the later part of this work. To avoid unnecessary repetitions, therefore, let us be satisfied with the much.

The Igbo see man as one who manifests God's goodness. Where does man manifest this goodness then?

---

[130] Ps 8: 4-6.
[131] Last respect here means that all the respect that is given to the person while he or she was alive will all be accorded to him or her for the final time. He or she will from thence be respected no longer as human person but as spirit and perhaps in the future as ancestor or ancestress.

## 1.4.4 Igbo Value of Community Life

In the traditional life of the traditional Igbo, the individual 'cannot' exist alone but corporately. He owes his existence to other people, including those of the past generations and his contemporaries. As L. Esomonu rightly puts it, "the strength of the individual is in his unity with the community."[132] The Igbo also say it that „*Igwe bu ike*" (Community is strength). The individual therefore, is simply part of the whole. To show how repulsive individualism is among the traditional Igbo, they say: „*Onye so nani ya no bu ozu* „(Only the dead[133] stays alone).

The community life of the traditional Igbo involves every person in a web of relationships. There is a high standard of attachment. An attachment which J. A. Sofola describes as a strong feeling that, „what we have we share in order to nurture, and all our actions will be calculated towards reinforcing rather than breaking the cord of human relationship."[134]

According to E. Ilogu, „Birth, death and memorials or any such occasions are the concern of all the members of the community."[135] J. S. Mbiti makes it clearer in these words: „When he suffers, he does not suffer alone but with the corporate group; when he rejoices, he rejoices not alone but with his kinsmen, his neighbours and his relatives whether dead or living. When he gets married, he is not alone; neither does the wife 'belong' to him alone. So also the children belong to the corporate body of his kinsmen, even if they bear only their father's name. Whatever happens to the individual happens to the group, and whatever

---

[132] Esomonu, L., Respect for Human Life in Igbo Religion and Morality, Rome 1981, 45.

[133] The dead here refers to the corpse, which decays and rottens away. But even at that the person whose body is the corpse still unites with the family in a mysterious way. This is the traditional Igbo belief. The Christian idea of the communion of the saints is not different or far from it.

[134] Sofola, J. A., African Culture and African Personality, Nigeria 1973, 69.

[135] Ilogu, 19.

happens to the whole group happens to the individual. The individual can only say: 'I am, because we are; and since we are, therefore I am'."[136]

Among the traditional Igbo in their community life, biological birth is not enough. It is the duty of the Community to make, create or produce the individual. The child must go through the rites of incorporation so that he becomes fully integrated into the entire society. To say more on this here will be considered crossing our bridge before reaching it because that is part of the main thrust of our work. At the appropriate time, we shall delve into it fully but suffice it to say that these rites of incorporation continue throughout the physical life of the individual, during which he passes from one stage of corporate existence into another. The final stage is reached when he dies and even then, he is ritually incorporated into privileges and his own responsibilities towards himself and towards other people.

The individual is so intimately and deeply united to the group. His problems are the problems of the group and vice versa. Likewise, his joys are the joys of the group and the joys of the group are at the same time his. Thus in the traditional Igbo society, „the truism that no man can be sufficient to himself is plain to all"[137], and crucial for this is the basic conception of the interrelatedness and order of everything, from which it follows that the individual can only be happy if all those around him including spirits are happy too.[138] In Scheler's words: „So wahr Ich bin, so wahr sind wir, oder gehöre ich zu einem wir."[139]

In which of the ways do the traditional Igbo express the value of community life? Where can one easily and commonly experience and

---

[136] Mbiti, African Religions, 108-109.
[137] Beattie, J., Other Cultures, London 1964, 194.
[138] Sempebwa, J. W., African Traditional Moral Norms and their Implications for Christianity, Rome 1983, 33.
[139] Scheler, M., Der Formalismus in der Ethik und die materiale Wertethik, München 1966, 532.

enjoy most the traditional Igbo value of community life? These form the basis for our next preoccupation below which we termed 'family bed-time stories'.

### 1.4.5 Family Bed-Time Stories

In traditional Igbo homes, storytelling is an art commonly performed and enjoyed by both parents and children. Usually after dinner, men and women regale one another until they are carried off by sleep.[140] The story ranges from creation or origin stories, explanatory stories, trick stories, contest stories and didactic stories.[141] These stories are informed by a candid wit and robust sense of humour. Attention to them gives one, sensitive insight into the philosophy of life and the foibles of all human beings.

Family bed-time story not only bring the traditional Igbo family always together, through it children also learn faster and more effective the family norms, simple courtesy, fundamentals of good training and good manners and they are better prepared for public and community life. It also helps them to retain whatever they learnt. It helps them to form future ideas as well as the application, knowing what to do in a given situation and how to do it successfully. Recalling the remark of Adalbert Balling correctly fits in here. He writes: „*In Fabeln, Mythen, Märchen und vor allem in köstlichen Sprichwörtern haben die Völker Schwarzafrikas ihre Lebenserfahrungen von Generation zu Generation weitergegeben. Ihre 'Philosophie' ist drastisch und plastisch.*"[142] We would not discuss about *köstlische Sprichwörter* now because it will have its proper place in the later part of our work. There, it will be given

---

[140] Cf. Egudu, R. N, The Calabash of Wisdom and other Igbo Stories, Eungu 1973, 13.

[141] Every story is by nature fundamentally didactic. Any other purpose or agenda is secondary.

[142] Balling, A. L., Lebensweisheit aus Schwarzafrika, Freiburg 1985, 2.

the attention it deserves. Three examples of traditional Igbo family bedtime stories[143] below will suffice to make our points lucid enough and to show the special role it has to play in the later part (the main body) of this work.

## Example 1
## The Origin of Day and Night

In the beginning of the world, before there was either Day or Night, a certain man had many wives. One of his wives was barren and the other wives tormented her. „You are an evil woman," they would say, „that is why you are cursed with barrenness." One day this unfortunate woman heard of a *dibia* (a traditional medicine man) who could make a woman fertile by rubbing his naked palm on her belly (stomach). Off she went to seek him out. She had to trek to a distant land beyond seven hills. When she arrived at the *dibia*'s shrine she told her woes to him. The *dibia* was sympathetic but told her she had to wait a little while because there was no child of good breed in his stock." All I have now are devilish babies and I do not want to bring you a curse. You should wait for a good baby." The woman was so anxious to have a baby that she insisted she have whatever was available. „Give me a child, good or bad, as long as it has the shape of a human being. I am tired of being insulted by my husband's wives," she said. „I shall give you what I have but I fear for you woman," said the *dibia* wondering at her impatience. It reminds me, he thought, of the proverbial little animal who although he had been trapped in a cesspool for many years first complained of the stench when he saw some people coming to help him out. Again the *dibia* said, „Woman it is a terrible gift you ask for." But the woman begged him.

---

[143] The Igbo expression of „Bed-Time Story or Stories" here in our use means Akiko Iho/Ifo. In English, it is expressed in many terms: Feeble, Myth, Fairy-tale (Märchen), Folk-lores and so on.

„Please give me a child ... please." The dibia rubbed his palm on her belly. At once it began to swell. Almost mad with joy, the woman hurried home. When the other wives saw her, they were filled with awe. But, they were suspicious too. Soon after, she gave birth to a male child who grew rapidly in height and in mischief. He insulted his seniors and bullied his juniors. But because he was the only child of his mother, his parents neither reprimanded nor punished him. The boy began to use his freedom most shockingly. With the aid of a charm given him by a magician, first he killed all the domestic animals in the kingdom. Then he killed all the people. Lastly, he killed his parents as well. Only an old woman escaped death from his hands. She had her own powerful charms with which she defended herself and tried to kill the boy. Whenever this old woman waved her charm in the air, there was darkness. Whenever the boy waved his charm, there was blazing light. As the battle continued it became apparent that their charms worked for twelve hours at a time. Soon both of them fell dead. Since then darkness and light have continued to appear alternately, each for twelve hours. And because there is nobody who knows the secrets of their charms, Day and Night have continued to appear on earth.[144]

Example 2
The Origin of Death

One day God threatened to destroy the world. All mankind was afraid and assembled to decide how to prevent this disaster. During the meeting there arose two opposing groups. One group said that men should not die at all. The other group said that Death was necessary as long as people died one after another. After endless arguments on both sides, God rose in anger and said that he would destroy everybody at once unless mankind reached an agreement within the next two days. It was clear to

---

[144] Cf. Egudu, 19-21.

mankind that they could not agree. Each group decided it would present its case directly to God. The group that did not want Death at all decided to send their memorandum through the Dog. The opposing group chose the Tortoise as their agent. It would be a long journey for the Dog and for the Tortoise. To reach God's kingdom they had to travel across seven seas and seven deserts. Those who did not want Death were confident that the Dog would be the first to reach God since he was faster than the Tortoise. As soon as the signal was given, the Dog dashed off amidst the cheers of those who did not want Death. At midday he entered the bush where he sought animal dung for his belly. The Tortoise went on slowly but steadily. Not once did he stop to eat or drink. The Tortoise reached God's kingdom before the Dog. He tapped at God's door and as soon as he was greeted, delivered his message. God accepted it and agreed that Death should take people one after another. Meanwhile, the Dog, who had fallen asleep after a heavy lunch, had stirred and was hurrying to God's kingdom. But he arrived after God had decided that Death should take men. No matter how he begged God would not accept his message. Since that day Death has been taking (people) men one after another.[145]

## Example 3
## Why the Tortoise Lives in River Swamps

The Tortoise and the Beetle lived, cooked, ate, and played together. Indeed they were very good friends even though the Beetle knew that the Tortoise was always scheming and cheating.

While hunting in the forest one day, they killed a big antelope and brought it home to cook. They made a sweet-smelling stew and sat around it, each with a keen appetite. The Tortoise began to cut the meat into small and big pieces. The Beetle knew what he was up to but did not say a word. The Tortoise threw out a few sprinkles of stew and two

---

[145] Cf. Egudu, 23-24.

pieces of meat as a libation to their *chi* (Personal God) for enabling them to kill the antelope. After this they began to eat.

Suddenly the Tortoise stopped eating and ordered the Beetle to do likewise. The Beetle stopped eating and looked up.

„Beetle," said the Tortoise looking furious, „you have no respect for me at all. Why do you dare to touch the big pieces of meat? Do you not know that they are mine for I am the bigger partner?"

„No, I do not know they are yours," the Beetle said calmly and went on munching the morsel in his mouth.

„They are mine and you must not touch them again," the Tortoise warned and reached for a big piece.

The Beetle dipped his hand in the dish and picked up an equally large piece and began to eat.

„Beetle," the Tortoise bellowed, „you must know yourself. You have no respect for your big partner. The small ones are yours."

„You are not my big partner," said the Beetle defiantly.

„We shall see," the Tortoise snorted. „Let us see!" the Beetle said.

Together their hands went into the stew dish and each came up with a large piece of meat. The Tortoise raised his hand and knocked the Beetle into the dish.

The Beetle did not move. He wanted to make the Tortoise think he was dead.

The Tortoise panicked. He touched the Beetle tenderly and pleaded with him to come out. „Friend, Beetle," he said shedding tears, „you are right. There is no bigger partner between us. We should share everything equally. Please come out and let us share the stew. Take whatever pieces you want."

But his pleas were of no use. The Beetle did not come out. Tortoise tiptoed out of the room and ran as fast as his short legs could carry him into the deep forest.

After he was gone the Beetle rose from the dish, cleaned his body of stew, took out some more meat, and ate to his fill. Then he took up a big axe and went to the same forest to which the Tortoise had fled. At the

forest he began to peck at a dry tree with his axe, *koi, koi, koi.*
"Who is that?" the Beetle asked disguising his voice.
"It is the Cow in search of firewood," the Beetle answered, also disguising his voice.
"Good evening Cow. I hope all is well at home."
"Well? Not in the least."
"What can it be?"
"What? Have you not heard of the tragedy of poor Beetle? What could one expect? That wicked friend of his killed him and threw him into a dish of stew they were both eating from."
"Now tell me good Cow, what are people saying about it?"
"Saying? You know the law of the land. The killer does not outlive his victim. All the town has spread out in search of the Tortoise. A prize has been promised to anyone who catches him and hands him over to the people. Oh God, how I wish that prize could be mine!"
There was no need for the Tortoise to ask another question. He turned and ran deeper into the forest. The Beetle cautiously followed him. Once again he hit a dry wood with his axe and the Tortoise asked who it was.
"It is the Giraffe in search of firewood," the Beetle replied. The conversation went on as before. Tortoise once again ran further and further into the forest. The Beetle closely but cautiously followed him until the Tortoise fell headlong into the swamp of a great big river. That is why to this day the Tortoise lives in the swamps of rivers.[146]

The above stories could be used to inculcate a lot of virtues and values into the young minds. They could be used in various forms or ways to teach the children the followings: Creation or origin stories, explanatory

---

[146] Cf. Egudu, 45-48. Also one notices other versions of the same stories as one moves from one part of the Igboland to the other or from one village to the other. However, the most important thing is the fact that such stories are meant for teaching purposes and most especially, children not only learn faster through such very effective teaching-learning method, they also retain what they have learnt almost for life.

stories or to inculcate some virtues into them, such as courage, not giving up easily in difficult moments (the case of the barren woman in example 1 story), always have hope that there is a way out of every problem. One only need to be patient.

The second example story could be used to teach the children that all the people may not agree on particular point all the time, that different people think differently („It was clear to mankind that they could not agree", as the story has it). Again, that it is not always the case that he who calls the police first, wins the case (The Dog was the first to run off as soon as the signal was given, but it was the last to reach the kingdom of God. The Tortoise was the last to move, but he was slow and steady; and he was the first to reach the kingdom of God and delivered the message of death). They should, therefore, learn to be virtuous because virtue stands in the middle.

The third example story could be used to teach them that trick is not good. You can maltreat your friend because you think that you know better than him, but it is not always the case. He can out-wit you and mercilessly subject you to a lasting bad condition, like that of the Tortoise. Let us be satisfied with the much so far because it is premature to be treated in full now. Later, we will have enough time for a detailed method of application of the family bed-time story as it is intended in this work.

There are many other values such as: Respect for Elders, Ancestor cult, Prayer and Sacrifices, Masquerade in its various forms, Community festivities, Music and Dance in all their fascinating and tantalising mellifluous embellishments. These and the other values that are not mentioned here and which we cannot go on enumerating now, (time and space being taken into consideration) could be seen from social point of view, from religious and (or) even from economic points of view, depending from which direction one looks at it. Interestingly enough, among the traditional Igbo there is no dichotomy in life. Life is one, though influenced greatly from religious perspective. We shall see the reason for this interesting and unique phenomenon when we shall discuss the World View of the traditional Igbo.

Before we get into the study of Igbo World View which will bring this chapter to its *terminus ad quem*, we will discuss, but briefly one of the most important rituals in Igbo traditional life. What is this ritual and why is it so important in Igbo traditional life?

### 1.4.6 Igbo Kolanut Rituals

Kolanut ritual is one of the most distinctive and distinguishing characters of the Igbo among the other African peoples. Its significant role among the traditional Igbo cannot be over-emphasised. Below is one of the superlative and cardinal functions of kolanut among the traditional Igbo.

### 1.4.6.1 A Mark of Igbo Socio-cultural and Religious Identity

Inspite of the current turbulent and violent wind of modernism and globalisation and their consequent catastrophic effects on African (Igbo) identity, tradition and culture, kolanut (and its elaborate rituals) still occupies and maintains its unique position and pride of place in Igbo culture and traditional religion. There is no official or important gathering among the traditional Igbo, which does not begin with kolanut and its consequent elaborate rituals.

Ritually, the kolanut is synonymous with the Igbo and its usage in Igbo traditional socio-religious life derives from its ability, as a ritual symbol, to manifest the sacred and to achieve social interaction.[147] As Turner rightly puts it: „symbols produce actions and dominant ritual symbols tend to become focuses of interaction."[148]

Among the ethnic groups in Nigeria, Nwahaghi observes with

---

[147] Cf. Nwahaghi, F. N., The Meaning of Kolanut Ritual Symbol among the Igbo of Nigeria, in: Sevartham, 21<1996>, 93. See also Nwahaghi F. N., The Kolanut as a ritual Symbol among the Igbo, Unpublished Ph.D. Thesis, University of Jos-Nigeria 1994.

[148] Turner, V. W., The Forest of Symbols, Ithaca 1967, 22.

meticulous exactitude that the Yoruba produce the kolanut most, the Hausa consume it most; but the Igbo ritualise it most.[149] Practically, kolanut becomes a powerful focus in the interaction of the Igbo. Its body of rituals envelops a cluster of Igbo values, norms, beliefs, social roles and relationships. From the socio-religious point of view, *Oji Igbo,* with a tranquil sublimity describes the kolanut as the „key which unlocks the hearts of men and the gods in Igbo traditional society."[150]

Among the Igbo, there are a number of activities that can never be performed without kolanut being presented. Nzeako expresses it better thus: „*O nwere otutu ihe o ga-abu ma a hughi oji, ndi mmadu agaghi eme ha. Ihe ndi a bu igbu ehi wee chie echichi, ikwasa ihe n'arusi, ita oji ala, ikpe ikpe ala na idozi okwu, ilu nwunye na ichi echichi*"[151] (There are many functions which in the absence of kolanut, nobody will venture to carry out. They include slaughtering a cow for title-taking, keeping/abandoning the property of a wicked person at the shrine of a deity, eating the Earth-Deity kolanut, settling disputes and peace-making, marriage and conferring of title and title-taking). Nzeako further enumerates other values of kolanut thus: „*Uru ozo di iche iche nke oji bara bu n'iji chere onye obia, ikwa onye nwuru anwu, ichu aja, igbu ichi, ikuputa nwa na omenala ndi ozo di iche iche*"[152] (Other various values of kolanut are for welcoming a stranger, burying the dead, offering sacrifices, tattooing, naming ceremony of a child and other various traditions).

One may then ask, what is this kolanut? What is its significance among the traditional Igbo or what special role does it play in the life of the traditional Igbo in general?

In Webster's Third new International Dictionary, kolanut is defined thus:

---

[149] Nwahaghi, The Kolanut as a ritual Symbol among the Igbo, 24.
[150] *Oji Igbo*, Cultural Division Ministry of Education and Information, Nigeria 1975, 18.
[151] Nzeako, J. U. T., Omenala Ndi Igbo, Nigeria 1986 (Reprint), 3.
[152] Nzeako, 3.

„the bitter caffeine-containing seed of a kola tree that is approximately the size of a chestnut and is chewed as a condiment and stimulant."[153] By physical appearance the size of kolanut could be approximated to that of a chestnut. Some are even smaller than a chestnut. But by function (the outward manifestation of what it is inwardly signifying)- the socio-religious significance, it is no doubt, mightier than a chestnut. When it is presented to a guest, it is never carried with one hand and accepting it with left hand[154] is considered a mark of disrespect, if not an actual offence.

Anigbo is right in his observation that among the Igbo, kolanut assumes a unique position as the only item of food the sharing of which has different commensal implications.[155] It is a ceremonial covenant of hosts and guests with benevolent ancestral spirits and deities in the presence of *Ani*, the Earth Deity. Its role and place in Igbo traditions and customs is very prominent. As we have noted somewhere before, no Igbo tradition or custom could be performed without kolanut. Never! Why so important then?

One of the cherished qualities is that kolanut symbolises friendship and if split and partaken of by others, constitutes a pact of loyalty and communion. C. A. Nwokocha articulates with great sentiments but with sobriety of mind, the significance of kolanut for the traditional Igbo. He writes: „The kola, for us, represents that – call it suprasensible, moral or psychological, social or religious visible sign in which a man, as it were, incarnates his whole being, nay, his heart stripped of hatred, rancour- when offered to a fellow human being invites the latter, in joy and unlimited love, to share with the host, the seat of his life – his heart-

---

[153] Webster's Third New International Dictionary, Vol. II, U.S.A. 1993, 1254.
[154] Throughout Igboland, and in fact in most of African countries, if not all, the use of left hand is abhorred. It is considered a great insult and disrespect to give somebody something with left hand.
[155] Anigbo, O., Commensality and Human Living Among the Igbo, Nsukka 1987, 156.

symbolically represented in the kola."[156]

The presentation and rituals of kolanut among the traditional Igbo is another point of pivotal importance and of great interest. This is done in four principal parts namely: *Iche Oji* (Presentation of kolanut), *Igo Oji* (Consecration of kolanut), *Iwa Oji* (Breaking of kolanut) and *Ike Oji* (Distribution of kolanut).

### 1.4.6.2 The Principal Parts of Kolanut Rituals

We have already mentioned somewhere earlier that there is no important gathering among the traditional Igbo which does not begin with the ritual of kolanut. It has to be recapitulated here again because of its pivotal importance. Further it must have to be distinctly and emphatically said also that in no gathering among the traditional Igbo is kolanut presented and people just begin to share it and to eat.

Below is discussed the ceremonial ritual sequence of kolanut among the traditional Igbo. It begins with *Iche Oji*. What is the process of *Iche Oji* (presentation of kolanut)?

### 1.4.6.2.1 *Iche Oji* (Presentation of kolanut)

The host presents kolanut to the guest(s) but before he hands over the kolanut to his guests, he first touches it with his lips signifying that it is about to be offered in good faith. This symbolic action proves him to be free from malice[157], then it is passed on to the guests with the words:

---

[156] Nwokocha, C. A., Kolanut: Igbo Symbol of Love and Unity (Unpubl. Doctoral Thesis), Rome 1969, 88. For other works on Kolanut see: Onwurah, E., The Igbo Social and Ritual Symbol, in: Sevartham, 15(1990); Onyeabo, O. N., Kolanut in Igbo Culture, in: Sunday Statesman, May 25, 1986, PTR 4; Ene, M. O., Kolanut Communion: Diaspora Dimensions, Internet: Nigeriaworld, May 9, 2001(1-6). It is not yet a finished article at the time it was read. Perhaps the author may finish it up later.

[157] Cf. Basden, G. T., Niger Ibos, London 1938, 162.

„*Ibe anyinu, Oji abila o*" (Brethren Kolanut has arrived) or „*Oha na Eze, anyi enweela Oji*" (lit. Public and king, we have kolanut) or some other similar expressions.

In some places, it is presented to the guests through the eldest relation or the closest neighbour (*Agbata obi*) of the host. He then offers it to his nearest relation or neighbour and it goes on according to this principle or order until every male representative of the communities present has closely seen the kolanut. In most cases, names are mentioned as the kolanut is being handed over to the next such as '*Mazi Okeke, Oji abiala*' (Mr. Okeke, kolanut has come). On receiving the kolanut he responds: '*Daalu Oji*' (Thanks for the kolanut) and then passes on to the next person in the same manner. Some times an appropriate proverb is given, which may set the theme of the gathering.

The mentioning of names as the kolanut is being passed round avails all present the opportunity to get acquainted with everyone present. By following a certain pertain of relaying kolanut, the people present find out who comes from where. For example, sons of women born in the kindred are given some priority over other guests; sons-in-law and their kindred also receive special positioning. By establishing who hails from where, they know who is who. Hence, whenever kolanut embarks on this 'relay race', it is said that *Oji agawala njem itu agbulu* (kolanut has embarked on a journey to establish lineage). It is in the course of this 'journey' that the whole lineages are linked.

The presentation of kolanut moves from the most senior and goes down the line in that order until it comes to the youngest. This movement often attracts some penalties when a person who is not familiar with the genealogical history of his community is handed over the kolanut and he passes it on to the wrong hands. To avoid this misfortune, an expert is looked for before hand, who performs this function accurately.

After the presentation of kolanut and all the accompanying fanfare, it is returned to the host with the words *Oji Eze di Eze n'aka* (The King's kolanut is in his hands). This saying is important; it confers supremacy on the host by popular proclamation. Subsequent to the next phase, the host must select at least one kolanut and hand it over to the guest from the most distant community for taking home with the saying: *Oji lue uno, okwue ebe osiri puta* (When kolanut reaches home, it will say from whence it has come).[158] This must be done before the kolanut is consecrated. Otherwise, if you give the guest a consecrated kolanut, what is he going to tell his ancestors and kindred deities? That the kolanut already offered to other deities is being 'recycled' to them? Why should a consecrated kolanut be re-consecrated at another ceremony?

If there are enough kolanuts, the celebrant could call each representative of states or nations or clans present, to come and take a kolanut for going home. Thereafter the remaining, are then consecrated, split and shared. Who consecrates the kolanut and how does he go about the consecration?

### 1.4.6.2.2 *Igo Oji* (Consecration of kolanut)

According to Igbo tradition, it is the privilege of the eldest male present at any occasion to consecrate the kolanut. This is not contested. He takes up a kolanut, clear his throat, for the Igbo say that „*Ikenye kwachaa akpili ya, ndi mmuo egee nti*" (When an elder clears his throat, the Spirits listen very well to hear him), raises it up towards heaven, calling on *Chukwu* (God) and throwing out some pieces in propitiation while beckoning on the ancestors and other friendly Deities and Spirits to come and partake of the kolanut. There is no written or stipulated formula for the consecration of kolanut.

In the prayer for the consecration of the kolanut, long life, good health, wealth, many children, progress and welfare of all are prayed for, among other needs. Wicked people and dangerous, vengeful spirits are wished

---

[158] Kolanut (*Oji*) does not actually move or speak. This expression means that when the person to whom the kolanut was given gets back to his home, he brings out the kolanut and say where it was given to him, that is, where he visited and was properly received.

disastrous end.
A typical prayer for the consecration of kolanut goes thus:
*Obasi bi n'elu, bia taa Oji o* – God in heaven come and eat kolanut!
*Nna nna anyi ha welunu oji taa o* – Our Ancestors take kolanut and eat!
*Igwekala bianu welu oji o* – Sky deity come and take kolanut!
*Umu Mmuo n'eche anyi, na ejekwara anyi ozi bianu taa oji o* – The spirits that guide us and run message for us come and eat kolanut!
*Anyi na-asi onye noro, ibe ya noro* – We are saying let everyone live!
*Egbe bere, Ugo bere, ma nke si ibe ya ebela, nku kwaa ya o* – Let Kite perch and Eagle also perch, anyone who refuses the other to perch, let its wings be broken to pieces! (fracture).[159]
*Onye si n'anyi agaghi ano, ya buru nwa-okuko uzo nakpue ura* – Let he who say we should not live, go to bed (die) before the chickens go in for sleep![160]
*Ogonogo ndu onye obula* – Long life for all!
*Onye wetara oji wetara ndu* – He who brings kolanut brings life!
*Anyi choro ndu, n'ife aga-eji zua ndu* – We want life and the things with which to maintain life!
*Anyi choro omumu, udo, oganiru, na aru ike* – We want many children, peace, progress and strong health!
Other requests then follow and those present always answer „*Isee o*"! (let it be so), as the petitioner prays. At the end of the prayer, one or two people from the group may spontaneously ship in the words „*Ka igolu ka olelu*" (as you have prayed so shall it be done), to give firm assurance that the prayers are heard. After this comes the breaking of the kolanut (*Iwa Oji*).

---

[159] Here one observes the traditional Igbo undiluted sense of value and respect for life, justice and fair play, live and let live. And to say the least, the value of harmony and community life.
[160] This means: let the person who would not want us to live any more, die so early, that is, at the prime of life.

What is the tradition for the breaking of kolanut and who breaks the kolanut among the traditional Igbo?

### 1.4.6.2.3 *Iwa Oji* (Breaking of kolanut)

There are various traditions for the breaking of kolanut in Igboland. It is not uniformed throughout the land. As Nzeako rightly explains, in places like Onitsha, Nnewi, Njikoka, Awka and some Riverrine areas, only the eldest present in the gathering has the honour and the privilege of breaking the kolanut. But in places like Ngwo, Nsukka, Owerri, Orlu, Abakaliki, some part of Umuahia and Ngwa, the youngest present in the group breaks the kolanut.[161]

In places like Ohaji-Egbema and Oguta, it is the inalienable right of title-holder to break kolanut in any gathering. When no title-holder is present, then the eldest or the host takes the function.

Generally, women do not break kolanut in Igbo custom and tradition. However, in some places like Asaba, Issele Ukwu, Ubulu Ukwu, their tradition allows titled women to break kolanut.

After the presentation, consecration and breaking of kolanut with its elaborate rituals, the people do not stop there and enter into another thing. No! The kolanut has to be eaten. And it is not 'a matter of serve yourself' system, it has to be served. In other words, it has to be distributed. What then is the process and how is it distributed and by whom?

### 1.4.6.2.4 *Ike Oji* (Distribution of kolanut)

The distribution of kolanut is in the order of *senioribus-junioribus*. It begins from the right hand side of the host or the elder, then goes to the left. The „right hand" (*Aka-nni* or *aka-nri* or *aka-nli*) signifies *Ikenga-* a symbol of dignity and respect. When it goes from the left hand side first, then it is considered odd and people scorn at it because it is believed that

---

[161] Cf. Nzeako, 4.

*"Oji gbara aka-ekpe na ebute ogbalu ufie"* (kolanut that passes from the left hand side during the distribution, brings along bad omen with it).

The men are served first before the women, where they are part of the gathering. In some places where the women are honoured with some traditional titles, such privileged women are allowed to take kola before the untitled men.

Generally the youngest male in the gathering passes the plate of kola to the members of the gathering community. Only on rare occasions are children permitted to partake of the kola. For example: at the naming ceremony of a new-born baby and (or) at the celebration of its one year of birth (birthday).

The distribution and eating of the kolanut (by all present except children as already indicated) mark the end of the kolanut ritual. Whoever is present and did not partake of the kolanut, and did not at least touch it, is seen as an enemy (in and) to this gathering or at least considered to have some 'skeleton in his cupboard'. And he is watched closely with utmost consternation in this gathering.

Nevertheless, it has to be noted at this juncture that in certain situations, kolanut do symbolise an idea in the mind yet to be communicated. Under such circumstance the normal is reversed. Instead of the host presenting the kolanut to the guest, the reverse is the case. For example, a guest who wishes to secure a favour or services from his host, may present kolanut to him. In such situation, while receiving such kolanut the host usually asks his guest: *"Kedu ije Oji a"*? (What is the purpose of this kolanut?). Until the guest discloses his intention for presenting it, the kolanut remains an idea in the mind.

However, the most important point, which we want to emphasise is the significant and pivotal role kolanut plays among the traditional Igbo throughout Igboland.

From what we have said so far, one notices another very important aspect, an essential value of kolanut. It is not just broken like that and people begin to partake of it. No! Prayers are said over it and the ancestors and other important spirits and deities are invoked. This would introduce us into the theme of prayer, which we would not like to get into specifically due to time factor, but at the same time we cannot avoid it because there is no dichotomy between social and religious life of the traditional Igbo. In the words of Van Gennep, among the traditional Igbo, "no act is entirely free of the sacred."[162]

Traditional Igbo religion is unlike, in the words of R. Hickey, „the Christianity of the enlightenment whose world-view had effected the distinction between the sacred and the profane, the material and spiritual, religion and science."[163] If prayer is part of religion and in deed 'a religion's primary mode of expression'[164], according to Heiler, and religion is part of the traditional Igbo life, it follows, therefore, that prayer is part of traditional Igbo life and vice versa. This point will be made clearer as we advance further in our work. From our next topic - Igbo World view, one understands the quintessential and fundamental clarifications underlying the traditional Igbo belief and life in general.

## 1.5 Igbo World-View

The world-view of a people is the „complex of the people's beliefs and attitudes concerning the origin, nature, structure of the universe and the interaction of its being with particular reference to man."[165]

Regarding the origin of the universe, the Igbo have a deep-rooted belief in the created universe (*Uwa*) and the Creator (*Chukwu* or *Chineke*). The Igbo attitude to these realities is that of complete and total dependence on what the Creator (*Chukwu* or *Chineke*) has in stock for him. This is clearly manifested in numerous typical Igbo names such as:

---

[162] Gennep, V. A:, The Rites of Passage, Chicago 1960, 3.
[163] Hickey, R. (ed.), Modern Missionary Documents and Africa, „Reports on Africa, at the 1974 Synod of Bishops Rome", Dublin 1982, 207.
[164] Cf. Heiler, F., Prayer: A Study in the History and Psychology of Religion, (trans.) McComb, S., Oxford University Press 1958, 358.
[165] Metuh, E. I., God and Man in African Religion, London 1981, 48.

*Odinakachukwu* (All are in God's hands), *Chinenye* or *Chinyere* (Only God gives), *Chukwuma* (Only God knows), *Nkechinyere* (Whatever God gives), *Ajuluchukwu* (Asked of God?), *Akachukwu* (God's help), *Akuchukwu* (Wealth from God), *Cheluchukwu* (Wait for God), *Chukwuebuka* (God is immensely great), *Chukwuadika* (God is marvellous), *Chukwuafugourum* (God has looked upon my affliction), *Chukwuagboso* (God does not run away), *Chukwuagozie* or *Chukwugozie* (God has blessed us or God bless!), *Chukwualuka* (God has done mighty things for me), *Chukwuamaka* (God is extremely good), *Chukwuanugo* (God has heard), *Chukwuatorapu* (God has freed us), *Chukwuazoputa* (God is salvation), *Chukwubawanye* (May God increase blessings).

As far as creation is concerned, God is central in the mind of the traditional Igbo and he (God) is the origin of the inter-relationship of beings in the universe. He is the origin, the beginning and the end (*Der Anfang und das Ende*) of man's life and he remains present and watchful over creation. P. Schineller, in no uncertain terms clearly affirms the above view thus: „Truly we are never far from the divine and its various manifestations. The world is God's creation, and God remains present and watchful over creation."[166]

For the Igbo, (*Chukwu*) God is the origin of all things. Everything comes from him and everything shall go back to him. They use the Ballard translated below to trace and prove that everything originated from God. It runs thus:

>What happened to Nwaniga?
>Breadfruit killed Nwaniga
>What happened to breadfruit?
>Wedge split the breadfruit
>What happened to the wedge?
>Termites ate up the wedge

---

[166] Schineller, 210.

What happened to the termites?
Hen ate up the termites
What happened to the hen?
Hawk carried the hen
What happened to the hawk?
Gun killed the hawk
What happened to the gun?
Blacksmith made the gun
What happened to the blacksmith?
God made the blacksmith.
In Igbo, the original version, it runs thus:
Gini mere Nwaniga?
Nwaniga-O! Nwaniga!
Na Ukwa dagbulu Nwaniga
Nwaniga-O! Nwaniga!
Gini mere ukwa ahu?
Na mkpo mawara ukwa
Na ukwa dagbulu Nwaniga
Nwaniga-O! Nwaniga!
Gini mere mkpo ahu?
Na akika tara mkpo
Na mkpo mawara ukwa
Na ukwa dagbulu Nwaniga
Nwaniga-O! Nwaniga!
Gini mere akika ahu?
Na okuko tara akika
Na akika tara mkpo
Na mkpo mawara ukwa
Na ukwa dagbulu Nwaniga
Nwaniga-O! Nwaniga!
Gini mere okuko ahu?
Na egbe buuru okuko
Na okuko tara akika

>    Na akika tara mkpo
>    Na mkpo mawara ukwa
>    Na ukwa dagbulu Nwaniga
>    Nwaniga-O! Nwaniga!
>    Gini mere egbe ahu?
>    Na Uzu kpuru egbe
>    Na egbe gbulu egbe
>    Na egbe buuru okuko
>    Na okuko tara akika
>    Na akika tara mkpo
>    Na mkpo mawara ukwa
>    Na ukwa dagbulu Nwaniga
>    Nwaniga-O! Nwaniga!
>    Gini mere Uzu ahu?
>    Na Chukwu kere Uzu
>    Na Uzu kpuru egbe
>    Na egbe gburu egbe
>    Na egbebuuru okuko
>    Na okuko tara akika
>    Na akika tara mkpo
>    Na mkpo mawara ukwa
>    Na ukwa dagbulu Nwaniga
>    Nwaniga-O! Nwaniga![167]

Concerning the nature and structure of the universe, the traditional Igbo have a vision of one world structured into two parts namely: the visible and the invisible. The visible is the world of man and other physical things while the invisible is the spiritual world.

For V.C. Uchendu, „The Igbo world is a real one in every aspect. There is the world of man peopled by all created beings and things, both animate and inanimate. The Spirit world is the abode of the Creator, the

---

[167] Ogbalu, F. C., Igbo Institutions and Customs, Onitsha (n.d.), 49-50.

deities, the disembodied and malignant spirits ...."[168] Beings in both visible world of man and other created things and the spiritual world interact, but in a mysterious way. Uchendu explains it this way: „There is constant interaction between the world of man and the world of the spirits, the visible and invisible forces."[169] D. Richards describes the constant interaction as that of interdependence. For him: „The spirits need us just as we need them, just as spirits need matter to give form, and matter needs spirit to give it force, being and reality."[170]

On account of the above vision of the world, the traditional Igbo take life as a continuous and dynamic process from the unknown to the known and vice versa. Thus life is no longer considered in a straight line of action in this world but as a cyclic movement in accordance with the rhythm of nature. A rhythm which according to Mbiti, includes: „Birth, puberty, initiation, marriage, procreation, old age, death, entry into the company of the departed and finally entry into the company of the spirits."[171]

The spiritual realm of the traditional Igbo world-view is a densely populated world. According to Madubuko however, it is not an amorphous or chaotic world. There is a discernible hierarchy of the spiritual beings- thus invalidating any polytheistic interpretation of the Igbo religion, polytheism as Paul Tillich has aptly remarked as „a qualitative and not a quantitative concept. It is not a belief in a plurality of gods but rather the lack of a unifying and transcending ultimate which determines its character."[172]

Space in the physical world, according to the traditional Igbo, is three-

---

[168] Uchendu, 11.
[169] Uchendu, 11.
[170] Richards, D., The Implications of African-American Spirituality, in: Asante, M. K. and Asante, K. W., (eds.), African Culture, New Jersey 1993, 209.
[171] Mbiti, African Religions, 19.
[172] Madubuko, 19.

dimensional.[173] Above is the sky (*Igwe* or *elu-igwe*). It is regarded as the dwelling place or the abode of God (*Chukwu*) and the invisible spirits[174]. In the middle is the earth (*Uwa* or better said, *Ala*), the habitation of human beings and other visible created realities. The third dimension of space is the earth beneath, *Ala mmuo* (the spirit world of dead human beings and other non-human spirits).

G. Parrinder wonderfully describes the Igbo world-view with a diagrammatical image of a triangle. At the top of the triangle is God, the head (and source) of all powers. On the two sides of the triangle are the next greatest powers, the gods and the ancestors. At the base are lower forces, with which magic and medicine are concerned.[175] He observes that man is in the middle and must live in harmony with all the powers

---

[173] Cf. Kalu, O. U., Precarious Vision, „The African Perception of his World", Readings in African Humanities, African Cultural Development, Enugu 1982, 40.

[174] As Metuh, E. I., properly and rightly noted in his book: African Religions in Western Conceptual Schemes, 10, there are in the traditional Igbo world, 'multiplicity of spiritual beings'. However these spiritual beings could be divided into two broad categories namely: the created spiritual beings and the uncreated spiritual beings. The created spirits could be further divided into three categories namely: i) The spirits who have once lived in human form in the physical world, but are now separated from human body and are living in the spiritual world. Within this category is also a group of spirits who, either because of their bad life while in human form, or because they were not accorded a befitting burial after death due to one reason or the other, their spirits are not welcome in the spiritual world. Consequently, they prowl and hibernate in the human world and afflict the human beings. ii) The spirits known as 'the personal *Chi*'. Each human being among the traditional Igbo is believed to have this personal *Chi* assigned to him by God (*Chukwu*) at the moment of conception, as guardian spirit. iii) The spirits that are connected with nature such as *Anyanwu* (the sun spirit), *Ala* (the earth spirit) and *Igwe* (the sky spirit).

[175] Cf. Parrinder, G., African Mythology, London 1975, 15.

that effect his life, family and work.[176] These powers, according to Parrinder, extend into the animal world, for animals have great forces, which need to be watched and harnessed if possible. Even supposedly inorganic nature is not dead, but may be the vehicle of power.[177]

A world-view also tells the society how it is to feel about, evaluate and react to the world and all reality. In other words, certain values, interests and attitudes are so basic to the culture that they trigger deep emotional reactions throughout most, if not all of culture. One of the ways through which the traditional Igbo express their ideas, feelings and (or) values of their world-view is proverb.

For A. L. Balling, „*Sprichwörter* (Proverbs) *sind Weisheitstropfen in einer Flut von Worten.*"[178] Proverb has been described to a great extent as an international wanderer.[179] Although we agree with Balling that „*Keine Kultur ist ganz ohne Sprichwörter, kein Stamm ohne 'geflügelte Worte' und gemeinverständliche Redewendungen,*"[180] but it must be

---

[176] Cf. Parrinder, African Mythology, 15.
[177] Cf. Parrinder, African Mythology, 15.
[178] Balling, *Lebensweisheit aus Schwarz-Afrika*, 13.
[179] Cf. Ojoade, J. O., Pareomiographical Evidences of Ethical Education in Traditional Africa with Christian and Islamic Analogues, in: Metuh, E. I., (ed.), Nigerian Cultural Heritage, Jos 1990, 15.
[180] Balling, 13. Balling is, however, not alone in this view. Kelso, with the same accolade and accustomed directness conveys a similar view thus: "Proverbs are of universal occurrence., there is no speech or language in which they are not found... no race, whether high or low in the scale of civiliasation, has been without them." With unparalleled intellectual boldness he formulated the idea that: "The pages of Aristotle and Plato are liberally sprinkled with terse, pithy sayings and Cicero's writings teem with proverbs. More than this, proverbs and gnomic literature were two of the seed-plots of Greek philosophy." And with abiding importance he observes that in Greek Philiosophy, "the number of proverbs was legion, and they were used by the learned rabbis, were current in social intercourse, and werefavourite means of imparting ethical instruction to the

known that in no part of the globe are proverbs as important as in the continent of Africa,[181] and among the Africans especially the traditional Igbo.

The observation of F. C. Ogbalu has never been disputed. He observes and reports thus: „Certain towns among the Ibos (Igbo) have the special reputation of being able to do all their conferences, and discussions in nothing but proverbs."[182] Ogbalu goes further to explain that: „Ibo (Igbo) proverbs are accumulation of Ibo (Igbo) experiences throughout the history of the Ibos (Igbo). In absence of any written history, they serve as the medium through which much can be learnt about the Ibos (Igbo). Their past history, their philosophy of life and family structure, their politics, and religion can best be learnt through the proverbs."[183]

Ogbalu makes no mistake as he says: „The proverbs too depict the Ibo (Igbo) man as being wonderfully observant; is it the references to the behaviour and life of both plant and animal world, human nature, and the physical world that the proverbs do not show the Ibo (Igbo) man as a mastermind?"[184] Here a few examples are very necessary so as to make the point clear. The Igbo say: „*Ijiji so anu anaghi ebu onu*" (Flies that stay close to dead animals do not suffer hunger); „*Oke soro Ngwere daa mmiri, o koo Ngwere, O gaghi ako Oke*" (When a rat enters into water with a lizard, lizard's body dries up easily but the rat will suffer cold before its body dries up); „*Achoba anya anu, e jee n'isi ya*" (When you want to see the eye of an animal, you look at its head); „*Nti di abuo, ma na odighi anu okwu abuo*" (lit. Man has two ears but he cannot hear two different things at the same time).

---

youth." See Kelso, J. A., "Proverbs", in: Hasting, J., (ed.), Encyclopaedia of Religion and Ethics, Vol. X, Edinburgh 1918, (412-415) 413-414.
[181] Cf. Ojoade, 135.
[182] Ogbalu, F. C., Ilu Igbo (The Book of Igbo Proverbs), Onitsha 1965, 2.
[183] Ogbalu, Ilu Igbo, 2.
[184] Ogbalu, Ilu Igbo, 2.

What area of the Igbo life did proverb not touch? Ogbalu also observes thus: „A thorough knowledge of the Ibo (Igbo) proverbs will enable any person to predict the reaction of the Ibo (Igbo) man to a situation; it will enable him to understand his attitude, his mind and those of his kinsmen generally."[185]

„Inspite of influence of the West, one cannot help breaking his speech in English in order to insert one or more Igbo proverbs here and there as there is a feeling that it is only by so doing that the point in question is completely driven home."[186] For the traditional Igbo,"*Inu bu mmanu Igbo ji eli okwu*" (proverb is the oil with which the Igbo eat/chew words/speech).

Proverbs are for the traditional Igbo, not only for rhetorical embellishment, they are also instruments of diplomacy for going through difficult situations of human interaction. The basket for euphemism and diplomacy are proverbs.[187] J. O. Ojoade enumerating the qualities, values and importance of proverbs for the traditional African says: „The fact that the proverbs express moral and value judgements, indicating what is right or wrong and what is good or bad, gives them an important place in African ethical teachings."[188] He explains further: „Proverbs are favourite vehicle for society-sanctioned ethical instruction for members of African society- youth and elders, the lowly and the high alike. No student of proverb can fail to notice the fact that the proverb is commonly utilised to reprove any member of the society who misbehaves, to praise or ensure, to give support to or withdraw support from a venture and to indoctrinate members concerning the acceptable standard of social behaviour."[189] Kelso goes steps further as he says: „So popular was it (Proverb), and so highly esteemed, that it was used to

---

[185] Ogbalu, Ilu Igbo, 2.
[186] Ogbalu, Ilu Igbo, 2-3.
[187] Cf. Madubuko, 19.
[188] Ojoade, 136.
[189] Ojoade, 136.

elucidate problems in almost every sphere and circumstance of life. Proverbs were considered efficacious in removing doubts and difficulties; they were quoted to elucidate names and obscure passages of Scripture; amid sorrow, they shed comfort, and in social gatherings they increased the good cheer."[190]

Kelso smartly observes that „with a proverb it was customary to speed the parting guest, and with one a literary man found an appropriate close for his book."[191] Every class of society takes delight in the proverb, from the emperor on his throne to the begger in his hovel.[192]

In races of advanced civilisation and culture, proverb plays no part in the teaching of formal schools, but continues to exercise a potent influence on popular ideals of conduct and conception of character. Proverbs continue to be employed by poets and religious teachers to impress upon the minds of the masses fundamental principles of morality and noble living. The authority of proverbs is acknowledged by the people generally because they constitute the hoard of a nation's wisdom, the silent unconscious accumulation that grows up in a long lapse of time.[193]

The above explanations are most practically seen in the life of the traditional Igbo of Africa. The nature of interaction in any society, at least in terms of ideal culture, is more often than not communicated to the members by the instrumentality of proverbs. This is exemplified in the traditional Igbo society. Hence F. Arinze succinctly declares: „For them (the traditional Igbo), to speak always in very plain and simple language is to talk like inexperienced little children ... Hence the uninitiated could be present when the hoary-headed discuss important matters, and yet understand absolutely nothing."[194]

In the presence of visitors or foreigners, the traditional Igbo can speak to

---

[190] Kelso, "Proverbs", 415.
[191] Kelso, "Proverbs", 415.
[192] Kelso, "Proverbs", 415.
[193] Kelso, "Proverbs", 415.
[194] Arinze, 3.

one another in proverbs and the wise will understand but the unwise will not. The Igbo express it this way: „*A tualu omanu, omalu. Ma atualu Ofeke, ofenye isi na ofia*" (when you speak in proverbs to a wise person, he will understand. But speak to a fool in proverbs, he will make mess of the whole thing). They also say: „*A tulu inu (ilu) ka ogbaa Ofeke ghalii* „ (It is spoken in proverbs so that the fool cannot understand).
Hence proverbs constitute one of the most valuable media of instruction and communication among the Igbo. They are also used by the Igbo to express what they like and what they do not like in certain directions in quite an unmistakable manner. Some of these proverbs expose the ironical wit of the people, they state what ought to be done, pretending that this is actually being done.[195]
Proverbs are also cited to indicate values such as humility, gratitude, carefulness in speaking, respect for parents and elders, adaptability, co-operation, hospitality, truthfulness and honesty, heedfulness, the golden rule and moderation. Some are used to rediculize gossips, rumour mongers and hypocrites.[196] For the Traditional Igbo then, proverbs touch upon every conceivable phenomenon under the sky. Put in other words, there is no conceivable situation in life for which the proverbial wisdom of the Igbo cannot furnish some apposite citation. In Igbo proverbs (and in proverbs in general) the greatest events are often told in the fewest words.

## 1.6 Conclusion

Up to this moment an attempt is made to present an idea of who the traditional Igbo are, (who form the centre around which this work revolves): their origin and location, demography, values and rituals, their world-view and how they express it in life. Because they form the basis

---

[195] Ojoade, 136.
[196] Ojoade, 136.

for this work, an adequate knowledge of the above mentioned become very necessary for the best result of our study.

From what we have seen so far, the history of the Igbo has been seen as a problem area and its present condition described as ropes of sand, for the reason that there have been no official written records *ab initio*. What obtained were mostly from oral tradition, usually from the elders.

But „in Africa more than anywhere else oral tradition is an integral part of the historian's basic material and greatly widens its scope."[197] Generally, African history and particularly the Igbo history cannot be written excluding from historical investigation the voice of the time represented by oral tradition.

Ki-Zerbo clearly explains that: „Oral tradition takes its place as a real living museum, conserver and transmitter of the social and cultural creations stored up by people said to have no written records. This spoken history is a very frail thread by which to trace our way back through the dark twists of the labyrinth of time."[198] He goes further: „Those who are its custodians are hoary-headed old men with cracked voices, memories often dim, and a stickler's insistence on etiquette (*vieillesse oblige!*), as behoves potential ancestors. They are like the last remaining islets in a landscope that was once imposing and coherent, but which is now eroded, flattened and thrown into disorder by the sharp waves of modernism. Latter-day fossils!"[199]

Bringing to limelight the pivotal importance of the said custodians (hoary-headed old men ...) of the oral tradition, Ki-Zerbo says: „Whenever one of them dies a fibre of Ariadne's thread is broken, a fragment of the landscope literally disappears underground."[200]

---

[197] Obenga, T., Sources and Specific Techniques used in African History; in: Ki-Zerbo, J. (ed.), General History of Africa, Vol.1, Heinemann-California-Unesco 1981, 82.
[198] Ki-Zerbo, J., (ed.), General History of Africa, Vol.1, 1981, 7.
[199] Ki-Zerbo, 7.
[200] Ki-Zerbo, 7.

He sees oral tradition as „by far the most intimate of historical sources, the most rich, the one which is fullest of the sap of authenticity."[201] Concluding, he sums up his clear argument with this simple but condensed time honoured African proverb: 'The mouth of an old man smells bad, but it says good and salutary things'.[202]

Anthropologists and historians who see the history of the Igbo as a problem area and describe its present condition as ropes of sand, should now ask themselves how far their knowledge of the Igbo is, how far do they know and understand the people, their language and their culture. Here L. E. Esomonu's testimony becomes *ad rem*. He testifies that „to learn a people's culture, to gain an adequate insight into their thought patterns, their beliefs, tradition and institutions, to understand their ... values, their philosophy of life and their vision, it is indispensable to know their language, and their proverbs which are part of the former."[203]

His conclusion that „language is the carrier of culture and the mother toung constitutes the warp and woof of the mental life of a given people"[204], has neither been disputed nor disproved.

Further in our study, it is mentioned that the Igbo people occupy geographically the south-eastern part of Nigeria, but they could be located in any part of the globe inhabitable. Their total population has been a matter of estimation but they are known to be 'a numerous nation'.

Values, Rituals and world-view and their importance to the Igbo, bring to limelight the dept and richness of the people's culture and traditional religion. Are all these not already very fertile ground for inculturating the Christian faith!

It is now mature to discuss Initiation in the traditional Igbo culture and religion and this forms the basis for our next chapter.

---

[201] Ki-Zerbo, 7.
[202] Cf. Ki-Zerbo, 7.
[203] Esomonu, 131.
[204] Esomonu, 131.

# Chapter Two

# Initiation in the Traditional Igbo Culture and Religion

## 2.1 Introduction

The term „initiation" usually possesses a special meaning, referring to male circumcision, female puberty rites, or induction into secret societies. There is, however, a wider context of initiation, the whole life-process of cultural (religious) education, which includes other social celebrations, as well as the socialisation of the young and the continuation of this learning process in adult life.[205]

However, our own situation here demands that we study initiation in the traditional Igbo Culture and Religion from a wider context and perspective. This is given to the fact that in African traditional life there is no dichotomy between religious, cultural and social life. It is without playing on sentiments but a statement of fact that Mbiti opened his well-known book 'African Religions and Philosophy' with equally well-known statement: „Africans are notoriously religious."[206] In similar vein, Shorter asserts with more clarity that: „Religion is interwoven with the entire fabric of African social and cultural life."[207] If the Igbo are part and parcel of Africa, then what is said of Africa applies automatically to the Igbo also, unless on some special issues, which will be then properly indicated. A proper example will be the Igbo idea of initiation, which will be studied immediately below.

---

[205] Cf. Shorter, A., Christianity And The African Imagination: After the African Synod Resources for Inculturation, Nairobi 1996, 87.
[206] Mbiti, J. S., African Religions and Philosophy, London 1969, 1.
[207] Shorter, A., Christianity And The African Imagination, 28.

## 2.2 Igbo Idea of Initiation

We have earlier mentioned about corporate existence in the Igbo world. In Africa, the sense of community is more than a place or common territory where people meet. It is more than a social organisation or a collection of individuals living in close quaters to each other.[208] Among the traditional Igbo, in their community life, biological birth is not enough. Nature brings the child into the world, but society creates the child into a social being, a corporate person. For it is the community which must protect the child, feed it, bring it up, educate it and in many other ways incorporate it into the wider community.[209] Mbiti says that „children are the buds of society".[210] For this reason the community takes it upon itself to 'make' or 'produce' the individual. The child must go through the rites of incorporation for him to be fully integrated into the entire society. This process of incorporation continues throughout the physical life of the individual, during which he passes from one stage of corporate life into the other, usually from a „lower" stage to a „higher" one. The final stage comes when he dies, and even then, he is further ritually incorporated into privileges and his own responsibilities towards himself and other people –his family (immediate and extended).

This process of incorporation from one stage of being to the other be it ontological, biological, social or religious, has been described by Van

---

[208] Cf. Townes, E. M., Searching for Paradise, in: Hopkins, D., (ed.), Black Faith and Public Talk, New York 1999, 110.

[209] Cf. Mbiti, African Religions and Philosophy, 110.

[210] Mbiti, African Religions and Philosopy, 110. He says: "Children are the buds of society, and every birth is the arrival of 'spring' when life shoots out and the community thrives. The birth of a child is, therefore, the concern not only of the parents but of many relatives including the living and the departed. Kinship plays an important role here, so that a child cannot be exclusively 'my child' but only 'our child'.

Gennep as 'Rites of Passage'.[211] It is interchangeably used with 'Life Crisis Ritual'.[212] But whatever the case may be, the main point of emphasis is that this process is a ritual one to earmark not just a change of position in the society or in life, from what may be considered a „lower" status to a „higher" one, but it is a transition. In the process of this transition, metamorphosis takes place after which the person in question becomes a new person in a new life circle.

This is however, not an easy process. Patrick Gesch makes it clear that „the sufferings of the candidates, which sometimes amount to torture, the possibility of severe personal disturbance, suicide, and attention to death from various means while in initiation enclosures, point further in the direction that initiation is not simply some admission to a club, but is the hope of a dramatic change, which cannot normally be presumed to happen, but in symbolic terms at least, is worth any price."[213] When once

---

[211] Van Gennep, A., The Rites of Passage, (trs.) Vizedom, M. B. and Caffe, G. L., London 1960.

[212] Cf. Metuh, E. I., Comparative Studies Of African Traditional Religions, Onitsha 1987, 197. Enyioha, U. B., says: "Although different terms are used for these rites-"transition rituals", "life-crisis rituals" or "initiation" – the common usage has been "rites of passage". See Enyioha, U. B., The Pastoral Significance of Traditional African Concept of Rites of Passage, 18 in: Ogbomoso Journal of Theology, No. 7, Dec., 1992. This is however his personal view. See also Amponsah, K., Topics on West African Traditional Religion, Ghana 1977, 60; Katonah, J., "Hospitalization: A Rite of Passage", in: Holst, L. E., Hospital Ministry: The Role of the Chaplain Today, New York 1985 (55-76), 55. The idea of the above writers are certainly influenced by their subject matter, and they are right in their individual specific directions. But we prefer to use the term "initiation" here because it is deeper in meaning than the other terms and it is most suited in our subject matter.

[213] Gesch, P. F., The Dynamic Element in Traditional Religion, 282-283, in: Piskaty, K., and Rzepkowski, H., (eds.), *Studia Instituti Missiologici*, No. 56, Germany 1993.

this process has taken place, it is irrevocable and it takes place only once in one's life time. For example, the biological birth of a particular child takes place only once. Puberty rite takes place only once in one's life time. One is initiated into *Ozo* title only once, and so on. This idea is also found among the Akan of Ghana. According to Kofi: „*Das menschliche Leben als solches ist ein Zyklus von Geburt, Pubertät, Ehe, Zeugung von Nachkommenschaft, Tod und Leben nach dem Tode. Der Mensch kann nicht für immer in einem Daseinszustand verharren, er muß sich auf den nächsten zu bewegen; zur Gestaltung eines fließenden überganges werden besondere Riten vollzogen, um sicherzustellen, daß keine Bruchstellen auftreten und wandel und Erneuerung unaufhörlich bestehen bleiben.*"[214] The view of Basu fits in here. He describes initiation as „the entry into a new stage of life with its appropriate duties and responsibilities, the successful discharge of which requires special training and also the rites marking this entry."[215]

From the above point of view, one sees that the inclusion of the passage of time or events such as New Year, new moon, planting season, harvest festivals and national liberation or independence, as 'Rites of Passage' according to Metuh[216], is not correct to be called initiation *qua tale*. Initiation as such has only one chance in a given situation and that is why its process takes time and in most cases, very hard and almost unbearable. 'Rites of passage' is a general term or idea but initiation is very particular.

Metuh's argument to support the fact that puberty rite is not excluded from initiation, confirms the above point. He argues: „The scope of

---

[214] Edusei, K., *Für uns ist Religion die Erde, auf der wir leben*, Stuttgart 1985, 26.
[215] Basu, A., Disksa, in: Bleeker, C. J., Initiation: Studies in History of Religions, Netherlands 1965 (81-86), 81.
[216] Cf. Metuh, Comparative Studies, 197. See also Bleeker, C. J., Some Introductory Remarks on the Significance of Initiation, 19; Mbiti, J. S., African Religions and Philosophy, 122.

initiation rites ... is not primarily to celebrate the physical changes brought about by adolescent life (though rites of this nature are sometimes included), but to make an individual a man or a woman, fit to be one ...."[217] For him, therefore, „characteristic features are rites which mark separation from the infantile asexual world, followed by rites of incorporation into the world of sexuality as a man or woman."[218] He goes further to explain that „these are rites which mark change from passive to active membership in the community with the attaching privileges and obligations. During these rites, candidates are taught the implications of community life –living together, obedience to the elders, public spiritedness, endurance, and entrusted with the secrets of the esoteric traditions and lore of the group. Above all they are introduced to the communion with the ancestors and other titulary spirits of the clan."[219] Finally, Metuh concludes: „These initiation rites prepare the young people for marriage and procreation which are means of implementing the sacred duty of perpetuating and strengthening the life-force of the clan."[220]

Initiation, therefore, has specific effective aims. But it occurs in juxtaposition and combination with rites of passage. Van Gennep attests to this thus: „all ... rites which have specific effective aims, occur in juxtaposition and combination with rites of passage."[221]

## 2.3 Typologies of Traditional Igbo Initiation Rites

Having seen Igbo idea of Initiation rites summarily as rites that mark change from passive to active membership in the community with the accompanying rights and responsibilities, we shall now advance further

---

[217] Metuh, Comparative Studies, 205.
[218] Metuh, Comparative Studies, 205.
[219] Metuh, Comparative Studies, 205.
[220] Metuh, Comparative Studies, 205-206.
[221] Van Gennep, 12.

to present types of traditional Igbo initiation rites. The first in the list according to the life cycle of the traditional Igbo is birth initiation rites.

### 2.3.1 Birth Initiation Rites

Metuh rightly asserts that: „Birth is the beginning of social life for an individual."[222] However, it is more than that. „It is the first step in the stages of life."[223] It is also the beginning of physical and spiritual life and every other life as a human being on earth. Seeing birth from another very important perspective especially for the traditional African, Shorter remarks, „child birth is the first and most fundamental of all African symbols, because it is the promise of future hope, the link in the chain of life transmitted from the ancestral spirits to their living descendants."[224] Is it then any wonder why so many rites and rituals accompany the birth of a child especially among the traditional Igbo!

In some African societies, as Metuh correctly put it, these rituals begin months before the child is born[225]. With great caution he makes it known that in some cases they begin as soon as the mother is sure that a human being has been formed in her womb. However, pregnancy rituals are directed more at the prospective mother than the expected child[226].

Among the traditional Igbo, before a child is born, some ritual sacrifices are offered to *Chi omumu* (the deity responsible for childbearing) to grant and assure the safe arrival of the expected baby into the family and

---

[222] Metuh, Comparative Studies, 200. See also Chibuko, P., *Die Liturgische Inkulturation Von Initiationsriten, Eine Igbo-Perspektive*; in: Schreijäck, T., (Hg.), *Menschwerden im Kulturwandel, Kontexte kultureller Identität als Wegmarken interkultureller Kompetenz*, Fulda 1999 (301-326), 304.
[223] Ishola, S. A., The Sociological Significance of the Traditional African Concept of Rites of Passage, in: Ogbomoso Journal of Theology, No. 7, Dec. 1992 (26-32), 26.
[224] Shorter, A., Christianity and the African Imagination, 125.
[225] Cf. Metuh, Comparative Studies, 200.
[226] Cf. Metuh, Comparative Studies, 200.

into the society. The family ancestor also receives his own sacrifice, so that the child will be received into the family and be allowed to live, have and enjoy good health, long life and prosperity.

When the child is born, the family, their neighbours, friends and other relatives rejoice. The question that is normally asked at the news of a new-born child is „O litelu gini"? (Which kind of baby has the mother given birth to?). If it is a baby-boy that is born, it is normally said: „O litelu soja"[227] (she gave birth to a soldier) and the joy is greater. When a baby-girl is given birth to, the people also rejoice, but not as much as they do when a baby-boy is born, especially if the baby-boy is the first child that is born in the family. The ancestral lineage is maintained through the males, while the females marry away to another family. That is why the joy is lesser when a baby-girl is born and more when a baby-boy is born.

From the above one can then understand Mbiti (as we have seen in the earlier part of our work) and especially Shorter when he talks of child-birth as the first and most fundamental of all African symbols, because it is the promise of future hope, the link in the chain of life transmitted from the ancestral spirits to their living descendants.

After the news of a new born child, the members of its family, their

---

[227] Before the Biafra-Nigerian Civil war, 1967-1970, the idea of soldier among the Igbo was positive. Any family that has a soldier was well respected and feared because of this soldier in their family. He fights for the protection of his family. Outside his family, his village was also respected and feared among other villages for the same reason. That was why when a boy was born in a family, there was great joy because only boys could become soldiers by then. The expression "*O litelu soja*" stems from this. But since after this 30 months Biafra-Nigerian War, the pogrom that lasted between 1967 and 1970, the Igbo idea of soldier changed and became negative for the simple fact of the massive organised massacre of the Igbo youth (soldiers) by the officials of the opponent group. The Igbo now express the negative idea thus: "*Nwanyi mutalu soja gba aka nwa*" (A woman that gave birth to a soldier, has no child).

neighbours, relatives and friends await with great expectation and joy, the day the child will be brought out for the public and be given a name. But before this, a diviner must have been consulted by the family of this new-born child, to know which of the ancestors reincarnated through the new baby. When this is known, then the family offers sacrifice accordingly. Other rituals like the burying of the umbilical cord and circumcision (*Beschneidung*) and shaving off the hair also take place. The shaving off the hair signifies that all bad things and ill lucks following this child have been cut off and thrown away. Through these steps, the child is being gradually initiated into the family circle. When the parents of the new born baby are now sure that the child has come to live in the family, arrangements to initiate him into the kindred and the larger community, that is, the naming ritual and ceremony begin. For convenient sake, we choose to title it here Igbo naming ritual and ceremony. When do the naming ritual and ceremony begin and how do they take place, and where?

## 2.3.2 Igbo Naming Ritual and Ceremony

The Igbo naming ritual and ceremony, which is always observed with feasting and great joy, takes place generally seven Igbo-weeks[228] (28 days) after the birth of the child. Both the male and the female relatives, neighbours and friends are invited and are well entertained.

Before the actual initiation of the new born-baby into the kindred and the larger group, kolanut is first and foremost presented. With the presentation of kolanut and its consequent rituals, the ancestors and other

---

[228] Igbo week is made up of four days named after the Igbo Traditional Markets. They include *Eke*, *Oye*, *Afo* and *Nkwo*. These make up one Igbo-week. One of the myths of origin has it that these names were the names of the four spirits sent by *Chukwu* (God) to Igboland and to the Igbo people. These spirits were deified and to immortalise their names, the four markets were founded and their names dedicated to these markets.

friendly deities are beckoned on and are invited to take their proper place in the celebrating community. With their presence in the gathering, their protection is assured and their blessings secured, the family, in the African sense, is complete and the ceremony begins in full swing.

The eldest in the kindred, who is taken to be closest to the ancestors, takes up the kolanut and consecrates it. During the prayer, he will not forget to mention the reason for the gathering, and making special prayers for the child who is about to be initiated and of course, his parents. After the consecration, the kolanut is split. He first throws some little pieces to the ancestors, then the rest are shared. During the feasting too, some lumps of fou-fou are also thrown away to them. Libation is also poured to them.[229] These take place in front of the „*Obi*"[230].

After the above, the new baby to be initiated is handed over to the eldest of the kindred, who carries the child outside the „*Obi*" and facing the baby heaven-ward, instructs him or her in these or similar words: „*Nne gi gwa gi okwu, nulu ife! Nna gi gwa gi okwu, nulu ife! Were efifie mulu anya! Ma gi were anyasi laru ula!*" (When your mother speaks to you, listen to her! When your father speaks to you, listen to him! Open your eyes in the day! And sleep in the night!).[231] At the end of this 'moral' instruction before all present and before the ancestral spirits also present, the child is given names. With the naming of a child, he or she is

---

[229] These are marks of strong communion between the Living and the departed (the living-dead). Mbiti clarifies that "libation and the giving of food ... are tokens of fellowship, hospitality and respect; the drink and food so given are sybols of family continuity and contact". See Mbiti, J. S., African Religions and Philosophy, 9.

[230] "*Obi*" here does not mean Igbo word for heart but the meaning is also not far away from the idea. In the sense in which it is used here, it refers to a ritual sitting room, normally separated from the main house. It is found in every traditional Igbo family. There, the head of the family together with all the members of his family gather together for ritual functions and performances. A better name for it is family shrine.

[231] Cf. Oranekwu, Sacrifice, 28.

initiated into the corporate community. „This ritual is the seal of the child's separation from the spirits and the living-dead, and its integration into the company of human beings."[232]

The essence of bringing the child outside the '*Obi*' and facing it heavenward before giving the first official 'moral instruction' and name is not only to introduce and to initiate the child to the cosmic realities. It is also that the Sky and Earth (*Igwe na Ala*) deities[233] can also see and bear witness that this child is well received and welcome into the family, and that he or she has been instructed to listen to the parents for him or her to have life, and emulate the correct ways of their ancestors. One finds here already one of the quintessential aspects and significant role of initiation among the traditional Igbo. But we shall give it a due attention at the appropriate time.

Two or more names may be given to the baby. The general name normally indicates the Igbo week-day on which the baby was born. Male children are given such names as „*Okeke*" or „*Nweke*" (meaning son or child of *Eke*), „*Okoye*" or „*Nwoye*" (son or child of „*Oye*", „*Okafo*" or „*Nwafo*" (son or child of *Afo*), „*Okonkwo*" or „*Nwankwo*" (son or child of *Nkwo*), when any is born on any of this day of the traditional Igbo week. Female children are named „*Mgbogo-eke*" or „*Mgbe-Eke*"[234]

---

[232] Mbiti, African Religions and Philosophy, 120.

[233] Sky and Earth (*Igwe na Ala*) deities are the highest deities before God, that the traditional Igbo calls for witness when one's innocense is at steck. To prove one's innocense, the accused person comes out at the open place and say: "*Igwe na Ala, bianu gbara m aka ebe*" (Sky and Earth come and bear me witness). Of course, no one who knows that he or she is guilty of the offence calls on these two powerful and most feared deities for witness. They do not spare any evil-doer and they render instant justice without delay. The measure is very drastic for any one who calls on them falsely.

[234] The prefix "*Mgbe*" refers to the time of the traditional Igbo week day on which the child was born. So that "*Mgbe-eke* " simply means 'at the time of Eke or during the Eke day'. The origin of these names has already been explained somewhere in the earlier part of this chapter.

(meaning daughter of *Eke* or simply child of *Eke*), „*Mgbogo-Oye*" or „*Mgboye*" –Short form of „*Mgbe-Oye*" (the daughter of *Oye*), „*Mgbafo*" and „*Mgbenkwo*" (the daughter of *Afo* and the daughter of *Nkwo* respectively).

Other names that follow this are always more significant and meaningful for the family and the relatives than the first name. Such names express remarkable events or circumstance very closely connected with the family or the birth of the child in question. The birth of a male child long expected and prayed for in the family is an event of great joy and satisfaction, so the child may be named „*Ifeanacho*" (we have received what we have been longing for) or „*Chukwuemeka*" (God has done much for us).[235] Some names also indicate future assignment to the child for his relatives and for the entire community. Such names include: *Onuorah* (Public speaker), *Ikemba* (The strength or power of the community), *Ochendo* (Giver of shade/protector at difficult times), *Ogbo-ogu* (Settler of disputes), *Ocho-udo* (Peacemaker), *Ngozi Chukwu* (God's blessing). This practise is also found among the Dagara people of Burkina Faso. According to Malidoma Some: „*Nach dem Glauben der Dagara tritt jeder Mensch mit einer bestimmten Aufgabe ins Dasein. Deshalb sind manche Namen programmatisch. Namen kennzeichen die Aufgabe ihres Trägers und erinnern schon das Kind an die späteren Lebenspflichten. Es ist also im Namen eines Menschen bereits die ihm aufgetragene Lebensaufgabe enthalten.*" [236]

What is the next stage of initiation after the naming ritual and ceremony among the traditional Igbo?

---

[235] Cf. Ezeanya, S. N., Handbook of Igbo Christian Names, Onitsha 1994, 7. (Henceforth "Handbook").

[236] Some, M. P., *Vom Geist Afrikas*, (trans.), Dietzfelbinger, K., München 1996, 7. The same idea is expressed by Miller, M., in his work: "The Shephard and Rock, Origins, Develpoment and Mission of the Papacy", U.S.A. 1995, 15-16.

### 2.3.3 Igbo Puberty Rites

Up to the moment of child delivery, most rituals are concentrated on the expectant mother. But right from birth one is surrounded by rituals: the circumcision, shaving off of the hair, and naming ceremonies through which the child is initiated into the human family, as has been already discussed. At the ripening age of maturity, formal initiation rites are celebrated which opens the way to the different traditional groups: the age-group, masquerade society, and if a girl, presents her as mature and ready for marriage. The most elaborate in the rites of passage is the traditional marriage.[237]

After the candidates must have been prepared by their parents and or those responsible for them, providing them with some food items and other necessary materials they would need, they are gathered in a special place far from their homes, to be alone and be prepared very well for the initiation. They go into this seclusion camp with a group of experienced leaders who are already initiated. It is in this lonely and secluded camp that these initiation candidates are taught in all quietude what community life implies, obedience to the elders, public spiritedness, endurance and all kinds of discipline and ascetic life. Towards the end of their training, they are entrusted with the secrets of the esoteric traditions and lore of the group and they are introduced to the communion with the ancestors and other titulary spirits of the clan. Before these candidates leave the camp for their individual homes, they are given names that introduced them to the new phase of life they have just entered. The names symbolise a change of status, in both physical, moral and social sphere. They are 'considered' completely a new people and no longer what they were before. A closer and clearer example of this is the Christian

---

[237] Cf. Onuh, C. O., Christianity and the Igbo Rites of Passage, Frankfurt 1992, 46.

sacrament of confirmation.[238]

Has Puberty initiation Rite any expressive aspects? What are they?

## 2.3.3.1 Expressive Aspects of Puberty Initiation Rite

Here we want to point out some standard qualities the society or community expects from one who has undergone puberty initiation rite as a 'finished product'.

## 2.3.3.2 Active Member Of The Society

As we have seen earlier, the scope of the initiation rite into what Metuh calls 'Social Puberty'[239] is not primarily to celebrate the physical changes brought about by adolescent life. The cogent element, which is most fundamental, is to make the individual (the initiand) a man or a woman, fit to be one. The rites involved are mostly and basically rites, which mark change from passive to active membership in the society or community, with the attaching obligations and privileges.[240] This however, characterises all initiations.

Puberty initiation rite acts as an 'opened gate' to active membership of and in the community. It presents one as a finished product, mature and fit for the community. As the Igbo express it: *O tolugo ife eji mmadu*

---

[238] At the Christian celebration of the sacrament of Confirmation, each of the candidates gets a new name called confirmation name, to distinguish it from baptismal name. Sacrament of Confirmation indicates that ' a baptised person is filled with the Holy Ghost for the inner strenthening of the supernatural life and for the courageous outward confession of faith.' See Ott, L., Fundamentals of Catholic Dogma, 4$^{th}$ ed., (trans.), Lynch, P., Illinois 1960, 361.

[239] See Metuh, Comparative Studies, 205.

[240] Some of the points here, which have been mentioned elsewhere earlier, may not be considered as repetition, but rather as strong points of emphasis for more and deeper elucidation.

*eme* (He or she is now worth somebody in the community). The person is now out of the group of *Akaliogheli, efulefu lere nma tulu obo,* good for nothing. The time of 'nothingness' and 'becoming' have gone. He or she is now a grown-up, a mature human being. Hence he or she now joins the 'bandwagon' of the active members of the community, having learnt the implications of community life and being entrusted with the secrets of the esoteric traditions and lore of the group. The privilege of being introduced to the communion with the ancestors and other titulary spirits of the clan (for boys) also plays a pivotal role. Often times, in most traditions, the group of candidates who underwent the puberty initiation rites together form and belong to one age group.
What then is Age group? What are their functions?

### 2.3.3.3 Age Group

The Igbo term for Age Group is *Otu Ogbo*. Another English synonym for the same term is Age Grade. An Age Grade (*Otu Ogbo*) is not simply a category of persons who happen to fall within a particular culturally distinguished age range, as C.R. Ember and M. Ember claim.[241] Not all persons who happen to fall within a particular culturally distinguished age range become members. One must be initiated into the group.[242]
For Williams Chancellor,"The age-group or age-set was the specific organizational structure through which the society functioned. Classification was determined by the period in which one was born."[243]
However, Hailey's description of Age Group brings out its major characteristics and functions. He writes: „Age-groups are formed by men of about the same age. They help to maintain law and order, bring suspected criminals before the elders, collect fines, and give general help

---

[241] Cf. Ember, C. R., and Ember, M., Cultural Anthropology, New Jersey, 4th ed., 1985, 205.
[242] Cf. Parrinder, G., Africa's Three Religions, London 1969, 80.
[243] Williams, C., The Destruction of Black Civiliazation, Illinois 1976, 175.

in public works."²⁴⁴

Qualified candidates are initiated into their respective Age Groups between the ages of fifteen and twenty. In some places this is done simultaneously with initiation into the masquerade society (*ima mmuo*) or sacred societies.²⁴⁵

As part of the initiation rite, there is the taking of a new additional name and motto of the Age Group. As soon as one is initiated into the group, he is launched into a responsible belonging to the Age Group in contributing his proper role to the community. Each Age Group gets a specific function and service for the community.²⁴⁶ It is up to them to distinguish themselves and make a recognisable impression, and project the good image of the group before the entire community. To attain and maintain such a high standard, each Age Group establishes means of control and discipline for its members.

Another cogent element of Age Group as Uchendu reveals is: „Besides serving as a social indicator which separates the seniors from the juniors, the age-grade association is a means of allocating public duties, guarding public morality through the censorship of the members' behaviour and providing companionship and mutual insurance for the members."²⁴⁷

Next to the Age-group is masquerade society. What is it all about?

---

[244] Lord. H., An African Survey, London 1957, 34.
[245] Metuh, E. I., sees the term 'secret societies' in the above connection as hardly adequate because entrance into them is open to all adult free born, male or female as the case may be. So that its secrets are secret only to the uninitiated. Entrance is also on a voluntary basis, but generally social pressure forces all who qualify to join. Though these 'secret societies' appear to be magico-religious in nature, the primary objective is more political and economic. See Comparative Studies, 206.
[246] See Eboh, 51.
[247] Uchendu, 42.

## 2.3.3.4 Masquerade Society

Masquerade society in the traditional Igbo community is a social as well as a secret association. Its function is essentially political; maintenance of peace and order. By its qualification as a secret society, it is meant that absolute secrecy is enjoined on its members. Any leakage of the secrets from any of the members attracts the culprit an unbearable punishment, which often times extends to a death penalty.

It is a closed association with many mysterious beliefs and practices and the membership is restricted only to males with initiation as the only possible condition. Though there are masquerades characterised and known as women masquerades, for example, *Nne nmuo* (Mother masquerade) or *Agbogho nmuo* (girl masquerade), women are not only absolutely prohibited from membership, but are also strictly debarred from appearing in the presence of a masquerade. However, women can watch and admire them from a far distance.

Entry into this secret society is by participating in a special initiation rite in which the mask's secrecy is unveiled to the novices. This initiation rite takes the form of passing through terrifying and excruciating ordeals of numerous and various types, meant to toughen and harden the young man, and to instil in him, a sense of manliness, courage and endurance. Often times, this is achieved by masquerades flogging the candidates mercilessly; giving them dry bone to chew, and then the unveiling of the mask to the aspirants, which secrecy one is now bound by oath under death to keep.[248]

The uninitiated is considered a woman equivalent and perjuratively called *Ogbodu* (literary meaning very weak person, unmanliness). He cannot take any heroic title in the community. This is understood because Masquerades function as means of social control, compelling

---

[248] Cf. Parrinder, G., West African Religion, London 1969, 133-134. See also Basden, G. T., Among the Ibos of Nigeria, 235-243.(Hence, Among the Ibos).

individuals in the society to comply to traditional standards and way of life, as well as guarding community property against intruders. They are enforcement agents within the traditional set-up. Isichei, therefore, correctly observes that: „... much of the function of these masquerades is to effect obedience to the sanctions of the town on a culprit. These could invade a culprit's home, and seize all his belongings until the owner pays the stipulated fine for his crime ..."[249]

After a successful admittance into masquerade society, one is now considered fully qualified for, and can enter into married life.

### 2.3.3.5 Married Life

Basden's observation that 'marriage has a foremost place in the life of the Igbo, and that it looms upon the horizon of every maid and youth as an indispensable function to be fulfilled with as little delay as possible after reaching the age of puberty'[250], is not a mere expression of sentiment. It is crystal clear and a statement of fact. The gate to responsible fatherhood and motherhood is opened after the puberty rite, the person having been adequately prepared for life and its consequent challenges and difficulties. He or she is now capable of managing and handling any situation in human life.

Having successfully entered into married life, the question of social status follows, that is, social recognition. How can one be socially recognised? How can a great rise in social status be secured?

### 2.3.3.6 Title-taking

„A great rise in social status", says Arinze, „is secured by entry into the societies, the most widespread of which is the *Ozo* title society."[251]

---

[249] Isichei, Igbo Worlds, 74-75.
[250] Basden, G. T., Among the Ibos 213.
[251] Arinze, 5. Eboh, S. O., devoted a whole work to *Ozo* Title Institution in Igboland. Though his treatment of *Ozo* Title Institution is not all-

People become influential and assume positions of honour in the community by entry into this institution.[252] The Igbo especially, consider various titles as marks of excellence. Consequently, an untitled person has virtually no say in the gathering of the community. Merely taking wife and having children, no matter how highly these two values are regarded among the Igbo, does not necessarily make one fulfilled. Title-taking is regarded as the crowning factor in one's personal fulfilment in life.[253] This is the only traditional way by which one is publicly proclaimed famous, and through which one is declared affluent and well-to-do.[254]

Unfortunately, however, not all who desire to become title-holder (*Ozo*) is admitted into the group. This is given to the obvious fact that a certain standard of conduct is required and must be maintained throughout life. As a result, admission into the group is only possible through initiation, after all other requirements have been met. Isichei describes the quality of an *Ozo* title-holder thus: „An *Ozo* title-holder is supposed to be an honest man. He must not enter into anything that is dirty, and the cord is a witness between him and the gods, that he is now different from other human beings. He is regarded as pure all through, and he wears a bell, so that wherever he goes the bell jingles .... He is no more a hidden person. He will never enter any secret thing."[255]

Through initiation, an *Ozo* title-holder is placed at the apex of the traditional society both in matters of social and religious affairs.

As Basden correctly put it: „... the members exercise a widespread

---

embrassive, but what is said of one community in some cases, could be applied to the other. For more details see Eboh, S. O., *Ozo* Title Institution in Igboland, Aachen 1993.
[252] Cf. Onuh, 40.
[253] Cf. Ubesie, T., Odinala Igbo, Ibadan 1978, 121.
[254] Cf. Green, M. M., Igbo Village Affairs, London 1964, 58.
[255] Isichei, Igbo World, 66.

influence and they administered all the affairs of the town. They were treated with utmost respect ... and ... feared .... They had the power of life and death, and were the fully accredited rulers of the town."[256] As Isichei also observes: „After the decisions of the Ozo, no more appeal. At times, they condemned somebody to death, and it was final."[257]

What we presented above are major expressive aspects of puberty initiation rites. We shall then advance further with marriage initiation rites.

## 2.4 Marriage Initiation Rites

Marriage for the traditional Igbo is considered a very delicate issue that must be handled and treated with utmost care and proper attention. It is not a child's play. For this reason, the traditional Igbo see marriage not as a private affair of a young man and a woman. „The two individuals are not merely married to each other, but to the two families of their origin, and extended families."[258] What Imasogie says about marriage in Africa is also applicable in a special way to marriage among the traditional Igbo of Nigeria. He says: „In Africa you do not marry an individual; you are married into a family because the individual is not human apart from his community."[259] Marriage for that traditional Igbo, therefore, is a family to family affair which even develops into village to village relationship when the marriage has been fully established.

Not only the living are concerned with marriage affairs according to the traditional Igbo belief, the 'departed' are also involved because they are still part and parcel of the family members.

The process of marriage among the traditional Igbo differs from village

---

[256] Basden, Among the Ibos of Nigeria, London 1966, 264.
[257] Isichei, Igbo World, 67.
[258] Ishola, S. A., The Social Significance...., 29.
[259] Imasogie, African Traditional Religion, 62.

to village, even in some places from clan to clan. But there are common elements that are found in all. There is marriage investigation, for example; there is a middleman who acts as agent between the families of both spouses; there is a trial time in which the wife to be go to the family of the would-be husband to find out if she can live in the family; there is bride-price[260]; and the proper traditional marriage.

The investigations are supposed „to ensure that the families have no records of social maladjustments (sic), or other problems that might affect a successful marriage."[261] The goal is not necessarily the survival of the new family alone, but the whole community to which it belongs. In other words, every step or precaution is taken to make the marriage survive. The stability of the nuclear family results in the stability of the extended families and the society as a whole.[262] „In that case, the marriage rituals", says Ishola, „must of necessity be properly performed, and all marriage protocols followed."[263]

Though during the puberty initiation rites, the young people (boys and girls) are prepared for marriage, when the girl eventually marries, before she goes in to settle in the family of her husband, she must go on another course. She goes to an elderly good woman who will give her the essentials and fundamentals of basic home training. She learns to be a good house-wife, how to please her husband, cooking good food, good relationship with the parents and other relations of her husband and their neighbours. These are the basic things that make for a happy and

---

[260] Bride price or Bride wealth among the traditional Igbo is known as and called "*Ego aku nwanyi*". For the traditional Igbo, it is the testamony that a marriage has taken place. It is a sign of respect for the woman. It does not mean, as most foreigners think, that the woman is bought or sold. This tradition is also found in the Jewish tradition (Cf. Gen 34:12, Ex 22:16).

[261] Ishola, S. A., Towards a Contextualized Missiological Approach to the Yoruba Religio-Cultural Milieu, Texas 1992, 154.

[262] Cf. Ishola, The Social Significance...., 29.

[263] Ishola, The Social Significance ...., 29.

peaceful home among the traditional Igbo family.

On the side of the boy, before he begins to look for a woman to marry, he must have learnt how to be a father in the family. He learns this through training some domestic animals like goat or sheep. These animals are considered stupid and senseless, and as a result, very difficult to rare, so that if he is able to control them and feed them well, then there is no doubt that he can 'father' his own family excellently well. Unfortunately, however, this practice no longer exists among the traditional Igbo. Perhaps, it is among the values that the catastrophic wind of modernism and western influence has blown off.

What then do they learn about marriage during the period of puberty initiation rites? During the period of puberty initiation, the candidates learn more through practice. Because the traditional Igbo believe that experience is the best teacher, practical example becomes inevitable. The principle then is, learn by doing.

On the night before the traditional marriage, the friends and colleagues of the boy, especially those of his age-grade who have not yet married, gather in his house to officially send him off from their group (bachelors group). This occasion is mostly characterised with eating, drinking, music and dancing throughout the night. The central aim of this 'ritual' celebration is to mark the end of bachelor-spinster time for both couples. They are separated from their age-group, and that night is a transition moment and on the traditional marriage day, after marriage, they will be incorporated into the married group. Hence they should only mind themselves as man and woman; to the exclusion of every other until death do them part.

What is death for the traditional Igbo and how does he go about it when it occurs?

## 2.5 Death and Funeral Initiation Rites

Death is the passage from this life to the life beyond.[264] Kalu says: „Death is a mere passage from the human world to the spirit world."[265] For the Igbo particularly, it is joining the spirits of the forefathers and the ancestors in the spiritual land (*Ala ndi mmuo*), the great beyond. But it is somehow a paradox because for the Igbo, death is bad (*Onwu di njo*). Though it is seen as a passage to a happy joining of the ancestors in the great beyond, yet it is bad because the person will no longer be seen physically among the living members of the family. „Death cuts the individual off from his or her group, in terms of personal or social contact."[266] For this reason the Igbo say: *Onwu di iwe* (death is sad or painful).

However, not all the dead go to join the spirits of the fore-fathers or the ancestors. Those who died a bad death[267], their spirits neither join the spirits of the fore-fathers nor the ancestors. They roam about in the domain of the living especially their relatives, and torment them. The spirits of some of the dead who belong to this group are known and addressed as *Akaliogheli*[268]. Because of their wickedness and

---

[264] We have already seen in the traditional Igbo World-view, the two-tier world view of the traditional Igbo.

[265] Kalu, O. U., Ancestral Spirituality and Society in Africa, in: Olupona, J. K., African Spirituality: Forms, Meanings and Expressions, N.Y. 2000 (54-84), 54.

[266] Wach, J., Sociology of Religion, Chicago and London 1966, 66.

[267] What the traditional Igbo considers a bad death is death through sudden accident such as falling down from a tree, being killed by thunder and lightening or being killed by some certain diseases as leprosy or protrusion of the stomach (dropsy).

[268] It refers here to those aimless rapacious and disgruntled spirits who neither belong to the ancestral spirits nor have place in the spirit land either because they died bad death or because they were not buried befittingly.

rapaciousness, they are very difficult to be pleased and to be satisfied. Consequently the Igbo also address them as *Amala emeta mma*[269].

To show how the Igbo are resentful of death and how they fear death, when a person falls sick, all kinds of remedies are tried, even the diviner may be called in all to make sure that death do not occur. Although for the Igbo, there is a firm belief in the spirit world, in joining the ancestors in the great beyond, that life is not preferable to this one here and now on earth. The world beyond is a place of shades and cold, although its organisation may be on much the same pattern as earthly life, this sunlit warm world is better.

However, the ultimate questions that surround the experience of death leaves one dumb-founded. If man is very meticulous and happy in welcoming the gift of life at its very beginning with the birth rites and rituals, he is even all the more careful and elaborate at the ultimate moment of the separation from the physical world of the living. This accounts for the presence of funeral rites in almost all the cultures of human race. Interesting enough and very important to take note of is that for the traditional Igbo, *Mortus non tolitur sed mutantur est* (death is not annihilation or destruction but a change). The traditional Igbo does not see death as the end of all. Hence he does not fear death for he names his child,"*Onwuatuegwu*" (death is not fearful). Death is rather seen and considered as a gate way into another life or better said, a transition from mortality to immortality. As Olupona puts it, a passage „from human plane to the spiritual/Ancestral world."[270]

Practically, in every culture of human race, death marks a physical

---

Consequently, they roam about in the physical world and trouble their living relatives.

[269] A description of a person who cannot be pleased. By its nature it is a negative expression. No traditional Igbo would like to be tagged with such derogatory and abusive term.

[270] Olupona, J. K., African Spirituality, *xxii*.

separation of the individual from other living members of human family. This is so radical that such separations are celebrated with funeral rites and ceremonies, which are intended to emphasise this fact of separation from the living members of the human family.

Generally, the *kern Punkt* of the functions of death and funeral rites are to ensure a permanent separation of the dead person's spirit from the survivors and an attempt to re-establish a solidarity of the dead person with the world of the dead and the ancestral spiritual world. Because the physical world of the dead has come to an end, he has to be initiated into another life – the spiritual life in the land of the spirits. Otherwise, this spirit of the dead which has been separated from the physical body will not have a place of abode, a place of rest. Parrinder rightly says: „There is much more ritual connected with death because these last rites of passage are intended to ensure that the dead person leaves this world with full ceremony and enters safely into the company of his fathers."[271]

## 2.6 The Peculiarity of the Igbo Initiation Rites

We have undergone a long and great task of ex-raying the fundamentals of the Igbo cultural system with special reference to the Initiation Rites. When one looks from the earlier stages of this work, one cannot but be convincingly appreciative of the very rich cultural heritage of the Igbo. Initiation rites among the traditional Igbo have their specific peculiarities, which one can categorise into religious, social and political dimensions.

Firstly, Igbo Initiation rites are deeply penetrated and intertwined by the deep religious sense of the people. Religion is noted to be the centre of the life, activity and psychology of the Igbo. Their life is their religion and their religion, their life. A.G. Leonard candidly bears eloquent testimony to this fact. He succinctly declares: „they (the Igbo) are, in the

---

[271] Parrinder, Africa's Three Religions, 82.

strict and natural sense of the word, a truly and a deeply religious people, of whom it can be said, as it has been said of the Hindus, that 'they eat religiously, drink religiously, bathe religiously, dress religiously, and sin religiously'. In a few words, the religion of these natives as I have all along endeavoured to point out, is their existence, and their existence is their religion."[272]

The above clear observation and remarks of Leonard is not only a strong support but more a concrete and practical example of Mbiti's general statement about Africans and the implications of their world view. Mbiti in his normal choice of adequate terms says: „It is religion, more than anything else, which colours their understanding of the universe and their empirical participation in that universe, making life a profoundly religious phenomenon. To be is to be religious in a religious universe."[273]

The religious aspect of the traditional Igbo Initiation rites, is rooted in the idea of 'all-comprehending' religious vision of the universe by the Igbo. In strategic transitional moments of life, the Igbo, overwhelmed by this religious sense, resort to what Mbiti calls 'Instant Religion'.[274] In such moments, the Igbo are constrained to turn to the traditional religion as a „genuine means of finding an outlet for their feelings of joy or tension generated by the particular crisis or important event."[275]

The Initiation rites have a deep religious meaning. For example, the physical and social ceremonies associated with pregnancies, birth, and

---

[272] Leonard, A. G., The Lower Niger and Its Tribes, London 1968, 429.
[273] Mbiti, African Religions and Philosophy, 262.
[274] "Instant Religion is that which shows itself mainly in moments of crisis like sickness, desperation, emergency, death and tragedy; and comes to the surface also at key moments of life like birth, wedding, death, or national events like independence celebrations, state funerals, the deportation or overthrow of one governing class." Mbiti, African Religions and Philosophy, 275.
[275] Mbiti, African Religions and Philosophy, 275.

childhood are, over and above the social implications, regarded with deep religious feelings. These rites are seen from the perspective „that another religious being has been born into a profoundly religious community and religious world."[276]

Regarding the social aspects, the peculiarity of the traditional Igbo Initiation rites is observable from the strict, unalloyed fidelity of the Igbo to the traditional social system with its laws and customs which has immediate relationship not only with the traditional religion, but also with the ancestral allegiance. The Initiation rites are deeply conceived as dictates of the traditional law –*Omenala* or *Omenani*. Every traditional Igbo is always cautious not to go against, or do anything contrary to these traditional dictates.[277] No wonder why such practices are taken very seriously and are regarded as obligatory.

The societal force behind the traditional Igbo Initiation rites arises from this link with the ancestors, who, through the *Omenala* or *Omenani* – traditional custom, dictate such rites to be performed. Is it any wonder then that each Igbo traditional Initiation rite is in one way or the other directly connected with the ancestors. In the pregnancy rituals, the ancestors have their peculiar place. They must be consulted and sacrifices are offered to them. At the birth of a child and before the naming ceremonies, the ancestors must be consulted to ascertain which of them reincarnated in the child, of course they must have their share of sacrifice. The same system is applicable to puberty, marriage, title-taking, death and funeral initiation rites.

Through the traditional Initiation rites, the traditional statues originated by the ancestors are further transmitted and perpetuated, and thus, the traditional standard set by the ancestors are maintained. Marriage rites insure a steady flow in the ancestral lineage by guaranteeing the flow in offspring (*Nach-wuchs*). Through marriage and procreation, therefore, a

---

[276] Mbiti, African Religions and Philosophy, 120.
[277] Cf. Meek, E., Law and Authority in a Nigerian Tribe, London 1937, 61.

physical prolongation and quantitative expansion of the lineage are actualised.

As one gets older, he becomes a veritable mouthpiece, through which the ancestors, who according to the Igbo belief, continue to influence the affairs of the living in the lineage, speak to the Igbo community. This is the reason why the authority in the traditional system rests in the hand of the oldest in the community (Gerontocracy). He is, as it were, the nearest link with the ancestors and even, physically speaking, he is nearest to the land of the ancestors. When one dies finally, he is received into the company of the ancestors, if other necessary requirements are met. From here one sees a strong relationship and solidarity of the traditional Igbo with their ancestors. Schineller makes a reference to this strong relationship and solidarity as he remarks: „A strong sense of solidarity exists in Nigeria between the living and the dead. Parents and grandparents who led good lives and died well are honoured and remembered, and their presence is felt in the family, in the lives of those who remain behind. They protect the living and mediate to them the power and love of God. Is not this precisely at the heart of Catholic belief in the communion of saints and in the veneration of saints?"[278]

The Ancestors are evoked as the source of the traditional authority. For the fact that it represents the absolute dignified values of the society in which the common good and common interest handed over by the ancestors, the traditional authority dispensed by the elders is supreme in the traditional community; hence the political implications of the initiation rites among the traditional Igbo.

Another peculiarity of initiation rites is that through the rites one establishes himself or herself as a true, authentic, responsible and active member of the community, as we have somewhere earlier indicated. Further, the birth initiation rites celebrate not only the gift of life but also the joy and fulfilment of parenthood, especially, the motherhood of the

---

[278] Schineller, P., A Handbook on Inculturation, New York 1990, 89.

bearer of the new-born child. This is the case mostly at the birth of the first child of the family. As Mbiti rightly observes: „In some African societies, marriage is not fully recognized or consummated until the wife has given birth. First pregnacy becomes, therefore, the final seal of marriage, the sign of complete integration of the woman into her husband's family and kinship circle."[279] Onuh rightly points out that „one needs only to consider the fact that for the Igbos, a woman who has no child is taken as someone useless in the community, or as one who is not in the good book of the ancestors, or may have attracted their hatred and hostility. That is why a woman feels fulfilled not only by the birth of a child, but only when she begets a male child."[280] „Unhappy is the woman who fails to get children", says Mbiti, „for, whatever other qualities she might possess, her failure to bear children is worse than committing genocide: she has become the dead end of human life, not only for the genealogical line but also for herself. When she dies, there will be nobody of her own immediate blood to 'remember' her, to keep her in the state of personal immortality: she will simply be 'forgotten'. The fault may not be her own, but this does not 'excuse' her in the eyes of the society."[281]

Metuh however, expresses the point with more cogent element as follows: „Motherhood is a much sought after .... It is the dream and self-fulfilment of every ... young woman. A woman who cannot or has not given birth is a social misfit. If she has never conceived she is openly ridiculed and told that she is not a woman."[282]

Also a man who has married and could not get children, especially at

---

[279] Mbiti, Africa Religions and Philosophy, 110.
[280] Onuh, 165.
[281] Mbiti, African Religions and Philosophy, 110.
[282] Metuh, E. I., Comparative Studies of African Traditional Religions, 200.

least a male child[283], is not free from the ridicule too. He is described as and called a 'woman' in the derogatory sense. Here also Onuh expresses it well: „A man who has no male child sees himself and is regarded in the community as useless. Consequently, in the birth rituals, one celebrates and appreciates this gift of life, and at the same time the parents are publicly recognised, acclaimed and boosted, more especially if it is a case of the first pregnancy, where these celebrations have also social and economic importance attached."[284] So there is a great desire to have children, no wife feels her marriage secure till she has born a child, and no man feels that his family can be continued and his own funeral rites ensured till a son is born.[285]

It can be summed up therefore, that for the traditional Igbo child is the basic contribution to the community. The child renews the community and strengthens it. The more healthy children there are, the better the service by the individual to the community, the greater the sense of self-worth by the bearer of the children. A person without a child can feel worthless and endangered. Worthless because he or she fails the community, and endangered because the community will not be strong enough to help him or her. So that a marriage without a child, is difficult to reconcile with the need for keeping the community young and strong.[286]

Even from the point of view of the Igbo communal and corporate life, one sees that the rituals not only concern the individuals on whom they are centred, but also mark changes in the relationships of all the people connected with them by ties of blood, marriages, political and economic

---

[283] Traditional Igbo idea of male child is in line with the Book of Ecclesiasticus –"Even when the father dies, he might well not be dead, since he leaves his likeness behind him." (Eccl 30, 4).
[284] Onuh, 165.
[285] Cf. Parrinder, Africa's Three Religions, 79.
[286] Cf. Mantovani, E., 317-318.

associations.[287] As Turner well puts it, their 'big moments' become the 'big moments' of others as well.[288]

Initiation rites among the traditional Igbo not only make one to be very mature, ripped and a balanced personality with nobility of character in all aspects of life of the community and the society at large, they make one to be in very close contact with the life and the activity of the community and the ancestors. In a short sentence, initiation rites bring the people nearer to beings and things.

There are three very significant and symbolical moments in the process of initiation rites. These three emphatic moments characterise all initiation rites there are among the traditional Igbo. What are these triadic moments in the process of initiation rites?

## 2.7 Triadic Moments of Initiation Rites

Studies in traditional initiation rites reveal three very symbolic and quintessential moments in the process of initiation. These three moments namely: separation, transition and incorporation moments have been conceived and presented by some scholars as levels or types of initiation rites. Hence S. Eboh combines two complimentary concepts of Van Gennep and Turner's triadic structure in initiation rites respectively as follows:

1) Rites of separation – pre-liminal rites
2) Rites of transition – liminal or threshold rites
3) Rites of incorporation – post-liminal rites.[289]

The term 'triadic structure' here refers to the three moments in the process of initiation rites. These moments are not rites in themselves. They only indicate different particular points or moments in the process

---

[287] Cf. Metuh, Comparative Studies of African Traditional Religions, 198.
[288] Cf. Turner, V., The Forest of Symbols, London 1970, 7.
[289] Cf. Eboh, 106.

of initiation rites, which are however, of pivotal importance because of their emphatic symbolic meaning, and what is done at each particular point or moment. Understood in this sense, we then examine the three moments in the above terms used by van Gennep and Turner.

## 2.7.1 Rites of Separation – pre-liminal rites

The rites of separation actually mark the first step in every initiation rites, after all other proper, fundamental and preliminary preparations have been completed. Symbolically they express that „one had left or no longer belongs to a particular 'state' , place, group or phase of life to which he formerly belonged and should no longer be associated with it."[290]

However, following the 'life-cycle' idea of the traditional Igbo, it does not mean or imply that when the person later eventually dies, for he must surely some time die, he cannot go back to the spirit-land (*Ala mmuo*) from where he came. It means rather that so long as the person still lives in this physical world, he cannot be associated with that particular 'state', place, group or phase of life from which he has been separated. The best examples that best illustrate this are the Christian sacraments of Baptism, Confirmation and Order, which are validly received only once in one's lifetime. Canon 845 of the Code of Canon Law, § 1 states: „*Sacramenta baptismi, confirmationis et Ordinis, quippe quae characterem imprimant, iterari nequennt.*" The English section of the same code and the same paragraph reads thus; „Because they imprint a character, the sacraments of baptism, confirmation and Order cannot be repeated."

There are different ways of expressing symbolically the rites of separation. A particular type of initiation determines the symbolical method of separation ranging from seclusion, shaving one's hair, stripping of clothes associated with one's state, passing between the

---

[290] Metuh, Comparative Studies of African Traditional Religions, 198.

parts of an object that has been two equal parts, or passing between two branches or under something. „These activities in the context of some rituals express that a person has left behind one world or stage in life, and is about to enter another."[291] This is the moment of separation. But the *terminus ad quem* is not yet reached. What comes next then?

### 2.7.2 Rites of transition – liminal or threshold rites

At this point the candidate has left one state and is at the threshold of entering another. Hence the term 'transition' or 'threshold'. It is a period or time (moment), state or position in society, in which the aspirant is, according to Metuh, „betwixt and between".[292] The candidate has left his former position or status but is not yet incorporated into a new status. The neophyte is at once no longer classified and classified. He is in a transition (*Übergang*).

Ekwunife describes liminal or threshold stage as „ a period of inter-structure, a kind of undefined structureless situation .... The neophyte in that situation cannot be said to belong totally to the new state, nor completely detached from the old one .... Like the Igbo mythical bat, he or she is hanging between two worlds (states)."[293]

---

[291] Metuh, Comparative Studies of African Traditional Religions, 198.
[292] Metuh, Comparative Studies of African Traditional Religions, 198.
[293] Ekwunife, A., Consecration in Igbo Traditional Religion, Enugu 1990, 143. For further details see also Metuh, E. I., Comparative Studies of African Traditional Religions, 198-199; Uzukwu, E., Traditional Initiation Rites: Anthropological And Religious Viewpoints, in Lucerna, Vol. 7, 1(Dec. 1986-June 1987), 31-33. About the experiences of the liminal stage Streck says: "*Die 'gemeinsame Grenzerfahrung' im Ausnahmezustand körperlicher Schmerzen rücke die Initianden in die Nähe des Außergewöhnlichen wie Tod, Unsichtbarkeit, Bisexualität, Asexualität, Zügellosigkeit, Sonnen- und Mondfinsternis, Wildheit, Nacktheit, Besitzlosigkeit und Anonymität. Alle Initianden seien gesellschaftlich nicht strukturiet d.h. in Rollen eingebunden, sondern schlichte Glieder einer communitas.*"

The group of candidates, if they are many, in transitional period or stage are sometimes designated by a group name different from the group they have left and the one they are aspiring to. Good examples here are converts to Christianity who have not yet been baptised. They are called 'catechumens'[294]. They are no longer non-Christians. But they are not yet Christians.[295] Similarly, candidates who are on training for membership of a religious Order are called novices. They have not become full members of the Order but they are not non-members. They are in the process of becoming.

In so far as they are no longer classified, the symbols that represent them are in many societies drawn from the imagery of biological death and other physical processes that have a negative import such as menstruation. The neophytes may be buried, forced to lie motionless or ritually swallowed by a monster. As Shorter puts it: „Liminal rituals recreate temporally, or institutionally, a „liminal" experience. Members surrender their identity and enter another „world". This helps them understand something fundamental about human existence. It is a

---

Streck, B., Initiation, in Streck, B., (ed.), *Wörterbuch der Ethnologie*, Köln 1987, 94.

[294] A Latin word derived from the Greek noun '*Kat e.ku men*' meaning one who is preparing to receive baptism. In the early ages of the Church a period of two years or more was usually required before the instruction was considered complete and the sincerity of the person was proven. See Broderick, R. C., Catholic Concise Dictionary, Chicago 1966, 47.

[295] The statement of Vatican Council II regarding the Catechumens is in no way contradictory to the above explanation. The Council states that the Catehumens "are already joined to the Church, they are already of the household of Christ, and are quite frequently already living a life of faith, hope and charity." *AG* 15, 5. It says further: "with love and solicitude the Mother Church already embraces them as her own." *AG* 14, 3; cf. CIC 206; 788,3. But they have not yet received into the Church with the Christian sacraments of initiation. And that is the point.

womb/tomb experience (a dialogue with the future)."[296]

The other aspect that they are not yet classified, is often expressed in symbols modelled on processes of gestation and parturition. The neophytes are linked to or treated as embryos, new-born infants, or sucklings by symbolic means which often varies from place to place. The essential feature of these symbolizations is that the neophytes are neither living nor dead from one aspect, and both living and dead from another. They are in transition, betwixt and between.[297]

What is discussed above is the transition moment and what is done in this period of time and its signification or symbolism. After this, comes then the arrival point, the *terminus ad quem*, the incorporation moment. What is it then?

### 2.7.3 Rites of Incorporation –Post-liminal rites

These are rites, which express the idea that the initiates have successfully achieved the new state of life or status to which they were aspiring. They have now arrived at the aiming and desired point. They are transformed like those before them and like those before them, they are to be united with those before them who are already in this state. „The ways in which this is ritually expressed vary from ritual to ritual and from one society to the other. It could be expressed by ceremonially handing over the tools, or paraphernalia associated with the new status. It may also be expressed by a public festivity to mark the end of the rites, ceremonial performance of some of the functions attaching to the new state, or just sacrifices and prayers of thanksgiving to mark the end of the ritual process."[298] A Good example of this aspect is the priestly ordination in Catholic Church.

---

[296] Shorter, A., African Culture: An Overview, Kenya 1998, 62.
[297] Cf. Turner, V., The Forest of Symbols, 95; see also Metuh, E., Comparative Studies, 198-199.
[298] Metuh, Comparative Studies, 199.

The three moments in the process of initiation rites among the traditional Igbo having been clearly presented, we shall now turn our attention to discuss who does what in the process of initiation rites among the traditional Igbo.

## 2.8 Agents of Initiation Rites in Igbo Traditional Religion

Previously, we have been concerned with Igbo idea of initiation. We saw major typologies of Igbo initiation and the three moments or structures of traditional Igbo initiation.

In this section, our focus is on the agents of initiation rites in Traditional Igbo Religion. The point of emphasis is on who does what in traditional Igbo initiation rites? Here there are three main recognised authorities namely the father of the family (or the eldest of the kindred), the traditional chief-priest and the eldest 'Ozo' or 'Nze' title-holder. Of course, there could be a delegation but in this case, it is always an exception. In whichever case however, the type of initiation determines the particular agent for it. We therefore, attempt the specification below.

### 2.8.1 The Father of the family

At the initiation of a new born child into the family and the community, it is the prerogative of the father of the child or the grand-father (often from the father's side) or the eldest male of the *Umunna*[299] to act as the

---

[299] *Umunna* here refers to the descendants of a common ancestor. He is the custodian of the ancestral shrine *Okposi*, the ancestral cult staff *Ofo* (a branch of the tree detarium elastica) which is the symbol of ritual authority and priesthood, and the ancestral cult spear *Otonsi* or *Alo*. Because of this, he is very important in every Igbo family. See also Metuh, E. I., African Religions in Western Conceptual Schemes, Jos 1991, 154; Okorie, C. P. A., Priesthood in Igbo Traditional Religion, St. Ottilien Germany 1997, 169.

agent of initiation. It is however, good to note at this initial stage (as in other stages) that there is no stipulated and written down rules and regulations regarding this. The system varies from kindred to kindred and from community to community.

The high point of a child's initiation into the traditional Igbo family (both nuclear and extended) is the naming ceremony. „When a child is named, he is both individualised and incorporated into society."[300] It is therefore, a major ritual of great traditional importance. Obiukwu describes it as 'the turning point in the history of the Igbo child'. He goes further: „... it has a double dimension; social and religious. With it a child is incorporated and received officially into 'umunna' (extended family) community."[301]

Obiukwu did attempt a description of how the eldest (Okpala or Onyeisi) of the family, the chief actor, assisted by the other heads of the nuclear family performs this very important ritual function. According to him, it takes place in 'Obi' ancestral compound, normally before the ancestral shrine of the extended family. The ceremony is witnessed by an invited cross-section of the community, (other friends and relatives from far and near). Obiukwu describes the ritual actions of the chief actor thus: „Having washed his hands, he takes up white chalk and draws some lines on the ground ... takes one of the kolanuts, ... gives thanks to Chukwu (God), to Ala, to the ancestors and all the good spirits of the community, prays for himself, ... the whole members of the family, for all present and finally for the child about to be received into the umunna. ... breaks the kolanuts throws some on the altar, and some pieces on the ground. He eats parts of this nut, breaks and shares the rest of the nuts to all present. The child is ... handed over to Okpara (or Okpala), who ... lays it with back flat on the ground. He consults the parents for the

---

[300] Van Gennep, 62.
[301] Obiukwu, S. C., 'Ala' (Earth Spirit) in Igbo Culture and Traditional Religious Beliefs, Rome 1978, 36.

choice of name for the child, then, picks it up, addresses it, recounts for it the accepted norms of conduct in the community."[302]

The ceremony is then concluded with a formal calling of the chosen name after which the child is publicly and fully received and incorporated into the family (nuclear and extended) and the community. Thanksgiving sacrifices are also made to 'Ala' deity, the ancestors and the guardian spirits and then the feasting and entertainment with music and dancing.

In traditional marriage, the chief actor is also the father (or the eldest-Okpala, where the father is no longer living).

Who is the chief actor in most initiation rites among the traditional Igbo?

### 2.8.2 The Traditional Chief-Priest

The traditional Chief-priest (Eze Mmuo[303]) is always the chief actor in most initiation rites among the traditional Igbo. He officiates at puberty initiation rites (but in some places there are specially trained people for puberty initiation), he officiates at the initiation rites of other traditional priests and in some places, at the initiation of traditional title-holders: Chiefs, 'Obis', 'Igwes', the 'Nzes' and 'Ozos' and other traditional rulers.

At the initiation of a traditional priest, for example, it is the chief priest who 'opens the eye' (*Iwa anya*) of the priest 'in the making' so that he will have the power to 'see' the spirits and foresee the future. „He is to be consulted by those who doubt the intentions of the spirits or are

---

[302] Obiukwu, 36-38.
[303] Traditional priests among the Igbo are called '*Dibias*'. But there are some suffixes attached to the name to indicate the particular function of the particular priest. Hence there are '*Dibia nchu aja*' (priest for the offering of sacrifices), '*Dibia ogba afa*' (priest-diviner), '*Dibia Ogwogwu*' (medicine man,-in a negative sense, or juju man,-also in a negative sense), '*Dibia Ogwo oya*', here in a positive sense (Herbalist). See also Oranekwu, G., 42-43. But *Eze Mmuo* is the chief priest, as indicated above.

molested by them."[304]

The rites of the above initiation, which vary from one Igbo cultural zone to another are very significant in the Igbo religious context. A common factor that is found almost in all cultural zones throughout Igboland is the *Nso* (a number of rules which the candidate for priestly initiation must observe throughout the initiation period). Among the *Nso* binding the candidate during this period are:

i. He must leave his entire family and live in absolute seclusion, often in a special grove, which is normally dedicated to an *Alusi*.[305] There in the woods, he spends the period in dry fasting and deep meditation.

ii. He is to abstain from sexual intercourse until he has offered the final thanksgiving public sacrifice marking the end of his initiation and the consequent installation.

iii. He has to keep off from water and oil. If he wants to wash his hands, he does it with sand.

We have said that the traditional chief priest is the chief actor in most initiation rites among the traditional Igbo. This still holds true. In most places in Igboland, the chief priest always comes from the class of the *Ozo* or *ndi Nze* group of title-holders.

Who then is an *Ozo* or *Nze* title-holder and what role does he play in initiation rites among the traditional Igbo?

## 2.8.3 'Ozo' or 'Nze' Title-holder

*Ozo* or *Nze* is the greatest title among the traditional Igbo. Eboh is correct to say: „There is no title in Igboland greater than *Ozo* title

---

[304] Arinze, 65.

[305] *Alusi*, also called *Arusi* by some group is one of the Deities in Igbo Traditional Religion. Its place of abode is called 'okwu' *Alusi*. In some places it is called '*nkwu*' *Alusi*. Big groves or very thick forests are often dedicated to this deity.

taking."³⁰⁶ He also observes that „the names, ceremonies, and requirements vary from place to place according to local needs."³⁰⁷

By the virtue of the fact that *Ozo* is the highest title in Igboland, makes the point very clear that only an *Ozo* title holder can initiate an aspirant to *Ozo* group into the college of *Ozo* title holders. In some parts of Igboland, it is a special right of the oldest *Ozo* man to crown kings. A special example is Nkpologwu town in Anambra State of Nigeria. Hanny Hahn-Waanders reports a witnessed case: „As *Ndichie*, EzeOfoma is also a member of the Irimmadunato. Within this 'Council of wise men' a group has emerged, whose speaker he is. Any resolution has to be announced by him, otherwise it is not valid. In the Obi's absence the Ezeofoma ensures the implementation of the resolutions."³⁰⁸ She reports further: „As the senior in rank of the *Ozo* society in the oldest village of Obinabo of Nkpoloogwu, he (Ezeofoma) enjoys the highest esteem amongst the population. On the day of the coronation it was he, who placed the crown on the head of the newly elected Obi."³⁰⁹

However, *Ozo* is not only a title, it is also an office. As an office, it has two major functions: one is religious and the other is political. Each of these functions has equally with it a social character. Some people, however, hold the view that *Ozo* office is essentially priestly and no more. For example, Okolo, in his foreword to Orakwue's Book, 'Onitsha Custom of Title-Taking', says: „Two factors are quite clear ..., that while *Ndichie* institution is purely political and social, the *Ozo* ... is rather sacerdotal and particularly confers on its recipient the character of a priest which, if removed, the *Ozo* ... would lose its essence and would therefore degenerate into a mere economic proposition."³¹⁰ Ilogu also maintains that Ozo grew out of the need for priests who would preside at

---

[306] Eboh, 61.
[307] Eboh, 61.
[308] Hahn-Waanders, H., Eze Institution in Igboland, Nimo-Nigeria 1990, 109.
[309] Hahn-Waander, 109.
[310] See Orakwue, J., Onitsha Custom of Title-Taking, (n.p.), (n.d.), 3.

the extended family and lineage worship and supervise the cult of the ancestors and keep the family *ofo*.[311] For Ilogu, the continuity of the lineage, clan or village depends on the existence of God-fearing men who share in the spirit of the land through their relationship with the Earth goddess (Ala), and also know how to placate the spirit of dead ancestors and uphold the ordinance of the land. „The *Ozo* title is said to be the religious means of achieving these ends."[312] Therefore, the individual who has taken an *Ozo* title „must live a holy life, uphold publicly and privately the morality of the land and observe all the taboos, religious ceremonies and rituals of all the gods and goddesses of his community."[313] In the same perspective Okorie says: „As a titled man, an *Ozo* is regarded as a symbol of moral and spiritual excellence in the community."[314]

The socio-political office of *Ozo* is well described by Okorie. He writes: „*Ozo* title holders enjoy a number of privileges. There is a special seat reserved for an *Ozo* both in the community and in his family. They are exempted from manual labour and are safeguarded against bodily assault. They acquire almost limitless authority in some areas and each of them holds a private council and exercise jurisdiction over traditional, civil and even criminal cases among his kindred. It is this juridical role that expresses the socio-political nature of the *Ozo* society."[315] Further privileges enjoyed by the *Ozo* title holders include respect from the people and „any unnecessary insult on an Ozo is seen as an insult on the community. They (Ozo titled men) are treated with due respect and care. They constitute the living symbol of justice and righteousness in the society."[316] Basden observes that „there is a small room where he (Ozo

---

[311] Cf. Ilogu, E., Christianity and Igbo Culture, Enugu 1974, 31.
[312] Ilogu, 31.
[313] Ilogu, 31.
[314] Okorie, 140.
[315] Okorie, 140. See also Nkwo, M., Igbo Cultural Heritage, Onitsha 1984, 46.
[316] Nkwo, 46.

titled man) eats and as he eats, a young man beats a special *ekwe* rhythm. In some areas, he eats only food prepared by his wife or daughter."[317] In some areas he does not cross a stream. In case an *Ozo* errs, his punishment is enormous, but he is not commonly disciplined in the open. Even with the event of colonialization which introduced a different system of government into the country, an *Ozo,* who is involved in a serious case may be arrested but may not be handcuffed or tied in any manner.[318] An *Ozo* is not allowed to climb a tree. He dares not touch another woman outside his wife or wives. When the *Ozo* dies, he is buried in a special way.[319] As Ilogu rightly puts it: „At death all the *Ozo* titles which a man has acquired, may be in a period of time extending for over fifteen years, are removed from him in a very solemn religious ceremony which involves the sacrificial killing of some goats, cocks and cows."[320] For Ilogu, „... the practice of removing the *Ozo* in symbolic religious rites is to teach people that no one should carry title or rank to the gods; for before the gods all men are equal, and the only title or rank to be awarded in the land of the dead, is what the gods themselves give, according to the quality of life a man has lived in this world."[321]

From what we have studied so far about initiation rites among the traditional Igbo, it is considered necessary to ask at this point: Are these rites of initiation still intact and active among the traditional Igbo today? If they are not, why? What and what constitute the obstacles to the initiation rites among the traditional Igbo?

---

[317] Basden, Niger Ibos, 263.
[318] Basden, 263.
[319] Cf. Ogbalu, F. C., *Omenala Igbo* (The Book of Igbo Customs), Onitsha, 118. Ilogu observes that when an Ozo titled man dies, especially in old age, his burial assumes pious and secred form which indicates the people's belief that his spirit has joined the gods and the ancestors, and that ha has become divine. See Ilogu, 32.
[320] Ilogu, 33.
[321] Ilogu, 33.

## 2.9 Obstacles To The Initiation Rites Among The Traditional Igbo

„Changes are rapidly taking place in Africa", observes Geoffrey Parrinder, „and the initiation rites are some of the areas of life mostly affected by modern changes."[322] This is „partly because," according to Mbiti, „Christian missionaries and some governments have attacked or discouraged the practices. Yet, where initiation rites were part of the traditional cycle of individual life, the practice still lingers on and often with some modifications or in a simplified form."[323] For Mbiti therefore, „that these initiation rites are extremely important in traditional life needs no further emphasis. If they are to die out, they will die a long and painful death."[324] He goes further, „they are at the 'middle' of life for the individuals concerned, not only because they coincide often with the puberty changes, but because they close a whole phase of life, childhood in the broad sense of that word, and open up a new and whole phase of life, adulthood with all its implications. Because of this radical change, many African societies mark the occasion with a dramatization and physical-psychological experiences that are hard for the individual to forget."[325]

Certainly before the advent of the so-called colonial masters and the Christian religion in Igboland and even many years after that, traditional initiation rites everywhere in Igboland, to a greater or lesser degree, fitted the pattern outlined above. But with the introduction of western civilization and the influence of Christian religion, a new attitude towards traditional values as a whole becomes apparent in almost all spheres of the Igbo traditional life. Chinue Achebe bemoaned and

---

[322] Parrinder, Africa's Three Religions, 80.
[323] Mbiti, African Religions and Philosophy, 131.
[324] Mbiti, African Religions and Philosophy, 131.
[325] Mbiti, African Religions and Philosophy, 131.

decried this unpleasant situation in his much celebrated work „Things Fall Apart" with the famous and much quoted statement: „Things fall apart: the centre cannot hold; Mere anarchy is loosed upon the world."[326] Achebe looks back at his Igbo society, specifically at the period the white man broke into it as missionary, trader and administrator, and that period throws into relief the relevance of the two lines above. This awareness of things falling apart is located by Obierika in his accusation of the white man: „Now he has won our brothers and our clan can no longer act like one. He has put a knife on the things that held us together and we have fallen apart."[327]

However, it is not to be taken or understood that Chinue Achebe has said it all for it must be recognised „that Europe did play a preponderant role in introducing Christianity to Africa"[328] over a hundred years ago. What then are the obstacles to Initiation in Igbo traditional religion?

---

[326] Achebe, C., Things Fall Apart, (reprinted edition) Ibadan 1998, *v*.
[327] Achebe, *v*.
[328] Cf. Obi, C. A., (ed.), A Hundred Years of the Catholic Church in Eastern Nigeria (1885-1985), Onitsha 1985, 1. Another very important work related to the above is "The Catholic Church in Onitsha, People, Places and Events (1885-1985)" edited by Nwosu, V. A., and also published in Onitsha in 1985. Also the article of Onunwa, U. R., "Christian Missionary Methods And Their Influence On Eastern Nigeria" (59-84) is very infomative. For further details on this article see Metuh, E. I., (ed.), The God's In Retreat, Enugu 1986.

## 2.9.1 Christian and Islamic[329] Religions

G. Parrinder writing on modern change, its influence on initiation among the Ashanti of Ghana says: "Similarly Islamic and Christian influences inevitably accompanied the political forces of the Berbers or the Europeans. These two religions are missionary forces but they have political effects. ... Christianity came into immediate conflict with the chiefs in Ashanti. The first converts were encouraged by their leaders to cut themselves off completely from 'heathen' customs, and in some cases separate villages were formed which removed Christians entirely from the traditional authority of the chiefs."[330] Even where such segregation was not practised Christians were liable to reject the jurisdiction of the chief, and even objected to libations and annual ceremonies to gods and ancestors.[331]

The above situation described by Parrinder did not feature in Ashanti alone, it featured also in Igboland and perhaps in many other parts of Africa and other mission countries. For example, Ajayi, in his work titled „Christian Missions in Nigeria" writes: „Christian villages were a Roman Catholic device made famous by the work of Jesuit Fathers on Paraguay, where the Fathers made mass conversions of Indians and established them in little theocratic states absolutely ruled by the Fathers ..."[332] C. A. Obi gave a somewhat detailed account of the so-called Christian village as an early missionary strategy for evangelisation in

---

[329] The traditional Igbo had little or no contact with Islamic religion in those early years except for those in business line. The Islamic (unfriendly) influence on the Igbo people became so pronounced and manifest in the Sixties, and this later developed into Nigerian-Biafrian war which lasted from 1967 to 1970.
[330] Parrinder, G., Africa's Three Religions, 95.
[331] Cf. Parrinder, Africa's Three Religions, 95.
[332] Ajayi, J. F. A., Christian Missions in Nigeria, 4th impression, Ibadan 1977, 114.

Igboland.[333] To get into details here is considered not too important, more still, time factor taken into consideration. The key point however, is that the Missionaries in question, did not understand the people, their culture, tradition and customs. Consequently, whatever is not like the European expression has been judged strange, pagan, devilish and unchristian.[334]

## 2.9.2 Schooling As A Factor Against Initiation

This is especially the case in urban areas where especially the young people attend school. Attendance at school at once puts a severe limitation on the time that can be allotted to the preparations of the ceremonies and the actual initiation itself. Though one can argue that the holiday period could serve the time but other factors must be taken into consideration also. For example, the farming season and most initiations do take place in dry season when the candidates could be off from their homes and camp in the wood for a period of time (seclusion).

Accompanying the undoubted advantages of schooling therefore are the disintegration of the traditional society and the wrecking of the strong bonds that existed between parents and their children. There is little or no time again for the family to stay together. There is no time for the bed-time stories and for learning family moral, good manners, respect for elders, traditional greetings, proverbs, riddles and other rudiments of elementary and simple courtesy.

Further still, many literate grown-ups (boys and girls) consider some of the rites to be, in the words of Sarpong, „ a remnant of 'savage

---

[333] Cf. Obi, C. A., The Christian Village as an Early Missionary Strategy for Evangelisation at Onitsha-Lower Niger Mission, 18-41, in: Nwosu, V. A., (ed.), The Catholic Church in Onitsha, People, Places and Events (1885-1985), Onitsha 1985.

[334] Cf. Oranekwu, G. N., The Christian Saints Vis-A-Vis Ancestral "Worship" in Igbo Traditional Religion, (Unpub. Thesis for Bachelors Degree in Theology) B. M. S. Enugu 1995, *iv*.

superstition' and are scornful of them."³³⁵ „For them the old supernatural sanctions have lost all their threatening force; and the application of the former social or physical deterrents ... is fast becoming impossible or impracticable."³³⁶

## 2.10 The Significant Role of Initiation in Traditional Igbo Culture and Religion

Initiation plays an important part in practically all types of religion. Every religion introduces its adherents to 'eternal truth' –into a spiritual happiness of high quality. Therefore, it is no exaggeration to contend that initiation is one of the key notions of religion. Initiation is the gate, which leads to the knowledge of the nature and of the will of the gods or the deity.³³⁷ This fact is very manifest and of significant importance in the traditional Igbo Culture and Religion. Further, initiation presupposes a religious secret, which is only known to the initiated. Actually, true belief always is a secret.³³⁸ True prayer takes place in the inner room.³³⁹ True belief belongs to the secret place of human life. It eludes the grasp of scientific research. One understands a religious truth only in so far as one is initiated into it.³⁴⁰ This means that the very essence of piety always escapes from scientific research and, moreover, that an outsider never fully manages to penetrate into the core of a religion which is not his own.³⁴¹

---

[335] Sarpong, P., Girls' Nubility Rites in Ashanti, Ghana 1977, 93.
[336] Sarpong, 93.
[337] Cf. Bleeker, C. J., Some Introductory Remarks, 15.
[338] Cf. Bleeker, Some Introductory Remarks, 15.
[339] Cf. Mtt 6, 6. Christ gave in the Sermon on the Mount, the well-known prescription concerning prayers.
[340] Cf. Bleeker, Some Introductory Remarks, 15.
[341] Cf. Bleeker, Some Introductory Remarks, 15. Bleeker contends that the above statement does not imply that the student of the history of religions

Initiation rituals carry much significance for the participants and for their communities. As Wayne Oates rightly puts it, they „help define and redefine the community's relationship to an individual and the individual's changing place in the community."[342] For the initiate in the traditional Igbo culture and religion, the eyes are opened so that he discovers a new level of truth and reality, which is unknown to the uninitiated. Far from being empty traditional rituals therefore, initiation rituals embody much spiritual and existential meaning for the people, and many times symbolise some kind of progress in the journey of life.[343]

Some beliefs and aspirations underlie traditional African practices of rites of passage (initiation rites). These include a recognition of the growth and development process in life, the need to prepare adequately for each new stage in life, and the necessity for a reaffirmation of community covenant during the major transitions of life. Other underlying cultural ideals or beliefs include the acknowledgement of the emergence of new identities, and of the sanctity and sacredness of life. Since life is seen as sacred, the spiritual dimension of the major transitions of life are taken seriously.[344]

Among the traditional Igbo, the key transitions of life are integrated with the people's religious belief and practices, and thus give the initiation rites associated with them a religious flavour. In addition to reflecting the people's history and embodying their values and aspirations, initiation rites also draw from their cosmology and religious philosophy.

---

is incapable of understanding the charateristic features of whatever religion may be the object of his research. He certainly is able to penetrate deeply into the very essence of different religions. See Bleeker, 16. This opinion of Bleeker is, however contestable.

[342] Oates, W. E., When Religion Gets Sick, Philadelphia 1970, 81.
[343] Cf. Enyioha, The Pastoral Significance, 18.
[344] Cf. Enyioha, The Pastoral Significance, 18.

Thus they are usually performed in the colour and language of religion. They represent, in some way, the sum total of the people's understanding of their existence.[345]

Initiation rites among the traditional Igbo take various forms and can have different significance in a different context. With the naming of a child, as we have seen before, the child is initiated into the corporate community. By identifying and calling him or her by this name he or she feels psychologically and socially accepted by the family and the entire community. Often times, this name brings positive influence and progress in the life of the child. Metuh rightly observes that „for the Igbo, as for the Romans, '*Nomen est Omen*' –a name is an omen. There is a strong conviction that there is a close connection between a person and his name. A name expresses a person's personality and in some circumstances some identity between a person and his name is recognised."[346] For example, if a persons name is *Ngozichukwu* (God's blessing), his presence always brings God's blessings and it is seen in whatever he does. If his name is *Nchekwubechukwu* (Hope in God), the trade mark of all his actions will be characterised by strong hope in God.

The youth are ritually introduced to the art of communal living. This happens when they are withdrawn from other people to live alone in the forest or in specially prepared huts away from the villages. They go through a period of withdrawal from the society, absence from home, during which they receive secret instructions before they are allowed to rejoin their relatives at home again. This is a symbolic experience of the process of dying, living in the spirit world and being reborn. The rebirth, that is the act of rejoining their families, emphasizes and dramatizes that the young people are now new, they have new personalities, they have lost (dropped) their childhood.[347] Here one also notices the value and

---

[345] Cf. Enyioha, The Pastoral Significance, 18.
[346] Metuh, E. I., Comparative Studies, 35.
[347] Cf. Mbiti, African Religions and Philosophy, 121.

quintessence of silence and quietude. These essential qualities are however, unfortunately disappearing very fast in our day.
The physical pain, which the children are encouraged to endure, is the beginning of training them for difficulties and sufferings of late life.[348] The frighteninig ordeal is a psychological device partly to emphasize the seriousness of the occasion, and partly to drive out fear from the candidates so that in time of danger, they do not flee away but take courage to defend themselves and their families. The initiates are now entitled to know every secret of tribal life and knowledge, apart from what is known to exclusive groups.[349]
Further significant role of the rites is that it is a means of introducing the young to adult life after which they are allowed to share in the full privileges and duties of the community. They enter into the state of responsibility: they inherit new rights, and obligations are expected of them by the society.[350] This incorporation into adult life also introduces them to the life of the living-dead as well as the life of those yet to be born.[351]
The initiation rites prepare young people in matters of sexual life, marriage, procreation and family responsibilities. They are henceforth allowed to shed their blood for their country, and to plant their biological seeds so that the next generation can begin to arrive[352], so that through initiation, „the corporate life of the nation is revived, its rhythm is given a new momentum, and its vitality is renewed."[353] As Mbiti rightly put it: „These initiation rites are like the birth of the young people into the state of maturity and responsibility. Initiation rites dramatize and effect the incorporation of the young into the full life of their nation. Only after

---

[348] Cf. Mbiti, African Religions and Philosophy, 123.
[349] Cf. Mbiti, African Religions and Philosophy, 125.
[350] Cf. Mbiti, African Religions and Philosophy, 121.
[351] Cf. Mbiti, African Religions and Philosophy, 121.
[352] Cf. Mbiti, African Religions and Philosophy, 121.
[353] Mbiti, African Religions and Philosophy, 131.

initiation, ... is a person religiously and socially born into full manhood or womanhood with all its secret, responsibilities, privileges and expectations."[354] „The ceremony is a deeply sacred one, for in it lies the survival of the nation. It is the solemn religious dramatization of man's conquest over death and disintegration."[355]

Initiation rites have great educational purposes. The occasion often marks the beginning of acquiring knowledge which is otherwise not accessible to those who have not been initiated. It is a special period of awakening to many things, a period of dawn for the young. They learn to endure hardships, they learn to live with one another, they learn to obey, they learn the secrets and mysteries of man-woman relationship.[356] They are introduced to the knowledge of the myth and to the rules and customs.[357] They learn something about the weather, about being industrious, about returning borrowed articles, about being kind and polite.[358] Parrinder notes well that „not only is instruction given by elders in traditional rituals and social duties, but boys have to learn endurance by sleeping out of doors and fending for themselves."[359] The incumbents or teachers instruct the girls in matters of house work and marital relations. This includes how to sleep with their husbands, when to refrain from sexual intercourse during pregnancy and up to the time the child begins to walk, how to be attractive wives, and how to bring up children.[360] Mbiti emphasizes that the „knowledge about bringing up children is considered the most important part of their education."[361]

One of the social significance of the puberty rites is the development of

---

[354] Mbiti, Africa Religion and Philosophy, 134-135.
[355] Mbiti, African Religion and Philosophy, 131.
[356] Cf. Mbiti, African Religions and Philosophy, 121-122.
[357] Cf. Bleeker, 18.
[358] Cf. Mbiti, African Religions and Philosophy, 131.
[359] Parrinder, Africa's Three Religions, 81.
[360] Cf. Mbiti, African Religions and Philosophy, 129.
[361] Mbiti, African Religions and Philosophy, 131.

self-concepts based on the expectation of the societal role models. This is actualized through participation in the puberty rites. The rituals provide opportunity for sensitivities to all-round balanced maturation expected of the 'young adults'. It is a ritually acceptable methodology for creating a healthy society in which the initiates live, and interact, as they too are expected to become role models for the next generation's healthy community.[362]

Puberty rites are graphic role-playing which are geared towards developing in the initiates, strong character and ability that will enable them to see matters beyond egocentric standpoint. The naivete of youth is supposed to be shattered and remodelled during the puberty rites.[363]

Initiation accompanies man's spiritual growth. Human life as such moves on in a succession of periods. The transition to new period always means the initiation into new truth –into a new domain of reality. These main turning points of human life are well known, that is, puberty, marriage, and death. These events are so highly important, that a man, who evaluates them in a religious sense, cannot remain passive. Therefore, he performs certain rites in order to further the transition. These ceremonies often function as rites of initiation. Initiation, therefore, marks the stages of the development of human life.[364]

Initiation is an indispensable factor in the process by which men really become human beings. Only by initiation does a man become a real man, a spiritual man, a man who knows the different dimensions of human life.[365] Initiation, in the words of Bleeker is „an introduction into unknown, hidden and fascinating regions of religious thinking and religious feeling. Each initiation is, in some respect an unmasking. A mysterious truth is deprived of its mask. The hidden world proves to be

---

[362] Cf. Imasogie, African Traditional Religion, 27.
[363] Cf. Imasogie, African Traditional Religion, 28.
[364] Cf. Bleeker, 19.
[365] Cf. Bleeker, 20.

otherwise than one thought and imagined."[366] It is interesting to note that what Schroeder holds about the importance of male initiation among the Wosera group of Papua New Guinea also holds among the Igbo people of Nigeria. According to Schroeder, „the system of male initiation is important for solidifying social identity, establishing leadership, reconciling inter-village and intra-village divisions, and forming responsible adults who can promote the cause of the village."[367]
For the traditional Igbo, transitional rites are not just educational or socialization process, they represent 'mile-posts' in a person's spiritual pilgrimage. They are ways an individual and his or her community may keep faith with their destinies. Through such rites the community acknowledges or reaffirms its belief in the sanctity and sacredness of life. This understanding of the underlying beliefs and goals of traditional Igbo initiation rites can serve as a bridge between the values and practices of the traditional culture and the Christian community.
At this point, we shall be satisfied with Igbo idea of initiation and the significant role of initiation rites in the traditional Igbo culture and religion. Our next attention will be focused on the other direction, the Christian initiation. What is it all about?

## 2.11 Conclusion

In the previous chapter is a frantic effort and an honest attempt to present an idea of the traditional Igbo, who formed the central point of this study. Most interesting and valuable aspects of their life especially in connection with our area of study were looked into. Those essential aspects namely their values, rituals, and world view contribute in no

---

[366] Bleeker, 20.
[367] Schroeder, R., Contextualization of Initiation in a Melanesian Community, in:
Piskaty, K., and Rzepkowski, H., *STM*, No.156, Nettetal 1993 (294-308), 297.

small measure in understanding and appreciating the depth and richness of the peoples' culture and traditional religion.

This chapter tries to illuminate as far as possible initiation rites in the traditional Igbo Culture and Religion. Among the traditional Igbo, no individual lives for himself alone but for the community, and the community also lives for the individual. For this reason, biological birth of an individual is considered not enough. He has to be 'reborn' by the community through some special rites into various stages of life and life's responsibility. These special rites culminate in incorporation (from the old state or position into the new). Because of what life itself entails and the amount of responsibility involved. Thus the three significant moments and the ordeal in initiation rites process. This is the sum total of the traditional Igbo idea of initiation.

Special areas high-lighted in initiation rites among the traditional Igbo include: Birth initiation rites, naming ritual and ceremony, puberty rites, expressive aspects of puberty rites, marriage initiation, death and funeral initiation rites. The chapter is concluded with the significant role of initiation in traditional Igbo culture and religion.

# Chapter Three

# Christian Initiation

## 3.1 Introduction

In the previous chapter we discussed 'initiation in the traditional Igbo culture and religion' and at the end elaborately presented 'the significant role of initiation in the traditional Igbo culture and religion'. In this chapter we are taking the same form as in previous chapters mentioned above in our study of Christian initiation.

In this section we would make some particular references to and include as our special source-material *Katiizim nke Okwukwe Nzuko Katolik n'asusu Igbo* (The Catechism of the Catholic Church in Igbo Language).[368] Committing in writing some part of the Church's doctrine for catechetical purposes regarding faith and moral in Igbo language and communicating (as well as inculcating) the same (in)to the people is already a proper step towards a proper direction. Our using *Katiizim nke Okwukwe Nzuko Katolik n'asusu Igbo* as a special source-material here, will therefore, help bring to lime-light the necessity and the urgent need for using traditional Igbo idea of initiation as a fundamental basis for pastoral catechesis of Christian initiation.

In the language of the history of religions, the salvific act that touches an individual human person and allows that person to begin the practice of Christian life can be designated as initiation.[369] Christian initiation is

---

[368] One of the greatest tools used by the Missionaries in spreading the Catholic faith and doctrine throughout the Igbo-speaking area of East of the Niger is Igbo Catechism Book. Though many of them never spoke the Language but through interpretation, progress was made.

[369] Cf. Vorgrimler, H., *Sacramental Theology*, 3$^{rd}$ ed., trans., Maloney, L. M., Minnesota 1992, 107.

rooted in the first three of the seven sacraments of the Church, as we shall see later.

Since Christian[370] initiation is based on the first three of the seven sacraments of the Church, it is considered rewarding to begin at this initial stage with a brief historical development of the concept 'sacrament' and other various teachings (of the Church and some renowned theologians of the Church) on sacrament.

---

[370] The name was originally applied to followers of Christ by outsiders, being first used according to the information in Acts 11:26 at Antioch (ca. *AD* 40-44). In Old Testament there is no trace of the name as is used in Acts of the Apostles. In New Testament it appears in only two other places namely Acts 26:28 (At this Agrippa said to Paul, 'A little more, and your arguments would make a Christian of me') and 1 Pet 4:16 (... but if any one of you should suffer for being a Christian, then there must be no shame but thanksgiving to God for bearing this name). Kasper, W., refers to the early Christians as "*Messiasleute*" (Messiah-People). See the original work in German: *Der Gott Jesu Christi*, 3.*Aufl.*, Mainz 1995, 205. English edition by the same author: The God of Jesus Christ, trans., O' Connell, M. J., New York 2000, 163. For more historical development of the name, see Cross, F. L., and Livingstone, E. A., (eds.), The Oxford Dictionary of the Christian Church, 2nd ed., London 1974, 278. For the Igbo Christians, the *Igbo* equivalent for the English word 'Christian' is "*Onye otu Kristi*". In the literal sense it means "*Onye Uka*" (a Church member or a Church fellow). In Igbo Catechism Book it is asked: "*Onye bu Onye otu Kristi*"? (Who is a Christian?) The answer runs thus: "*Onye otu Kristi bu Onye kwerenu a baptizie ya. O bia kwe na-emeputa n'omume ya nkuzi nile nke Jeeso Kristi*" (A Christian is one who believes and is baptised and he puts into practice all the teachings of Jesus Christ). See Nwosu, J. A., (ed.), *Katikiizim nke Okwukwe Nzuko Katolik n'asusu Igbo*, Onitsha 1996, q.113. (Hence referred as *KOKI*).

## 3.2 A Brief Historical Development of the Concept 'sacrament' and other various teachings on sacrament

As already mentioned above our preoccupation here is to make a brief but condensed historical excursus of the development of the concept 'sacrament'. The concept was not originally Christian, but it was such an important, meaningful and above all significant word, especially in the ancient Roman 'pagan' world. But since its 'inculturation' and inception into the Church's vocabulary, it has occupied a pride of place. To put it in a clearer form, it has been identified with the Church.
What then is the historical development of the concept of 'sacrament' and how was it transferred into the ecclesial-theological vocabulary?

### 3.2.1 A Brief Historical Development of the Concept of the Term 'Sacrament'

We have to recapitulate here again that the concept of the term 'sacrament' was not initially Christian. There was no concept of sacrament in the early Christian era, as it is understood today. Though in this era (early Christian centuries) baptism and Eucharist were primary and also penitential practice, the imposition of hands, and anointing were mentioned, there is no single unified term under general concept as sacrament.[371] Attempts to form such a concept developed at certain important stages in history.[372]

According to its etymology the word '*sacramentum*' means a 'sacred' or 'holy thing' (*res sacrans* or *res sacra*). In Roman profane literature the oath of loyalty taken by the soldiers and the oath in general were called

---

[371] Cf. Vorgrimler, Sacramental Theology, 43.
[372] For the history cf. Finkenzeller, J., "*Sakrament*", in *LThK* IX, 220-225. See also Cross and Livingstone, The Oxford Dictionary of the Christian Church, London, 1218-1219.

*sacramentum*. In Roman legal language the word *sacramentum* means a pledge deposited in the temple by disputing parties.[373]

In the Vulgate, *sacramentum* is the rendering of the Greek *mysterion* which means 'something hidden', 'secret' (*mysterium*); in the sphere of religion it signifies the secrets of God (Wis. 2, 22; 6, 4): and in particular the mystery of the Redemption by Jesus Christ (Ep. 1, 9; Col. 1, 26). It has the further meanings of: sign, symbol, type of a mystery (Eph. 5, 32; Marriage is a symbol of the mysterious bond of Christ with His Church. Cf. Apoc. 1, 20; 17, 7).[374]

According to its history, the transfer of *sacramentum* to ecclesial-theological vocabulary was accomplished by the African theologians Tertulian (+ ca.220), Cyprain (+ 258) and Augustine (+ 430). In their interpretations of *mysterion* in Ephesians and Colossians, the realization of the plan of salvation, Jesus Christ, the incarnation (*sacramentum incarnationis*), the Church (Cyprian: *sacramentum unitatis*), faith, and the creed are all called *sacramentum*.[375]

It appears that the first to refer to baptism and Eucharist as *sacramenta* was Tertulian. In the case of baptism he pointed to its similarity to the religious-ethical self-obligation in the recruit's oath. In general, it can be said that the widest possible variety of rites are referred to as *sacramenta* in the writings of the Church Fathers.

The Roman Catechism (II 1,8) defines a Sacrament as „ a thing perceptible to the senses, which on the ground of Divine institution possesses the power both of effecting and signifying sanctity and righteousness."[376]

---

[373] Ott, L., Fundamentals of Catholic Dogma, 4th ed., trans., Lynch, P., Illinois 1960, 325.
[374] Ott, Fundamentals of Catholic Dogma, 325.
[375] Cf. Vorgrimler, Sacramental Theology, 44.
[376] See Ott, Fundamentals of Catholic Dogma, 326.

## 3.2.2 Other various Teachings on Sacraments

The theme of sacrament is so vast and too deep that no single word or sentence or expression or even a book can encapsulate all the meaning and what it is, all together. Our effort here is, therefore, only an attempt to collect and put together some important descriptions and statements from the teaching Office of the Church, the Catechism of the Catholic Church (CCC) and some renowned theologians on sacrament.[377]

### 3.2.2.1 The Vatican Council II (1962-1965) on the Sacraments

The teaching Office of the Church, in the Second Vatican Ecumenical Council, in the Constitution on the Sacred Liturgy, sees the sacraments from the point of view of their purpose. In the above mentioned document she (the teaching Office of the Church) outlined three outstanding functions of the sacraments namely: „To sanctify men, to build up the Body of Christ, and, finally, to give worship to God."[378] The Document further explains: „Because they (the sacraments) are also signs they also instruct. They not only presuppose faith, but by words and objects they also nourish, strengthen, and express it. That is why they are called 'sacrament of Faith'. They do, indeed, confer grace, but, in addition, the very act of celebrating them most effectively disposes the faithful to receive this grace to their profit, to worship God duly, and to practise charity."[379]

Elsewhere the teaching Office of the Church clearly declares that „the Church, in Christ, is in the nature of sacrament –a sign and instrument,

---

[377] This also testifies how vast the subject of sacrament is. Not even the teaching Office of the Church has the last say, the contributions of some renowned theologians are also very important, and as such are recognised by the Church.
[378] *SC* 59.
[379] *SC* 59.

that is, of communion with God and of unity among all men ..."³⁸⁰

In another section it says: „Yet he (God) frees all of them (men) so that by putting aside love of self and bringing all earthly resources into the service of human life, they can devote themselves to the future when humanity itself will become an offering accepted to God (cf. Rom 15: 16). The Lord left behind a pledge of this hope and strength for life's journey in that sacrament of faith where natural elements refined by man are changed into his glorified Body and Blood, providing a meal of brotherly solidarity and a foretaste of the heavenly banquet."³⁸¹ In this particular section, the Church was explaining human activity and its fulfilment in the *paschal mystery*.

### 3.2.2.2 The Catholic Catechisms on Sacraments

a) *Roman Catechism* (1566)
„*Sacramentum est invisibilis gratiae signum ad nostrarum iustficattionem institutum.*": „A sacrament is a visible sign of inward grace instituted for our salvation" (Pars II, cap 1, 3; cf. Augustinus, De cat. rud. 26).³⁸²

b) *Catholic Catechism* (1847)
„A sacrament is a visible sign instituted by Jesus Christ through which we share invisible grace and inner healing."³⁸³

c) *Catholic Catechism for German Dioceses* (1955)
„To a sacrament belongs 1. The visible sign, 2. The inner grace, 3.

---

[380] *LG* 1.
[381] *GS* 38.
[382] Cf. Biemer, G., *Symbole Des Glaubens Leben*, Ostfildern 1999, 53. (Hence Biemer only).
[383] Deharbe, J., *Katholischer Katechismus*, Mainz-Freiburg 1863, 147; quoted by Biemer, ibid, 53.

Instituted by Jesus Christ."[384]

d) *Faith – life – act* (1969)
"The Lord is with his people; the sacraments are signs of his nearness. They work what they signify."[385]

e) *Good-News of Faith: A Catholic Catechism* (1978)
"Sacraments are holy signs that work through Jesus Christ what they signify. – Word and sign that show the grace on behalf of the Lord belong to a sacrament."[386]

f) *Catechism of the Catholic Church* (1993)
Jesus Christ „seated at the right of the Father" and pouring out the Holy Spirit on his Body which is the Church, Christ now acts through the sacraments he instituted to communicate his grace. The sacraments are perceptible signs (words and actions) accessible to our human nature. By the action of Christ and the power of the Holy Spirit they make present efficaciously the grace that they signify."[387]

g) *Katikiizim nke Okwukwe Nzuko Katolik N'asusu Igbo* (1996)
In the Igbo Catechism Book (named above) the meaning of sacrament is close to the translation of the English definition from the Catechism of the Catholic Church. In question 351 of the said catechism book it asks: „*Gini bu Sakramenti*"? (What is sacrament?) to which it answers:

---

[384] Cf. Biemer, 53.
[385] Cf. Biemer, 53.
[386] Cf. Biemer, 53.
[387] CCC 1084. The German edition reads: *Christus, der "zur Rechten des Vaters sitzt" und den Heiligen Geist in seinem Leib, der Kirche, ausbreitet, handelt jetzt durch die Sakramente, die er zur Mitteilung seiner Gnade eingesetzt hat. Die Sakramente sind durch die Sinne wahrnehmbare Zeichen (Wort und Handlungen), die unserer Menschennatur zugänglich sind. Kraft des Wirkens Christi und des Waltens des Heiligen Geistes bewirken sie die Gnade, die sie bezeichnen.* (KKK 1084), 1993, 309.

*„Sakramenti bu Akara doro anya, nke na-agba ama maka grasia Jeeso Kristi na-esi na ya bu Akara ehunye na mkpuruobi anyi"* (lit. Sacrament is a clear sign, which reveals the grace by which Jesus Christ through this sign pour into our soul).[388]

### 3.2.2.3. Expressions of Some Renowned Theologians on the Sacrament

a)   *Michael Schmaus*

In 1957 Schmaus expressed that the sacrament is a gift from Jesus Christ which he entrusted to the Church and because it is a gift from Jesus Christ, it is an effective symbol of salvation.[389]

b)   *Karl Rahner*

Rahner explained in 1964 that when and where the Church in her commitment with absolute engagement of her being leaves a mark as original sacrament of salvation (also in the name of Jesus Christ) gives a part in the individual salvation situation of each person and this on her particular being through their ultimate actualisation is then „what we call sacrament."[390]

c)   *Joseph Ratzinger*

Ratzinger sees the meaning of sacrament in the placement of the (human) person in the historical context of the coming Christ. To receive the Christian sacrament for him means: Entering into the history of Christ, .... First it expresses anew the vertical dimension of human existence, it points to God's call which makes a person human. Over and above all it points out the horizontal dimension of history of faith from

---

[388] *KOKI* 351 (translation mine).
[389] CF. Shmaus, M., Katholische Dogmatik IV/1, München 1957, 11.
[390] Cf. Arnold, F. X., (hrsg.), Handbuch der Pastoraltheologie 1, Freiburg 1964, 324.

Jesus Christ.[391]

d)    *Edward Schillebeeckx*

The being of Jesus Christ is a constitutive sign of God's gift of grace. (To encounter him means) to encounter God himself directly.[392]

e)    *Hans Urs von Balthasar*

The conversion of a person in pure faith to God has a necessary complement in the conversion of the individual to the community of the Christian Church; this represents the realised love of Jesus Christ to the world, each receives it, which the faith-love to Jesus Christ as one of them clearly heralds. So is the initiation sacrament, Baptism is two in one: Giving oneself to the death and resurrection form of Jesus Christ for the life of the world as accepted form of existence (Rom 6:3-12; Col 2:12) – giving oneself to the existence form of love and membership in the Body of the Lord (Eph 4:4-5). In Christ himself Baptism was both ritual (Mk 1:9 par) and existential (Lk 12:50: Baptism of the Cross), and he gives it for his own (followers) in the two equal level of meaning (Mtt 28:19; Mk 10:38f); already in the opinion of the baptizer, the Christian baptism of Spirit and fire supercedes water baptism ritual (Mtt 3:11), one must be concious of the whole paradox of a sacramental giving of Spirit (Acts 1:5;11:16), in order to see in the New Testament the inseparability of the objective gift and the subjective acceptance, as well as turning to God and turning to the community.[393]

f)    *Walter Kasper and Karl Lehmann*

Jesus Christ in his humanity, in his life and death is a sign of God for the people, he is the original sacrament in which all other sacraments must be founded. The making presence of the experienced salvation in and

---

[391] Cf. Ratzinger, J., Die sakramentale Begründung christlicher Existenz, Meitingen 1965, 18f.

[392] Schillebeeckx, E., Personale Begegnung mit Gott, Mainz 1964, 73.

[393] Von Balthasar, H-U., Spirit Creator, in: Skizzen zur Theologie, Bd. 111, 1967, 334.

through Jesus Christ, in the midst of human life happens through the Church. It is already a sign of its power of existence in the world, through the witness of her faith, her hope and her love, she can be a sign and sacrament of unity and salvation to humanity. ... In the sacraments a decisive basic human situation is made present and moreover the effective power of the Word of salvation from God in Jesus Christ is expressed.[394]

g) *Herbert Vorgrimler*

The sacrament is a symbolic action in which human beings are engaged as believers, as those who celebrate liturgy, as narrators, as persons who act symbolically; but the divine Spirit uses this human action as a means and a way by which to make Jesus Christ, with his historically unique saving activity, memorially, really, and actually present. – This making-presence thus does not happen without human beings, but neither does it happen simply through them (as happens from the point of view of religious studies or history of religions). Instead, it is the Spirit of God who takes the initiative and supports the whole event, causing the effects in the human persons; but instead of depriving those human persons of their own activity, the Spirit actually strengthens them for what they do.[395]

Günter Biemer briefly put together the major points of the structure elements of the sacrament according to the teaching of the Church:

a) Jesus Christ, the exalted Lord, founded through the effective work of the Holy Spirit in dialogue of history with individual and the nation his mystical Body- the Church- the sacrament of salvation.

b) The Church is the sign and instrument for our unity with God and

---

[394] Kasper, W., and Lehmann, K., Die Heilssendung der Kirche in der Gegenwart, Pastorale, Mainz 1970, 78.

[395] Vorgrimler, Sacramental Theology, 71. (It is originally written in German with the title "Sakramentaltheologie", Düsseldorf 1992, 88f).

for the unity of the whole humanity.
c) The Spirit of God works in the Church through the seven sacraments whose sign addresses the fundamental situation of life process, the salvation of the faithful.
d) The fullness of the sacrament contains the gifts of the Grace of God to every individual and the yes of the people as a response of his/her faith in God. Sacraments are experience of turning to God through the community's turning of the Church to the individual.
e) Through the sacraments, the faithful at the peak and turning-point of their lives, God's infallible creative love will become effective for salvation.
f) The sacraments initiate the recipient into the salvation history from Jesus Christ, which leads to the resurrection, to judgement and to everlasting life.[396]

What are the Sacraments of Christian Initiation and why are they referred to as Christian Initiation?

### 3.3 The Sacraments of Christian Initiation

The Church recognises as the Sacraments of Christian Initiation Baptism, Confirmation and the Holy Eucharist.[397] They are referred to as Sacraments of Christian Initiation because they „lay the foundations of every Christian life."[398] Pope Paul VI teaches: „The sharing in the divine nature given to men through the grace of Christ bears a certain likeness to the origin, development and nourishing of natural life. The faithful are

---

[396] Cf. Biemer, 56-57.
[397] See *Deutsche Bischofskonferenz (hrsg.), Katholischer Erwachsenen Katechismus*, *(KEK)*, 1. *Bd.* Styria-Köln 1985, 330., 339., cf. also *SC* 71.
[398] The Catechism of the Catholic Church (CCC) 1212.

born anew by Baptism, strengthened by the sacrament of Confirmation, and receive in the Eucharist the food of eternal life. By means of these sacraments of Christian initiation, they thus receive in increasing measure the treasures of the divine life and advance toward the perfection of charity."[399] In a copious manner Kathleen Hughes succinctly says: „The three sacraments of initiation – baptism, confirmation, and Eucharist – combine to bring us to the full stature of Christ and to enable us to carry out the mission of the entire people of God in the Church and in the world. These sacraments commit us to a vocation: to live as children of God, brothers and sisters of one another, freed from sin and the power of evil; joined to Christ; empowered by the Spirit; within a community of disciples, a priestly people, all of whom owe our allegiance to God in Christ and all of whom are witnesses to these realities before the world."[400]

In the early centuries of the Church, when only adult baptism was practised (at the time of great trials and persecution of the Church) these sacraments of Christian initiation were administered and received at a stretch. Kathleen Hughes describes the situation thus: „To the Liturgical baptismal core of water and word had been joined an all-night vigil, readings and instruction, a prayer over the water, renunciations, several anointings, triple questions and immersions, a final anointing, clothing, episcopal laying on of hands with prayer, another anointing and singing, prayers of the community, the exchange of peace, and participation in the Eucharistic banquet."[401] But after the Church has been freed and officially recognised as a state religion and with the increase in number of the converts there was a separation of the sacraments of initiation in

---

[399] Paul VI, *Divinae consortium naturae: AAS* 63 (1971) 657., cf. RCIA Introduction 1-2.

[400] Hughes, K., "Baptism: Pastoral-Liturgical Tradition", in: Stuhlmueller, C., (ed.), (et.al.), The Collegeville Pastoral Dictionary of Biblical Theology, Minnesota: The Liturgical Press, 1996, (70-74) 73.

[401] Hughes, "Baptism: Pastoral-Liturgical Tradition", 72.

the West.

Increase in number of the converts implies also increase in the number of parishes and also the distance. Kathleen Hughes again gives an extensive description: „As exemplified in the *Apostolic Tradition*, laying on of hands and prayer, the ritual which followed baptism, was an episcopal ceremony. Full ritual immersion in baptism took place under the direction of presbyters and deacons apart from the community because of the nudity entailed."[402] Hughes goes further, „Those baptized quasi-privately were clothed and led to the bishop who waited with the community to complete their incorporation publicly with prayer, laying on of hands and then participation in the Eucharistic banquet. As numbers increased, it became impossible for the bishop to be present at every celebration of initiation. In his absence, baptism was followed by Eucharist; the episcopal ceremonies simply were postponed by days or weeks until the bishop could complete the ceremony. Eventually even more time elapsed, and a rite of episcopal laying on of hands with prayer, now quite independent of baptism, demanded a theological rationale."[403] Hughes continues: „Thus, confirmation became a distinct sacrament, and gradually it lost its initiation moorings entirely as it was called a sacrament of Christian maturity, or, in this century, a sacrament of Catholic Action. „Strengthening" became the language associated with confirmation –strengthening to preach the gospel, to give witness, to maintain one's baptismal purity in the face of the sinfulness of the world. Confirmation, then, was deliberately postponed until the age of reason, variously computed between seven and the end of adolescence. And, in a final dismemberment of the ancient unity of the three sacraments of initiation, the Eucharist, too, was also postponed out of exaggerated medieval reverence for the sacred species."[404] However,

---

[402] Hughes, "Baptism: Pastoral-Liturgical Tradition", 72.
[403] Hughes, "Baptism: Pastoral-Liturgical Tradition", 72.
[404] Hughes, "Baptism: Pastoral-Liturgical Tradition, 72. See also *KEK* 340.

recently some scholars have started questioning the origin of Confirmation. They argue that in some early communities what became confirmation through various historical accidents and developments was simply the way that the baptismal rite itself was concluded and the Eucharist begun. Later its separation from baptism brought with it a whole host of theological and pastoral problems.[405] But time is not on our side for us to go further deep into the argument, moreover, it is not necessary in our study, at least for the moment.

Certainly the above description of Kathleen Hughes are historical facts. The Church till date retains officially as the sacraments of Christian initiation Baptism, Confirmation and the Eucharist. It is good to note here, however, that the idea that „today in all rites, Latin and Eastern, the Christian initiation of adults begins with their entry into the catechumenate and reaches its culmination in a single celebration of the three sacraments of initiation: Baptism, Confirmation and the Eucharist"[406], is only obtainable and functional in the Eastern (Church) rite. Though Christian initiation of adult still begins with the entry into the catechumenate also in the Latin (Church) rite, the 'culmination in *a single celebration* of the three sacraments of initiation (Baptism, Confirmation and the Eucharist)'[407] is practically lacking.

What is today practical in the Latin (Church) rite is that for adult Christian initiation, baptism and the Eucharist are conferred simultaneously at a single celebration, and Confirmation at later

---

[405] See Johnson, E. M., "The Role of Worship in the Contemporary Study of Christian Initiation: A Select Review of the Literature", in: Seasoltz, R. K., (ed.), Worship, Vol. 75, Nr.1, January 2001, (20-35) 25. For further arguments on the historical origin of confirmation see Kavanagh, A., "Confirmation: A Suggestion from Structure", in: Worship 58(1984) 386-395; Kavanagh, A., Confirmation: Origins and Reform, Collegeville-Pueblo 1988; Johnson, M., (ed.), Living Water, Sealing Spirit, 148-158.

[406] CCC 1213; cf. *AGD* 14, CIC 851; 865; 866.

[407] Cf. CCC 1213.

(proximate or remote) time. „In the Eastern rites the Christian initiation of infants also begins with Baptism followed immediately by Confirmation and the Eucharist, while in the Roman rite it is followed by years of catechesis before being completed later by Confirmation and the Eucharist, the summit of their Christian initiation."[408] An important observation worthy of note at this stage is that in practice, in the Latin Church the order of the sacraments for the Christian initiation is: Baptism, the Eucharist and then Confirmation, Confirmation being the seal of the Christian initiation.

Let us now concentrate our attention on these particular three sacraments of Christian initiation in the previous order mentioned above, in the next section of our work.

### 3.3.1 The Sacrament of Baptism

Baptism is the act in which Christian existence is grounded.[409] It is the fundamental (*grundlegende*) sacrament of Christian initiation (*Einführung, Einweihung*).[410]

The word baptism is derived from the Greek term *baptizein*, which means to „plunge" or „immerse".

The sacrament is so called after the central rite by which it is carried out. The „plunge" into the water symbolises the catechumen's burial into Christ's death, from which he rises up by resurrection with him as „a new creature."[411] This symbolic initiation gives to the newly baptised a new orientation and provides a new meaning to his or her life, in his/her relationship to him/herself and to others, to his/her whole environment,

---

[408] CCC 1213; cf. also CIC 851 §2; 868. In practice, however, the Eucharist comes before the sacrament of Confirmation.
[409] Kasper, The God of Jesus Christ, 246.
[410] *KEK* 334.
[411] 2 Cor 5:17; Gal 6:15; cf. Rom 6:3-4; Col 2:12.

to history and to God.[412]

Through one baptism we are received into the community of the Church of all times and places. The reception into the Church finds its concrete expression in the reception into the worshipping community; in a community then, which can be lawfully named with any name, which is the sign (mark) of one and complete people of God, the Church.[413]

The Sacrament of „Holy Baptism is the basis of the whole Christian life, the gateway to life in the Spirit (*vitae spiritualis ianua*)[414], and the door which gives access to the other sacraments."[415] Through Baptism the believer is freed from sin and reborn as a child of God; becomes member of Christ, is incorporated into the Church and is made sharer in the mission of the Church. It is that sacrament in which man being washed with water in the name[416] of the Three Divine Persons is spiritually reborn. According to the Roman Catechism: „*Baptismum esse sacramentum regenerationis per aquam in verbo* (Baptism is the sacrament of regeneration through water in the word)".[417]

In the Eastern Church, baptism by water (*Baptismus fluminis*) is done by immersion, that is, by plunging (the person being baptised) three times into the water in the name of the Three Divine Persons. But in the Latin Church, the circumstances vary. Mostly it is done by pouring of the water on the head (of the person being baptised) also three times and in

---

[412] Cf. Quasten, J., (ed.), Christian Initiation (Studies in Christian Antiquity), Vol. 17, CUA, Washington 1974, 1.
[413] *LG* 28., see *KEK* 335.
[414] DZ 1314
[415] CCC 1213
[416] The Roman Catechism expressly instructs that we are baptised not in the names but in the name of the Father and of the Son and of the Holy Spirit. See Catechismus Romanus II, 2, 10., quoted by Kasper, W., The God of Jesus Christ, 294.
[417] Roman Catechism II, 2, 5; cf. DZ 1314; CIC 204 §1; 849; CCC 1213. For further definitions see Biemer, 52-56.

the name of the Three Divine Persons.

Apart from the above two named methods of Baptism, there are also two substitutes for Sacramental Baptism:

a) Baptism of desire which is the explicit or implicit desire for sacramental baptism (*votum baptismi*) associated with perfect contrition (contrition based on charity);

b) Baptism of Blood (*Baptismus sanguinis*) which signifies martyrdom of an unbaptised person, that is, the patient bearing of violent death or of an assault which of its nature leads to death, by reason of one's confession of the Christian faith, or one's practice of Christian virtue.

What happens at Baptism? In other words how is Baptism administered?

### 3.3.1.1 The Administration of Baptism

The consideration of how Baptism is administered (Liturgy of Baptism) is very important at this point because it will help to bring to limelight the necessity and urgent need for the fundamental basis of pastoral catechesis of the Christian initiation in Igboland.

Concerning the Liturgy of baptism or how baptism is administered, the Igbo Catechism Book (*Katikiizim nke Okwukwe Nzuko Katolik n'asusu Igbo*) did not give any further or extensive description. In question number 370, it is asked: „*Kedu ka e si eme mmadu Baptizim*"? (How is Baptism conferred onto a person?). And it answers: „*Ka e si eme mmadu Baptizim bu site na ina-atakwasi ya mmiri n'isi na-ekwu si: Emee m gi Baptizim N'Afa Nna na nke Nwa na nke Mmuo Nso*" (lit. „Baptism is conferred on a person by pouring water on the head saying: I baptise you in the Name of the Father and of the Son and of the Holy Spirit").[418] More in this respect was not mentioned. However, baptism should normally take place in the parish (Church) during the Sunday celebration, that is, within the Eucharistic celebration. This is with regard to the infant baptism. But for the teenagers and adults, it is

---

[418] The translation is mine.

suitably celebrated within the liturgy of the Easter vigil.[419]

## 3.3.2 The Sacrament of Confirmation

After Baptism, the second sacrament of the Christian initiation according to the traditional order is Confirmation. The English word Confirmation is derived from the Latin verb-root *Confirmare*- „to make firm", „to strengthen". It constitutes one of the most essential parts for the completion of the sacraments of Christian initiation. This means that without the Sacrament of Confirmation administered, the Christian initiation though valid and efficacious, remains incomplete.[420] According to the teaching of Vatican Council II: „Incorporated into the Church by Baptism, the faithful are appointed by their baptismal character to Christian religious worship .... By the sacrament of Confirmation they (the baptised) are more perfectly bound to the Church and are endowed with the special strength of the Holy Spirit. Hence they are, as true witnesses of Christ, more strictly obliged to spread the faith by word and deed."[421]

Confirmation is, therefore, „that Sacrament in which, by the imposition of hands, unction and prayer, a baptised person is filled with Holy Ghost for the inner strengthening of the supernatural life and for the courageous outward confession of Faith."[422] Thomas Aquinas defines Confirmation as a Sacrament of the fullness of grace and as „that Sacrament in which strength is conferred on the regenerate":

---

[419] Cf. *KEK* 335.
[420] As we have somewhere earlier mentioned Baptism, Confirmation and the Eucharist constitute the Sacraments of Christian initiation. They form a unity so that without any of them, the Christian initiation is considered not yet completed.
[421] *LG* 11; cf. *OC*, Introduction 2.
[422] Ott, Fundamentals of Catholic Dogma, 361.

(*sacramentum, quo spirituale robur regenerato confertur*).[423] At the Confirmation the confirmand receives the „mark", the seal of the Holy Spirit. A seal is a symbol of a person, a sign of personal authority, or ownership of an object.[424]

In the early centuries of the Church, Confirmation generally comprised one single celebration with Baptism. Among other reasons, the multiplication of infant baptisms all through the year, the increase of rural parishes and the growth of dioceses often prevented the bishop from being present at all baptismal celebrations. In the West, the desire to reserve the completion of Baptism to the bishop caused the temporal separation of the two sacraments. The East has kept them united, so that confirmation is conferred by the priest who baptises. But he can do so only with the „myron" (sacred chrism) consecrated by a bishop or patriarch.

A custom of the Roman Church facilitated the development of the Western practice: a double anointing with sacred chrism after Baptism. The first anointing of the neophyte on coming out of the baptismal bath was performed by the priest; it was completed by a second anointing on the forehead of the newly baptised by the bishop. The first anointing with sacred chrism, by the priest, has remained attached to the baptismal rite; it signifies the participation of the one baptised in the prophetic, priestly and kingly offices of Christ. If Baptism is conferred on an adult, there is only one post-baptismal anointing, that of the Confirmation.

The practice of the Eastern Churches gives greater emphasis to the unity of Christian initiation. That of the Latin Church more clearly expresses the communion of the new Christian with the bishop as guarantor and servant of the unity, catholicity and apostolicity of his Church, and hence the connection with the apostolic origins of Christ's Church.[425]

---

[423] Aquinas, T., *ST* III. 72, 1 ad 2.
[424] Cf. Gen 38:18; 41:42; Dt 32:34; *CT* 8:6.
[425] Cf. CCC 1290-1292.

### 3.3.3 The Sacrament of the Eucharist

The Latin word *eucharistia*, meaning, 'giving thanks' brings to completion the celebration of the Christian initiation. This 'thanksgiving' (*eucharistia*) is also an invitation to participate in 'the table of the Lord'[426] together with the already Christian community.[427] The Catechism of the Catholic Church explains: „The holy Eucharist completes Christian initiation. Those who have been raised to the dignity of the royal priesthood by Baptism, and configured more deeply to Christ by Confirmation, participate with the whole community in the Lord's own sacrifice by means of the Eucharist."[428] As a result of its role, the Eucharist has been described as „the source and summit of the Christian life"[429], the soul of all Christian life[430] because „the other sacraments, and indeed all ecclesiastical ministries and works of the apostolate, are bound up with the Eucharist and are oriented toward it.... For in the Blessed Eucharist is contained the whole spiritual good of the Church, namely Christ himself, our Pasch."[431]

The inexhaustible richness of the sacrament of the Eucharist, the summit of Christian initiation,[432] shows itself in the different names given to it. It is called:

---

[426] John Paul II, On The Mystery And Worship Of The Eucharist, *Dominae Cenae*, February 24, 1980, 11., (hence *DC*).

[427] This is shown in the Liturgy when the Priest-celebrant says: "This is the Lamb of God.... Happy are those who are called to his supper"(Jn 1:29; Rev 19:9. It is also shown by the familiar Gospel parable about the guests invited to the marriage banquet (Lk 14:16ff).

[428] CCC 1322.

[429] *LG* 11: *AAS* 57 (1965), 15; *SC* 10: *AAS* 56 (1964), 102; *PO* 5: *AAS* 58 (1966), 997f; *CD* 30: *AAS* 58 (1966), 688f; *AGD* 9: *AAS* 58 (1966), 957f.

[430] *DC* 5.

[431] *PO* 5.

[432] *CIC* 851, 2; 866.

a) *Eucharist*, while it is an action of thanksgiving to God. It is a Jewish feast of thanksgiving commemorating Jahweh's countless blessings and his mighty deeds on Israel, his chosen people. Jahweh, the God of Israel freed his people with mighty hands from the hands of their enemies, from the bondage of slavery in Egypt, led them through the desert and brought them into the Land flowing with milk and honey.

b) The *Lord's Supper*, while it is connected to the last supper which the Lord took with his disciples on the night before he suffered, and while it points to an eschatological foretaste of the wedding feast of the Lamb in the heavenly Jerusalem.[433]

c) The *Breaking of Bread*[434], while Jesus at the Last Supper[435], when as Master of the table he blessed and distributed the bread.[436] By this action (of breaking the bread), his disciples will recognise him after his Resurrection,[437] and it is this expression that the first Christians will use to designate their Eucharistic assemblies;[438] by so doing they signified that all who eat the one broken bread, Christ, enter into communion with him and form but one body in him.[439]

d) *Holy Communion*, while by partaking of it we united ourselves to Christ, who makes us sharers in his Body and Blood to form a single body.[440]

Other names include: The Eucharistic Assembly; the memorial of the

---

[433] Cf. 1 Cor 11:20; Rev 19:9.
[434] Part of the Jewish tradition, especially at meal.
[435] Cf. Mtt 26:26; 1 Cor 11:24.
[436] Cf. Mtt 14:19; 15:36; Mk 8:6, 19.
[437] Cf. Lk 24:13-35.
[438] Cf. Acts 2:42, 46; 20:7, 11.
[439] Cf. 1 Cor 10:16-17.
[440] Cf. 1 Cor 10:16-17.

Lord's Passion, Death and Resurrection; the Holy Sacrifice;[441] the celebration of the Sacred Mysteries; the Most blessed Sacrament; the bread of angels; the bread from heaven; *viaticum* and the Sacred Liturgy. Pope John Paul II refers to the Eucharist as 'a pledge of eternal life'[442], 'a pledge of the eternal Passover'[443], 'Holy Sacrifice of propitiation'[444] 'Sacrament of love by which the disciples will be known'[445] (cf. Jn 13:35), 'Sign of unity and bond of Charity'[446], 'Source of charity'[447], 'Sacrament of Bread and Wine'[448], 'the Bread of the Lord'[449], 'the Sacrament of Church's unity'.[450] It is also referred to as Liturgy, which is the primary and indispensable source from which the faithful are to derive the true Christian Spirit.[451] It is also called the „Sacrament of sacraments" because „all the other sacraments are ordered to it as to their end."[452]

---

[441] Terms that are also used are: the Holy Sacrifice of the Mass or simply the Mass, "sacrifice of praise", "spiritual sacrifice", "pure and holy sacrifice". Cf. Heb 13:15; 1 Pet 2:5; Ps 116:13, 17; Mal 1:11. On his letter 'To All the Bishops of the Church' Pope John Paul II explains: "The Eucharist is above all else a sacrifice of the Redemption and also the sacrifice of the New Covenant...." See *DC* 9; cf. Also *SC* 2, 47: *AAS* 56 (1964) 83f; *LG* 3, 28: *AAS* 57 (1965), 6, 33f; *UR* 2: *AAS* 57 (1965), 91; *PO* 13: *AAS* 58 (1966), 1011f.
[442] *DC* 4.
[443] *DC* 4.
[444] *DC* 4, 7.
[445] *DC* 5, 12.
[446] *DC* 5. Cf. also 1 Cor 10:17; *LG* 7: *AAS* 57 (1965), 9.
[447] *DC* 7.
[448] *DC* 7.
[449] *DC* 11.
[450] *DC* 12.
[451] *SC* 14.
[452] Aquinas, T., *ST*. III, 65, 3.

## 3.4 The Effects of Christian Initiation

The effects of the Christian initiation seen from the three sacraments (Baptism, Confirmation and the Eucharist) that constitute the Christian initiation are multi-dimensional. It could be seen from the vertical-horizontal dimension, from the Ecclesiological-Christological dimension, and from sociological-Anthropological dimension. None of these could work perfectly in isolation of the others.

In the sacraments of Christian initiation, the recipients are freed from the power of darkness and are joined to Christ's death, burial, and resurrection. They receive the Spirit of filial adoption and are part of the entire people of God (the Church) in the celebration of the memorial of the Lord's death and resurrection.[453]

Through the sacrament of Baptism, the recipients receive the forgiveness of sins (original and personal sins committed before baptism),[454] are incorporated into Christ,[455] made members of the Church[456] and thus are formed into God's people. They (the baptised) are brought into the dignity of adopted children,[457] as a new creation through water[458] and Holy Spirit. Hence they 'are called and are indeed the children of God'.[459] The sacrament of baptism imparts the grace of justification,[460] sanctifying grace and indelible spiritual character (*unauslöschliches*

---

[453] Cf. *AGD* 14; see also 'RCIA' Introduction 1.
[454] See *KEK* 331.
[455] Cf. DZ 3802, 1314, 1671.
[456] Cf. DZ 780-781, 1621, 1627.
[457] Cf. Col 1:13; Rom 8:15; Gal 4:5; DZ 1524.
[458] The Conference of the German Catholic Bishops explains: "*Das Wasser ist Symbol der Reinigung wie Symbol des Lebens. Es bringt die doppelte Frucht der Taufe zum Ausdruck: Reinigung von der Sünde und Geschenk des neuen Lebens.*" *KEK* 331.
[459] Cf. 1Jn 3:1.
[460] Cf. DZ 1311, 1515, 1529, 1668. See also *KEK* 331.

*geistiges Prägemal)*[461] that is, the mark of ownership, on the recipient. In the context of the liturgical community is experienced the expression of the relationship of the Trinitarian God with the baptised individual and with the community of the faithful, and of the relationship with one another among the faithful of the community. The vertical dimension of the sacrament is seen in the sense of becoming the adopted children of God the Father, in his Son, Jesus Christ through the Holy Spirit, and the horizontal dimension is seen in so far as all the baptised become brothers and sisters (*Geschwister*) to one another as members of God's family, the Church.[462] In other words, this is called the sanctifying grace and the sacramental character.

Through Baptism we share in the life of Jesus Christ himself and become members of his Body, the Church. We become, in the language of St. Paul, 'new creation', which entails, new life[463], which is the life of Christ himself made possible by the power of the Holy Spirit.[464] The 'new life' is understood to be sharing in the life of the Trinitarian God, reception of a new heart and a new Spirit, life of love in Jesus Christ, life of witness, walking as the children of light, life of unity and equality, birth to new life, life of grace and imitation of Jesus Christ. Paul writing to the Romans says: „when we were baptised, we died with Christ, so that , as Christ was raised from the dead by the Father's glory, we too might live

---

[461] *KEK* 333.

[462] The Ecclesiological-Christological and sociological-Anthropological dimensions find their root and meaning in the same sense. In the ecclesiological dimension the Church is the centre and is fully involved, and because Christ is the head of his Body the Church brings in the Christological dimension. Also because man is involved, and man being a social being sets in the question of sociological and anthropological dimension. So there is a web of interrelatedness in the dimensions of the three sacraments of Christian initiation.

[463] Cf. Col 3: 10.

[464] The Prophet Ezekiel expresses thus: " I shall pour clean water over you. I shall give you a new heart and put a new Spirit in you.... See Ezek 36: 25ff.

a new life."⁴⁶⁵

Sharing in the life of Christ through baptism also entails participation in the paschal mystery of Christ. This is an active process of transformation, made possible by the grace of God, taking place in the person being baptised dying to sin and rising to grace, which means a process of change from death to life, which is signified and made present by its essential rite of washing the person in the name of the Triune God. Through this rite the reality, that God gives new life of the risen Christ and makes the baptised his own is made manifest. It also expresses clearly the active role of the Trinity in Baptism. Through baptism, God the Father makes the baptised his own child and Jesus shares his life with the baptised person and the Holy Spirit empowers him or her to love God and the neighbours.

By signing us with the gift of the Spirit, Confirmation makes us more completely the image of the Lord and fills us with the Holy Spirit, so that we may bear witness to him before all the world and work to bring the Body of Christ to its fullness as soon as possible.⁴⁶⁶ Through the sacrament of Confirmation the person confirmed receives the grace to become strong in faith and to witness Christ personally.⁴⁶⁷ As Karl Rahner explains, the grace of Confirmation is the grace of the Church for her witnessing mission to the world and for proclaiming the world's transfiguration.⁴⁶⁸ He refers to Confirmation as the sacrament of strength in faith and in professing the same faith with personal commitment before the world. It should not be understood that the Christian receives the Holy Spirit to privatise it to defend his faith and to save himself in

---

[465] Rom 6: 3-4.
[466] *AGD* 36; see also 'RCIA' Introduction, 2.
[467] Cf. DZ 1311, 1319.
[468] Cf. Rahner, K., Foundations of Christian Faith: An Introduction to the Idea of Christianity, (trans.), Dych, V. W., London 1978, 416-417. The Original work is in German: *Grundkurs des Glaubens: Einführung in den Begriff des Christentums*, Freiburg 1976.

the world as if the whole world were sinful, rather the comprehensive meaning of confirmation should be understood as the strength for personal and effective participation in the Church's apostolate of faith-witnessing function, a function of not asserting and saving herself but of saving and transforming the world through her service into the kingdom of God.[469]

Through the Eucharist we are spiritually nourished to grow in the Christian faith[470] and are fully incorporated into Christ.[471] The grace Christ earned through his self-sacrifice on the cross, effects in the individual the forgiveness of sins and punishments due to sins.[472] Coming to the table of the Eucharist, we eat the flesh and drink the blood of the Son of Man so that we may have eternal life[473] and show forth the unity of God's people. By offering ourselves with Christ, we share in the universal sacrifice, that is, the entire community of the redeemed offered to God by their High Priest,[474] and we pray for a greater outpouring of the Holy Spirit, so that the whole human race may be brought into the unity of God's family.[475]

Thus the three sacraments of Christian initiation closely combine to bring us, the faithful of Christ, to his full stature and to enable us to carry out the mission of the entire people of God in the Church and in the world.[476]

Having gone so far in our exposition of the quintessence of sacraments of Christian initiation, the next issue of great importance is: who

---

[469] Rahner, K., The Church and the Sacraments, (trans.), Hara, W. J. O., Freiburg 1963, 92-93.
[470] Cf. DZ 1311, 1312, 1638.
[471] Cf. DZ 1322.
[472] Cf. DZ 1638, 1655.
[473] Cf. Jn 6:55.
[474] Cf. *LG* 11, *PO* 2.
[475] Cf. *LG* 28.
[476] See *LG* 31, 'RCIA' Introduction, 2.

administers these sacraments of Christian initiation? At what time and in which place are these sacraments celebrated? And if possible, how are they celebrated?

## 3.5 Ministers of Christian Initiation

Ministers of Christian initiation could generally be majorly categorised into two parts namely primary-divine and secondary-human ministers.[477] While primary-divine minister is the actual cause of the sacraments, the secondary-human minister is the instrument[478] or the channel through which the sacraments are conferred. St. Paul calls the secondary-human ministers of the sacrament the „ambassadors for Christ."[479] The secondary-human minister could be further classified into ordinary and extra-ordinary ministers. However, there is no provision for such minutest details here. Any attempt towards that direction will certainly take us beyond our scope. We, therefore advance further to consider in a condensed form, the primary-divine and secondary-human ministers.

### 3.5.1 Primary-Divine Minister

The primary-divine (and invisible) minister of the sacraments of Christian initiation is the God-Man, Jesus Christ. He is also the actual and efficient cause of the sacraments. It is he who effects grace in the recipients *via* the sacraments. He alone is the source of all graces. God's grace is the fruit of the passion and death of Jesus Christ, not the fruit of human work. The human minister has a role to play as far as he is the instrument of God. He prays for the grace of God to the recipients in the name of the Church.[480]

---

[477] We can as well say, invisible and visible ministers.
[478] Cf. Cor 4: 1.
[479] 2 Cor 5: 20.
[480] Cf. Aquinas, T., *ST.* III. q. 64, a. 1.

As the instrument of God, the ordinary ministers of Christian initiation include the bishop and priest, and in Latin Church, the deacon also.[481] This is however, in normal situation. There are provisions and specifications for emergencies, which are not so necessary to be explained here to the minutest details, time and limited space taken into consideration. The next classification is the secondary-human minister.

### 3.5.2 Secondary-Human Minister

The divinely instituted ecclesiastical ministry is exercised in different degrees by those who even from ancient times have been called bishops, priests and deacons.[482] In the ancient Church however, it was the privilege of the bishop alone to confer the sacraments on the recipients. Later it was first extended to the priests, and further to the deacons.[483] As ambassadors for Christ,[484] the secondary and visible[485] human minister of Christian initiation, therefore 'acts in the person of Christ' (*in persona Christi*) and in the name of the Church. To understand the expression '*in persona Christi*' here requires calling to mind the very important teaching of Pope John Paul II 'On The Mystery And Worship of The Eucharist. He teaches that: „The priest offers the holy Sacrifice *in persona Christi*; this means more than offering „in the name of" or „in place" of Christ. In persona means in specific sacramental identification with „the eternal High Priest" who is the author and principal subject of this sacrifice of His, a sacrifice in which, in truth, nobody can take His place."[486] He further explains: „Awareness of this reality throws a certain light on the character and significance of the priest celebrant who, by

---

[481] Cf. *CIC* 861 § 1; *CCEO* 677 § 1.
[482] *LG* 28.
[483] Cf. *KEK* 335.
[484] 2 Cor 5: 20.
[485] Cf. *LThK* Vol. 9, 86.
[486] *DC* 8.

*confecting the holy Sacrifice and acting „in persona Christi"*, is sacramentally (and ineffably) brought into that most profound *sacredness*, and made part of it, spiritually linking with it in turn all those participating in the eucharistic assembly."[487]

### 3.5.2.1 The Minister of Baptism

The teaching and practice of the Church in the early centuries was that the administration of baptism was regarded as a privilege of the Bishop.[488] To this fact St. Ignatius of Antioch warned: 'Without the Bishop, it is not allowed to baptise or to celebrate the agape' (cf. Symyrn 8,2). Tertullian named side by side with the Bishop and in subordination to him, also the priests and the deacons as regular ministers of baptism. However, he made the provision that in the case of necessity, only the baptised laity (and only men) can administer baptism. This invariably meant that women were prohibited from the administration of baptism (even in case of danger).

Witnesses were found for the permissibility of lay minister of baptism in emergent cases in the synods of Elvira.[489] It was in the Middle Ages that express testimonies for the permissibility of baptism by women were found. The intrinsic reason for the validity of Baptism administered by anyone lies in the fact that baptism is necessary for salvation.[490] Also the Fourth Lateran Council (1215) declares that baptism is available unto salvation no matter by whom it is administered, provided that it is correctly administered according to the form laid down by the Church.[491] From what we have seen above, it can be said then, that the official

---

[487] *DC* 8.
[488] See *KEK* 335.
[489] See Can. 38; DZ 52d.
[490] Cf. Aquinas, *STh* III 67, 3-5.
[491] "*Sacramentum baptismi... in forma Ecclesiae a quocumque rite collatum proficit ad Salutem*," DZ 430.

function of administering the sacrament of baptism belongs to the hierarchy of the Church (the Bishop, priest and deacon). But in case of necessity (for example, danger of death), a layman or woman, even a pagan or a heretic can baptise, provided the person adheres to the form of the Church, and has the intention of doing what the Church does.[492]

The mandate: „Go, therefore, make disciples of all nations; baptise them in the name of the Father and of the Son and of the Holy Spirit ..."[493] is addressed to the Apostles. This mandate was later transferred to the Bishops, the successors of the Apostles.[494] However, according to the testimonies of the Bible, the Apostles already transferred the full power to baptise to others.[495]

The Igbo Catechism Book sums up the above points in a few words thus: „It is the duty of the Priest or the deacon to baptise but anyone can baptise when necessary in the absence of a priest or a deacon."[496]

### 3.5.2.2 The Minister of Confirmation

By the very fact of its nature, the ordinary minister of Confirmation is the Bishop. This is based on the testimony of the Acts of the Apostles where the rite of the communication of the Spirit was performed by the Apostles,[497] whose successors are the Bishops.[498]

However, in the Eastern rite, since Fourth Century the priests are

---

[492] Cf. DZ 696.
[493] Mtt 28: 19.
[494] Cf. *LG* 28.
[495] Cf. Acts 10: 48. See also 8: 38 and 8: 12, Philip the deacon administered baptism.
[496] *Katikiizim nke Okwukwe Nzuko Katolik n'Asusu Igbo*, q. 369. In the original lauguage : "*Onye o bu oru ya ime mmadu Baptizim bu Ukochukwu ma o bu Dikim, mana oyne obula nwere ike ime mmadu Baptizim ma o di na mkpa mgbe Ukochukwu ma o bu Dikim anoghi nso.*"
[497] See Acts 8: 14ff; 19: 6.
[498] See *LG* 28.

allowed to confer the sacrament of Confirmation togather with Baptism and the Eucharist in a single celebration, but under the condition already mentioned.[499]

In the West, the conferring or the administration of the sacrament of Confirmation has been always considered to be the privilege of the Bishop. But there is provision in which the Bishop for some cogent and special needs or reasons can confer the power and delegate a priest to administer the sacrament of Confirmation.[500] According to the indult of the Apostolic See, special power was given, with effect from 1$^{st}$ January 1947 to the following category of priests to administer the sacrament of Confirmation:

a) Parish Priests within their own territory;
b) Permanent Vicars (can. 471), administrators of vacant parish (can. 472);
c) Priests to whom, in a definite territory with a definite Church the full spiritual cares with all parochial rights and duties has been exclusively and permanently transferred.

These are empowered personally to confer the sacrament of Confirmation on those of the faithful who live in their territory but under the following conditions:

a) in consequence of serious illness, in actual danger of death;
b) If the Diocesan Bishop is not available or is lawfully prevented from being present, and another Bishop is not to be had.[501]

Considering it from the above view, the teaching of the Igbo Catechism on the administration of the sacrament of Confirmation has to be updated. It teaches that „it is the duty of the Bishop to confer the sacrament of Confirmation, but where the Bishop is unavailable, the priest gets

---

[499] See chapter 4.3.2.
[500] Cf. *KEK* 342.
[501] Cf. Ott, Fundamentals Of Catholic Dogma, 369.

permission from the Pope to confer the sacrament."[502]

### 3.5.2.3 The Minister of the Eucharist

The power for the consecration of the Eucharist resides only on a validly and legitimately ordained priest.[503] Against the Waldenses, who rejected the hierarchy and claimed equal powers for all the faithful, the Fourth Lateran Council (1215) declared: „This Sacrament can be consecrated by a legitimately ordained priest only."[504] Against the Reformers' teaching of the general lay priesthood, the Council of Trent defined the institution of a special priesthood, to which the power of consecration is reserved solely.[505] The Priest here, therefore, refers to the ministerial priesthood to which the Bishop is the head. The command by Jesus: „do this in remembrance of me",[506] was given only to the Apostles and their successors.

## 3.6 The Significant Roles of the Sacraments of Christian Initiation

### 3.6.1 The Baptism

The first and foremost significant role of baptism is that it is the only avenue, the gate-way to the Church and to other sacraments of the Church and it imprints in the recipient, the indelible spiritual mark (character) of his belonging to Christ, which no sin can erase, even if the

---

[502] *Katikiizim nke Okwukwe...* q. 388. In the original language: *O bu Bishop ka o diri inye ndi mmadu Sakramenti nke Konfameshon, ma o buru na Bishop a nogh nso, Ukochukwu anara ike n'aka Poopu were nye.*
[503] Cf. DZ 430, 424.
[504] DZ 430. Cf. DZ 424.
[505] Cf. DZ 961, 949.
[506] Lk 22: 19., 1 Cor 11:24. This is also said during the consecration: *"Hoc facite in meam commemorationem."*

sin prevents baptism from bearing the fruits of salvation.[507] Thus making baptism unrepeatable. By baptism, the water symbol (either by immersion or by pouring) signifies not only death and purification, but also regeneration and renewal. Hence the two major effects are purification from sins and new birth in the Holy Spirit.[508]

Baptism not only forgives all sins, original as well as personal, it removes also punishment due to sin.[509] Though it removes all sins and punishment due to sin, it does neither destroy nor remove „the tinder for sin" (*fomes peccati*). Since concupiscence „ is left for us to wrestle with, it cannot harm those who do not consent but manfully resist it by the grace of Jesus Christ."[510]

Another significant role of Baptism is that it makes the newly baptised „a new creature", an adopted child of God, who has become a „partaker of the divine nature,"[511] member of Christ and co-heir with him,[512] and a temple of the Holy Spirit.[513]

Through Baptism we participate in the life of the divine Trinity. „That (life) which has its origin in the Father and its centre in the Son (and) reaches its completion in the Holy Spirit."[514] The Holy Trinity gives sanctifying grace to the baptised, the grace of justification which enables them to believe in God, to hope in him and to love him through the theological virtues; he gives them (the baptised) the power to live and act under the prompting of the Holy Spirit through the gifts of the Holy Spirit; allowing them to grow in goodness through the moral virtues.[515]

---

[507] Cf. Rom 8: 29; DZ 1609-1619.
[508] Cf. Acts 2: 38; Jn 3:5.
[509] Cf. DZ 1316; (Council of Florence 1439).
[510] Cf. CCC 1264; 2 Tim 2: 5.
[511] 2 Cor 5: 17; 2 Pet 1: 4; cf. Gal 4: 5-7.
[512] Cf. 1 Cor 6: 15; 12: 27; Rom 8:17.
[513] Cf. 1 Cor 6: 19.
[514] Kasper, W., The God of Jesus Christ, 198.
[515] Cf. CCC 1266.

Baptism incorporates us into the Church, the Body of Christ and makes us „members of one another."[516] As St. Paul writes to the Corinthians, „For by one Spirit we were all baptised into one Body."[517] Baptism makes us share in the priesthood of Christ, in his prophetic and royal mission. It makes the baptised „a chosen race, a royal priesthood, a holy nation, God's own people that declare the wonderful deeds of him who called (them) out of darkness into his marvellous light.[518] It empowers them to profess before men the faith they received from God through the Church and to participate in the apostolic and missionary activity of the people of God.[519]

## 3.6.2 The Confirmation

One of the most significant roles of the sacrament of Confirmation, the out-pouring of the Holy Spirit, is for the completion of baptismal grace. For by the sacrament of Confirmation, the Baptised are more perfectly bound to the Church and are enriched with a special strength of the Holy Spirit. Hence they are, as true witnesses of Christ, more strictly obliged to spread and defend the faith by word and deed.[520]

In the West, Confirmation suggests both the ratification of baptism, thus completing Christian initiation, and the strengthening of baptismal grace and both are fruits of the Holy Spirit.[521]

The sacrament of confirmation is a special seal which marks our total belonging to Christ, our enrolment in his service for ever, as well as the promise of divine protection in the great eschatological trial.[522]

The Out-pouring of the Holy Spirit which brings an increase and

---

[516] Eph 4: 25.
[517] 1 Cor 12: 13.
[518] Cf. 1 Pet 2: 9.
[519] Cf. *LG* 11, 17; *AGD* 7, 23.
[520] Cf. *LG* 11, also CCC1285.
[521] Cf. CCC 1289.
[522] See Rev 7: 2-3; 9: 4; Ezek 9: 4-6.

deepening of baptismal grace roots more deeply in the divine filiation which enables us cry, „Abba, Father!"⁵²³ Confirmation unites us more firmly with the Church and thus with Christ; increases the gifts of the Holy Spirit in us; renders our bound with the Church more perfect⁵²⁴; gives us a special strength of the Holy Spirit to spread and defend the faith by word and action as true witnesses of Christ, to confess the name of Christ boldly, and never to be ashamed of the cross.⁵²⁵

In connection with baptism which it completes, confirmation is received only once, for it too imprints on the soul of the recipient an indelible mark, the „Character", which is the sign that Jesus Christ has marked a christian with the seal of his spirit by clothing him with power from on high so that he (the Christian) may be his (Christ) witness.⁵²⁶

### 3.6.3 The Eucharist

The Eucharist, whose first announcement divided the disciples of Jesus: „This is a hard saying; who can listen to it"⁵²⁷, just as the announcement of the passion appeared to them as scandal, never ceases to be an occasion of division: „Will you also go away"⁵²⁸. Paradoxically, the question echoes through the ages, as a loving invitation to discover that only he (Jesus Christ) has „the word of eternal life"⁵²⁹, and that to receive in faith the gift of his Eucharist is to receive Jesus Christ himself. Therefore, the Eucharist auguments our intrinsic union with Christ.⁵³⁰ He

---

[523] Rom 8: 15.
[524] Cf. *LG* 11.
[525] DZ 1319; *LG* 11; 12.
[526] Cf. DZ 1609; see Lk 24: 48-49; *STh* 111, 72, 5 ad 2.
[527] Jn 6: 60.
[528] Jn 6: 67.
[529] Jn 6: 68.
[530] St. Thomas regards the Eucharist as the "Sacrament of Church unity" (*STh* III 82, 2 *ad* 3).

who eats my Body and drinks my Blood abides in me and I in him.[531]
„As the living Father sent me, and I live because of the father, so he who eats me will live because of me."[532]

The Eucharist, therefore, is communion. Communion with the flesh of the risen Christ, a flesh „given life and giving life through the Holy Spirit"[533] preserves, increases and renews the life of grace received at baptism.

Jesus Christ is not only the way and the truth, he is also the light.[534] He is the light of the world.[535] What has come into being in him was life, life that was light of men; and light shines in darkness, and darkness could not overpower it.[536] Therefore, to receive the Eucharist is to receive Christ who is the life; and life that is light of men, light that scatters darkness. The Eucharist, therefore separates us from sin by indirectly weakening evil concupiscence through the deepening of charity, and by reinforcing the power of the will, so that it can withstand the temptations of sin. It is „an antidote by which we are preserved from grievous sins."[537]

It binds us in close union with the Church as we are called in baptism to form but one body.[538] The Eucharist fulfils this call: „The Cup of blessing which we bless, is it not a participation in the blood of Christ? The bread which we break, is it not a participation in the body of Christ? Because there is one bread, we who are many are one body, for we all partake of the one bread."[539]

---

[531] Cf. Jn 6: 56.
[532] Jn 6: 57.
[533] *PO* 5.
[534] Cf. Jn 14: 6.
[535] Cf. 8: 12; see also 9:5.
[536] Jn 1: 4-5.
[537] DZ 875; see also *STh* III 79, 6.
[538] 1 Cor 12: 13.
[539] 1 Cor 10: 16-17.

The Eucharist nourishes us, especially our soul and maintains our supernatural life. It strengthens us in our spiritual journey through this valley of tears to our heavenly Jerusalem. It is, therefore, food for spiritual journey, „*viaticum*". Above all, it gives us a pledge of eternal life.[540]

## 3.7 Conclusion

It has been an attempt to expose the idea of what Christian initiation is, and what it means. Because Christian initiation comprises of the first three of the seven sacraments of the Church, this section began with a brief historical development of the concept, and other various teachings on sacrament of the Church.

Under the historical development of the concept of sacrament, it was discovered that the idea of sacrament was not originally Christian. There was no concept of sacrament in the early Christian era, as it is understood today.[541] It was rather borrowed from the ancient Roman 'pagan' practice and was introduced into the ecclesiological vocabulary by some outstanding African theologians in the early centuries of the Church. And since its 'inculturation' and inception into the vocabulary of the Church, it has occupied a very important place. It has been identified with the Church.[542]

In 'Other various Teachings on Sacrament', the Teaching Office of the Church, that is, the Second Vatican Ecumenical Council, (1962-65) was mentioned first. The Council states unequivocally the triadic prominent functions of the sacraments in general, which include: „To sanctify men, to build up the Body of Christ, and, finally, to give worship to God." Other details of the Council's teaching on sacraments could be found in

---

[540] Jn 6: 54.
[541] See section 4.2.1.
[542] See section 4.2.

'The Constitution on the Sacred Liturgy': *Sacrosanctum Concilium* 59, 'Dogmatic Constitution on the Church': *Lumen Gentium* 1, and 'Pastoral Constitution on the Church in the Modern World': *Gaudium et Spes* 38. The Catechism of the Church at various times and from some particular Churches was considered and also some very important teachings of some eminent theologians of the Church. All these various considerations indicate how vast the term of sacrament is. Before attention was directed to the Christian initiation as such, we looked into the structural elements of the sacrament according to the teaching of the Church, as briefly put by G. Biemer.

In our study of Christian initiation, it is noted that Baptism, Confirmation and the Holy Eucharist are referred to as sacraments of Christian initiation because they „lay the foundations of every Christian life."[543] They combine to bring all the initiated to the full stature of Christ and to enable them to carry out the mission of the entire 'people of God'[544] in the Church and in the world. They commit the initiated to a vocation to live as children of God, brothers and sisters of one another, freed from sin and the power of evil; joined to Christ; empowered by the Spirit; within a community of disciples, a priestly people, all of whom owe allegiance to God in Christ and all of whom are witnesses to these realities before the world.

Our study further reveals that Christian initiation was formerly one single cerebration, and only for the adults, and was only performed by the Bishop. But with the increasing pastoral needs,[545] the cerebration was divided and performed at different times. However, this case is peculiar only in the West. In the East, it is still one single cerebration (Baptism, Confirmation and the Eucharist), and it can be performed by a priest but

---

[543] See section 4.3.
[544] *LG* 28.
[545] Such needs as increase in number of Christians, infant baptism, growing number of parishes and the distance, so that it becomes impossible for the Bishop to administer the sacrament alone.

the oil for the sacred anointing (myron) must be the one consecrated by the Bishop.

Each of the sacraments of Christian initiation was studied and the effects of these sacraments were also tersely presented. Before this conclusion, proper attention was also given to the study of the ministers of Christian initiation. Considered also was the significant roles of the sacraments of Christian initiation.

The above chapter reveals that Christian initiation has much in common with the traditional Igbo idea of initiation. The question of some differences notwithstanding, both can complement each other. In deed both has much to enrich the other with. Let us then move further to consider the common characteristics shared by traditional Igbo and Christian initiations on the one hand, and on the other hand, the dissimilarities.

# Chapter Four

# Traditional Igbo Initiation vis-à-vis Christian Initiation

## 4.1 Introduction

From what we have studied so far in traditional Igbo and Christian initiations, one notices already a lot of similarities and dissimilarities. Our main concern here therefore, is to bring out the major outstanding similarities and dissimilarities from both sides and place them side by side. The aim for this comparison however, is not to show which one is superior or inferior to the other. Rather, it is to see what they have in common, where they differ from each other and how to bring them together for a fruitful and fundamental inculturation basis of pastoral catechesis of Christian initiation. We first consider their common characteristics.

## 4.2 Common Characteristics of Traditional Igbo and Christian Initiations

Our study states with overwhelming clarity that the idea of initiation is common and fundamental to both traditional Igbo and Christian religions. In both traditional Igbo and Christian lives, initiation is considered the only gateway, the only 'passport' (in)to active and recognised membership and participation, together with all its rights and privileges. This however, does not mean that the uninitiated cannot live within the same environment with the initiated. It means, among other things, that the uninitiated has no claim or obligation from the community, be it the traditional or Christian. Though he lives in the midst of the community, he is alone, as we have said in the earlier part of our study.[546]

Apart from popular or public recognition, identification and responsible maturity with all the accompanying rights and privileges, another outstanding characteristic common to both traditional Igbo and Christian initiations, is the idea of death and resurrection (to new life) symbol. One of the practical ways (among many others) in which this is expressed is the giving of a 'new' name. Consequently, name becomes very important to both the traditional Igbo and to the Christian. Both have the belief that names give „a new identity"[547] and assign „a new position in the community."[548] In this sense, therefore, the idea of initiation as 'passage' from one phase of life to the other is common to both traditional Igbo and Christian.

Both traditional Igbo and Christian initiations have 'salvation' orientation. Both have the idea that through initiation, a happy and everlasting life will be gained. This needs a little further explanation. The Christians believe in salvation through Jesus Christ. Through his suffering and death, he brought salvation to the world and whosoever 'believe in him will be saved'.[549] This is the teaching and belief of the Church. But before the advent of Christianity, the Igbo already knew the existence of God whom he calls *Chi-ukwu,* as we have seen before. And he believes strongly in this 'Great Being' who also manifests himself in, and through the nature. Is it then any wonder that in Africa, nature is held very sacred and treated with utmost respect! Even sacrifices are offered „to" great Mountains, extra ordinary big Trees, the Sky, special Rivers and Seas, and the Earth. It is believed that God manifests himself through those, and that respect could be paid to him (God) through any

---

[546] See Chapter One.
[547] Cullmann, O., "Petro, Kephas", in: Friedrich, G., (ed.), trans., Bromiley, G. W., Theological Dictionary of the New Testament, Vol. 6, Grand Rapids 1968, 103.
[548] Cullmann, 103.
[549] Cf. Jn 3:16, see also Acts 16:31.

of these. Also petitions could be made to him through them, and favours received also through them.

The death, resurrection and 'salvation' idea found in both traditional Igbo and Christian initiations show that both also share in common, the concept of life-after-death. And the common concept of life-after death presupposes the common concept of sin, judgement, reward, Supreme Judge, heaven and hell, among other things.

Another very important and inevitable material in both traditional Igbo and Christian initiations is water. Water is a symbol of new life. It refreshes, and it is used to wash away dirts and keep things clean. It has other numerous symbols and functions (which are not to be enumerated here due to space and time limit) which are shared in common among the traditional Igbo and the Christians. These common characteristics of water found among the traditional Igbo and the Christians (as mentioned above) are also found among the Jewish people. For the Jews water signifies, among other things, penance, readiness for repentance, and cleaning away dirts.

On the other hand, however, it must be mentioned that water is also an instrument of destruction. This immediately calls to mind the Flood in the Old Testament[550] which 'lasted for forty days on earth'[551], and was 'to destroy all living things having the breath of life under heaven; everything on earth is to perish.'[552] Such untold experience has been occuring now and then in some part of the globe but it is not the aim of this work to go deep into such awful 'story'. But in Christian religion, the destructive role of water is a 'welcoming' and 'happy one'. The water of Baptism, for example, destroys all sin committed before baptism, the power of death and darkness, frees and brings the baptised

---

[550] Gen 6: 17; 9: 11; 9: 15. The term 'Flood' appears in the Bible 39 times, 32 times in Old Testament and only 7 times in the New Testament. In Genesis alone, it appears 11 times.
[551] Gen 7: 17.
[552] Gen 6: 17.

into the wonderful and marvelous light and 'new life'[553] of Christ. In baptism, the believer dies with Christ to live with him.[554] „... unless a wheat grain falls into the earth and dies, it remains only a single grain; but if it dies it yields a rich harvest."[555]

Naturally, the candidates for initiation are to be initiated by some special ministers whose duty among other things, is to initiate the new candidates into their group, as members of the group. This idea is found in both traditional Igbo and Christian initiations.

After the initiation rites and ceremonies, there are certain signs and symbols that show the initiated that they are now qualified and are full-fledged members of the group into which they are initiated. This is common in the initiations of the traditional Igbo and that of the Christians'. Whatever this sign or symbol may be depends on the type or the level of initiation. But for the traditional Igbo, it varies from community to community while for the Christian, it is the same everywhere, that is, it is always universally uniformed.

Initiation rites and ceremonies are not just performed anywhere and at any time. There are specific and special times and special places for this all-important function. This is also a special character found in both traditional Igbo and Christian initiations.

We could go on enumerating the endless list of similarities but we have got sufficient and very important ones that are very necessary and useful to us for the moment. Therefore, we shall be satisfied with the much so as to have the time and the space to glance also at the other 'side of the coin'.

What are the differences between traditional Igbo and Christian initiations, in other words, what are the dissimilarities between them?

---

[553] Cf. Rom 6: 4.
[554] Cf. Rom 6: 8.
[555] Jn 12: 24.

## 4.3 Dissimilarities in Traditional Igbo and Christian Initiations

On the above is the attempt at presenting the common features that are found in both traditional Igbo and Christian initiations. Here our attention is turned on the other direction, which is the differences in the two initiations, in other words, the dissimilarities.

The name (Igbo) did not only point out the dissimilarity but also indicates, with logical clarity, a glaring difference between the two initiations in question. The Igbo initiation is traditional. Unlike the Christian initiation, the form of its rites has no text where they are written down, and there are no rigid rules and regulations regarding which words are to be used and how they are to be used. In Christian initiation, both the form and order are properly written out and has to be followed *stricte dictum*.[556]

Every phase of the traditional Igbo life has a type of initiation peculiar and particular to it. There is also a type of initiation for the dead, but not every one is privileged to have this particular initiation performed on his or her behalf. It is mostly performed for the elderly ones (mostly men in most communities). The aim is to enable them join their clan and community ancestors (in the spirit-ancestral world) in ruling and caring for their living ones. This idea is foreign to the Christians. It is believed that dying with Christ and rising with him in baptism is enough. Therefore, there is no need for another initiation for the Christian after corporeal death. Moreover, Christ did not die twice. He only died once, therefore, what is then the need for the second initiation for the dead?

Christian initiation, therefore, means a 'passage' from death to life, from darkness to light, from slavery to free born. Death is destroyed once and for all, and the believers are freed forever. But for the traditional Igbo,

---

[556] The special manual for the Christian initiation is referred to as Rites for Christian initiation. They are in two parts; one for the infants and the other for the adults.

initiation is a continuous upward advancement towards joining the good ancestors in the spiritual world. For this reason, after death initiation rites are to be performed in other to be assured that nothing withholds the dead from joining the ancestors in their spiritual abode.

From the above, one sees the clear difference between the traditional Igbo concept of salvation and that of the Christian. The Christian concept of salvation is Christ centred while that of the traditional Igbo is ancestor centred. The aim and all efforts of the traditional Igbo in the life struggles are directed towards being able to join the blissful company of his ancestors in their spiritual world. And from there, he is able to help and pilot the affairs of his living ones. The consciousness of this 'life-aim' makes the traditional Igbo to observe all the traditions and rules of the Land (*omenala*); be at peace with the ancestors and fellow human beings and treat nature with absolute respect. He believes that if he breaks any of the traditions or rules of the Land, it is an offence against the earth deity (*Ala*) and invariably against the ancestors. This already shows the traditional Igbo concept of sin.[557]

The major difference between the traditional Igbo and the Christian concept of sin lies in the fact that for the traditional Igbo, there is no manual where what are to be done and what are not to be done are recorded. Everything is based on the tradition and '*nso Ala*'.[558] But for the Christians, there is the book of commandments, and the book of Church laws.

With regard to judgement, reward, heaven and hell, the traditional Igbo believes in the popular maxim: *vox populi, vox dei*.[559] One, who breaks

---

[557] To explain fully the traditional Igbo concept of sin, judgement, reward, Supreme Judge, heaven and hell amount to writing volumes of books. This is however, beyond the scope of this study. Other scholars are therefore, invited and challenged to explore these areas.

[558] The English word equivalent for the Igbo term '*nso Ala*' is abomination.

[559] The Igbo say: "*Onu mmadu bu onu Chukwu*" (The voice of the people is the voice of God).

the laws and the traditions of the land, can never taste the 'gate' of the ancestral spirit world. The punishment and the reward for the breakers of the laws and traditions especially those who commit abomination, is that their spirit will never be admitted into the ancestral spirit world. Such are the wicked spirits who hover and wander aimlessly in the physical world. They are the *Akaliogheli* spirits, who wander about and torment their living ones. Their restlessness and not having a place of abode, which is the punishment for their 'sins' and evil deeds, are referred to as being in hell. The blissful world of the good ancestors is referred to as heaven.

Initiation among the traditional Igbo more or less has nothing to do with belief or faith in contrast to the Christian initiation where faith is a *sine qua non*. For the Christians, 'without faith, it is impossible to please God'[560], and only those who believe will be baptised.[561] The apostles and their collaborators offer Baptism to anyone who belived in Jesus: Jews, the God-fearing, pagans.[562] Always, Baptism is seen as connected with faith.[563] However, for the adults who can decide for themselves, there may be no problem, but what of the infants who have not reached the age of reason and as such cannot decide for themselves? On the side of the traditional Igbo, initiation is not a matter of personal decision. It is the society or the community that decides for the individual. Here one sees the gerontocratic nature of Igbo community.

Taking a look back at what we have studied before, one observes that unlike traditional Igbo initiation, Christian initiation appears to deal more with dry and abstract principles that end up only in theory. The method of catechesis of Christian initiation appears to be more of indoctrination, merely an intellectual activity of mechanical memorisation of some doctrines and prayer. These are, however, not bad

---

[560] Heb 11: 6.
[561] Cf. Acts 16: 31, Mk 16: 16.
[562] Cf. Acts 2: 41; 8: 12-13; 10: 48; 16: 15.
[563] Cf. CCC 1226.

in themselves, but the practical aspect seems to be conspicuously lacking. If theology is *cognitio* or *scientia pratica*, theological knowledge enjoys a practical significance and is a determinative factor in human action.[564] Any fruitful and effective pastoral catechesis of Christian initiation, therefore, must include all human life existential situations: social, religious, political, economic and cultural environment. And above all, cognitive, effective and operative faculties must be taken proper note of. When it is only a mere indoctrination, it is not only boring, the participants also become very passive. On the other hand, unlike Christian initiation, traditional Igbo initiation has no written text for the rites and no document for references as regards the rules and regulations for a proper and valid initiation. This makes a great difference between traditional Igbo initiation and that of the Christian.

## 4.4 Conclusion

In this chapter, we have made an honest attempt to study side by side traditional Igbo and Christian initiations. It is made clear from the beginning, that the aim for this comparative study is not to show which is superior or inferior to the other. It is rather to see what they have in common, where they differ from each other, and how to bring them together for a fruitful and fundamental inculturation basis of pastoral catechesis of Christian initiation.[565]

Our study clearly spelt out the common characteristics shared by initiation of the traditional Igbo and that of the Christian. Where they differ from each other are also clearly presented. Thus providing useful materials, which can help construct a formidable, fundamental inculturation basis for pastoral catechesis of Christian initiation.

---

[564] Kretschmar, G., Recent Research on Christian Initiation, Studia Liturgica, Vol. 12, 1977, 87/106, 87.
[565] See the introductory section of this chapter.

What then is the inculturation basis for pastoral catechesis of Christian initiation? Our next chapter will be busied with this question.

# Chapter Five

# An Inculturation Basis for Pastoral Catechesis of Christian Initiation

## 5.1 Introduction

The earlier part of this work spells out clearly the main thrust of this study and what motivates it. This same thought still prevails up to this moment and will carry us throughout this endeavour.
Christianity in Igboland has been regretably noted as not being deep-rooted (Oberflächlich Verwurzelt). A phenomenon that is also found in other parts of the globe where 'Christian culture' is different from the peoples' traditional culture. This situation can be described as a 'sandwich' Christianity having a very flamboyant, Christian external features with an internal underlying cravings for fundamental cultural roots. Samuel Ruiz Garcia refers to such mere superimposition of a layer of Christianity as „sandwich religion", which according to him, „is the best possible 'culture medium' for the growth of religious syncretism."[566] The need to remedy this ugly situation, therefore, is not only necessary but also very urgent. And the solution must be Inculturation –understood as „missionary work based on the principle of incarnation –a challenge both anthropologically and theologically."[567] For this reason, the question of Inculturation becomes very necessary to be discussed at this point.

---

[566] Garcia, S. R., "The Incarnation of the Church in Indigenous Cultures", in: Missiology, vol. 1, No. 2 April 1973, 23.
[567] Garcia, S. R., "The Incarnation of the Church in Indigenous Cultures", 21.

## 5.2 What is Inculturation?

Our major preoccupation here is not just only to give classical theological definition(s) of the term 'Inculturation'. What are involved are theory and practice. Based on this fact, we begin our study of inculturation from its historical development, that is, how the whole idea and concept of inculturation originated and why?

### 5.2.1 A Brief Historical Origin of Inculturation

Inculturation is nothing new in the Church's mission.[568] Its historical origin and the practice of Inculturation could be traced back to the first signs of God's revelation of himself to mankind even in creation. The divine self-revelation in creation at the very beginning, by which a definite shape is given to the formless void –"tohuwabohu"[569] is already a sign of Inculturation. Therefore, „inculturation may be seen as similar to the incarnation of Christ which is a primal model of contextualization. Christ was deeply inculturated with his people. Thus God embraced humanity with incarnational self-donation. The Logos, Word of God, 'did not count equality with God, a thing to grasp but emptied himself, taking the form of a servant (Phil. 2: 6-8)."[570] In an intrinsic way, Jesus

---

[568] Cf. *RM* 52.
[569] Cf. Gerhard von Rad, Genesis, SCM Press Ltd 1972, 49-50.
[570] Nasimiyu-Wasike, A., 'Acceptance of the total human situation as a precondition for authentic inculturation', in: Turkson, P./ Wijsen, F., Inculturation: Abide by the Otherness of Africa and the Africans, Kampen 1994, 48-49. Also Roland Gradwohl once put it: "*Jesus von Nazaret hat seinen jüdischen Glauben und seine Zugehörigkeit zum jüdischen Volk nie in Frage gestellt. Als Rabbi, als Interpret der Heiligen Schrift, zieht er durchs Land, um den unter Roms Herrschaft leidenden Juden Trost zu spenden. Die Zeit ist nicht mehr fern, so spricht er, da die endgültige Erlösung beginnen wird: das Gottesreich der messianischen Friedenszeit. Jesus will die Gesetze der jüdischen Lehre nicht aufheben, sondern erfüllen*

became one of us, and as Eugene Hillman with laudable fidelity reflects: „So, Jesus of Nazareth is not a disguise used by God, not a human outer garment covering the divinity, not something foreign or extrinsic to what we are. He really is one of us, like ourselves in our everyday experience of life, circumscribed by the particularity of time, place, ethnicity and culture while thinking, acting and loving with a human mind, will and heart."[571]

The act of bringing the human culture 'ex nihilo' into existence, is the effect of God's decision to communicate himself to humankind in 'spacio et tempora'. This unique act was fulfilled in Christ, who is the centre of salvation. Therefore, God's election and interaction with the people of Israel in the Old Testament are steps leading up to the ultimate self revealing of God (Offenbarung Gottes) in the incarnation of Christ[572].

The manifestation of God to man, his creature, according to the record of revelation, is always made within the spacio-temporal and cultural conditions of man. Therefore, issuing from the Incarnation as the original source (Urquelle), have flowed all inculturational tendencies up to the present moment. The document of Second Vatican Council makes this point crystal clear: „There are many links between the message of salvation and culture. In his self-revelation to his people culminating in the fullness of manifestation in his incarnate Son, God spoke according to the culture proper to each age. Similarly the Church has existed through the centuries in varying circumstances and has utilized the resources of different cultures in its preaching to spread and explain the

---

(Mt 5,17), *d.h. in ihrer ganzen Fülle sichtbar werden lassen.*" See Gradwohl, R., *Was ist der Talmud?: Einführung in die 'Mündliche Tradition' Israels*, Stuttgart 1999, 41.

[571] Hillman, E., 'Mission Approaches to African Cultures Today', in: AFER, Vol. 23, 1981, 343.

[572] Cf. Heb 1:2

message of Christ, to examine and understand it more deeply, and to express it more perfectly in the liturgy and various aspects of the life of the faithful."[573]

In the decree on the Church's Missionary Activity, the Church advises her members thus: „They must give expression to this newness of life (bearing witness to Christ) in their own society and culture and in a manner that is in keeping with *the traditions of their own land*."[574]

For a fruitful and enduring evangelization (bearing witness to Christ), the Church further makes it elaborately clear and even mandatory to all her members that: „They must be familiar with this culture, they must purify and guard it, they must develop it in accordance with the present-day conditions, they must perfect it in Christ so that the faith of Christ and the life of the Church will not be something foreign to the society in which they live, but will begin to transform and permeate it."[575]

The term Inculturation has been described in the past by various people and in various theologico-anthropological terminologies. It is considered appropriate here to present some of these terminologies.

### 5.2.1.2 Previous Terminologies for Inculturation

From the above short historical excursus, one sees that although the term 'Inculturation' may seem to be new (being formed by some circle of theologians in the seventies), the idea (even the practice) is as old as Christianity itself (if not older than Christianity), seen from historico-logical perspective and sequence.

It is of great interest to note here that most of the terms associated with the idea of inculturation by some theologians are socio-anthropological by origin, but have been given theologico-missiological accentuation within the circle of theology. Some of these terms include: adaptation,

---

[573] *GS* 58.
[574] *AGD* 21. (Emphasis mine).
[575] *AGD* 21.

interculturation, enculturation, acculturation, transculturation and accomodation. In relation to Africa, some say: 'Africanization'.[576] Fundamentally, these terms are terms associated with cultural anthropology. However, using them in theological and missiological circles does not remove their original meaning. They only acquire new meaning and dimension, along with their original meaning. A few examples will illustrate the point better. In Anthroplogy, adaptation means the process whereby a population establishes means of existing and surviving in a specific environment.[577] In theologico-missiological field, it is portrayed as an adjustment process whereby a selection of certain rites and customs are made, purified and inserted within apparently similar Christian rituals in order to meet up with the cultural requirements of an area.[578] The meaning of adaptation is also not far from the above, though Luzbetak defines it as: „the respectful, prudent, scientifically and theologically sound adjustment of the Church to the native culture in attitude, outward behaviour, and practical apostolic approach."[579]

While 'Indigenisation' refers to the 'quest for cultural revival, not only in the secular but also in the religious domain', Nzomiwu defines it as: „an attempt to take more seriously a people's cultural background in discussing and imparting religious beliefs, commitments and attitudes."[580] But seen from another angle, indigenisation projects the necessity of promoting the native personnel for playing leadership role in

---

[576] See Metuh, E. I., African Inculturation Theology: Africanizing Christianity, Onitsha 1996.
[577] Cf. Kottak, C. P., Cultural Anthropology, New York 1975, 371.
[578] Cf. Waliggo, J. M., (et al.), Inculturation: Its Meaning and Urgency, Africa 1986, 11. See also Chupungco, A. C., Cultural Adaptation of the Liturgy, New York 1982, 48.
[579] Luzbetak, L. J., The Church and Cultures, California 1970, 341.
[580] Nzomiwu, J. P., "The African Church and Indigenisation Question: An Igbo Experience", in: AFER, Vol.28, No.5 (Oct. 1988), 324.

the local Church, and it is seen as a very good means for carrying out authentic adaptations.

Herskovits defines enculturation as: „the aspects of the learning experience which mark off man from other creatures, and by means of which, initially, and in later life, he achieves competence in his culture."[581] It is a technical term in cultural anthropology, which indicates the learning experience by which an individual is initiated and grows into his culture, and thereby acquires a culture.

Further 'acculturation' refers to the phenomenon, which results when groups of individuals having different cultures come into continuous first-hand contact, with subsequent change in the original culture patterns of either or both groups.[582] In the field of liturgy, there is what is referred to as 'liturgical acculturation' which is the „process whereby cultural elements which are compatible with the Roman liturgy are incorporated into it either as substitutes or illustration of euchological and ritual elements of the Roman rites."[583]

On the level of cultural concept are 'transculturation' and 'interculturation'. 'Transculturation' means the transference of cultural traits, symbols, meanings, patterns, values, or institutions of a specific culture to almost all other cultures[584], while 'interculturation' is the interdependence of cultures for mutual enrichment.

'Contextualization' is a term, which implies the knowledge of a particular real situation; it is an effort to adapt the Gospel message to the man of today in a dynamic and convincing way- taking into cognizance the human concrete situation. It is defined as: „all endeavour aimed at

---

[581] Hershovits, M. J., Man and His Works, New York 1952, 39.
[582] Cf. Luzbetak, 214.
[583] Chupungco, A. J., Cultural Adaptation of the Liturgy, New York/Ramsey 1982, 81.
[584] Cf. De Carvalho Azevedo, M., Inculturation and the Challenges of Modernity, Rome 1982, 7-8.

making the Christian message relevant to the local context."⁵⁸⁵ It is therefore, to be seen as a communicational exigency, and as such, cannot be equated to inculturation which is something more than communication.

Further still, there is the term 'africanization'. Considered from a general point of view, this term sounds a little bit 'parochial'. But in the context in which it is used, it means incarnating Christianity within the African culture. Therefore, it may serve to refer to inculturation. This is the idea the Holy Father expresses when he writes about 'making Christianity to be truly African in a way that it becomes a part of their thinking and way of life', which requires to be realised, in the words of the Holy Father, „that ... African souls become imbued to its depths with the secret charism of Christianity, so that these charisma may then overflow freely, in beauty and wisdom, in the true African manner."⁵⁸⁶

Finally, is the term 'incarnation', which is borrowed from the mystery of the Incarnation, as we have seen before. It aims at applying the principle of incarnation to evangelisation process, which means that the Church has to „implant itself among all peoples in the same way that Christ by his incarnation committed himself to the particular social and cultural circumstances of the men among whom he lived."⁵⁸⁷

## 5.2.2 Examining the Previous terms for Inculturation

From what we have studied so far about inculturation, one sees that its central focus is about evangelisation of cultures. For this, some theologians to describe the phenomenon of inculturation have previously used a number of terms. Consequently, it becomes necessary to examine

---

[585] Ukpong, J. S., "Contextualizing Theological Education in West Africa: Focus on subjects", in: CHIEA, Vol. 3, Sept. 1987, 60.
[586] Paul VI, Address to the African Bishops, in Kampala, Uganda 31 July 1969. *AAS* 71 (1969), 573-578.
[587] *AGD* 10.

some of those previous terms with the concept of evangelisation. This will definitely make for clearer understanding of the whole idea of inculturation.

Pope Paul VI defines evangelisation to mean „affecting the standards by which people make judgements, their prevailing values, their interests and thought patterns, the things that move them to action and their models of human living."[588] In other words, this means „the intimate transformation of authentic cultural values through their integration in Christianity."[589] If this meaning is accepted as a guide, one observes that most of those previous terms fall short of the essential elements.

Indigenisation, in as much as it is one of the best means of effecting adaptation, has a very restricted meaning. It, however, remains a means of effecting the objective. Adaptation and accommodation give the impression of an external, and therefore, superficial tolerance of culture. The terms lack that intimate relationship which should exist between the two values in contact.[590] Enculturation, however, seem to have more potentiality than other concepts in the process of inculturation. Given to the fact that it is a gateway into a culture, and that it lasts the whole lifespan of an individual, it ought to be applied in inculturation. It should play an assisting role. It is very important to recall here again that, while enculturation deals with the insertion of an individual into his culture, inculturation concerns the insertion of Christianity into the culture.

---

[588] *EN* 19.

[589] Lucien, R., "Mission and Inculturation: The Church in the World", in: Lucien, R., (*et al.*), Vatican II: The Unfinished Agenda, New York (nd), 103.

[590] The Bishops of Africa observe that: "… inculturation is different from a simple external adaptation, because it means the intimate transformation of authentic cultural values through their integration in Christianity in the various human cultures." THE EXTERODINANARY SYNOD OF BISHOPS, 1985, Message to the People of God, St. Paul's Editions, Boston 1985, 63.

Christianity is supranational. It is not identified or attached to any earthly culture. This is a fact the Church Fathers of Vatican Council II have unmistakably and solemnly made clear, as we have earlier seen. Based on this fact, therefore, one sees that acculturation cannot stand for inculturation. On the same hand, transculturation and interculturation do not fit in for proper and appropriate inculturation.

The term 'Incarnation' supercedes all other concepts in all its ramifications, including inculturation itself. Inculturation only tries to approximate the idea of the Incarnation. If evangelisation is an effort to realize by expansion in space and time the fruits of the Incarnation, then the Incarnation cannot but be seen as the origin and model of all evangelisation. Frans Wijsen and Harrie Hoeben correctly testify that the basis and justification of inculturation is surely the theology of incarnation.[591] They rightly observe that: „ *'Gaudium et Spes'*, Pope Paul VI's speech at the first meeting of the Symposium of Episcopal Conferences of Africa and Madagascar at Kampala, 1969, and *'Evangelii Nuntiandi'* provide indeed the first principles."[592] The teaching Office of the Church, in the document of the Vatican Council II presents the mystery of Incarnation as the primary motivation and pattern of inculturation.[593]

---

[591] Cf. Wijsen, F./ Hoeben., H., 'We are not a carbon copy of Europe', in: Turkson, P./ Wijsen, F., (eds.), Inculturation: Abide by the Otherness of Africa and the Africans, Kampen 1994, 74.

[592] Wijsen/ Hoeben, 'We are not a carbon copy of Europe', 74.

[593] Cf. *AGD* 10. Here it states: "If the Church is to be in a position to offer all men the mystery of salvation and the life brought by God, then it must implant itself among all these groups in the same way that Christ by his incarnation committed himself to the particular social and cultural circumstances of the men among who (sic) he lived." See also AG 22ff and LG 13. Chupungco also expresses the same opinion as follows: "As Christ became a Jew in all things save sin, so should the Church become not merely a Church in, but the Church of a particular locality." See Chupungco, A. J., Liturgical Inculturation…, 17

Nevertheless, one can still ask: 'if the situation is so as described above, why not use the term 'Incarnation' instead of 'Inculturation'? This idea, however, is not altogether completely out of place, but there appears to be a possible danger in using the term, a danger which Lucien Richard meticulously points out. For him: „... the main reason for hesitation in using the incarnation as a model is that the incarnation applies to the relation between the human and the divine, while inculturation applies to the passage of culture into culture."[594] But for Rayan: „Some would reserve the word 'incarnation' for the basic mystery and insist on clarity and distinction of ideas. Others find incarnation the aptest language and symbol for understanding and expressing reality as seen by Christian faith."[595] He is then of the opinion that „we take incarnation, both word and thing, sign and reality, seriously in all its rich and endless resonances."[596] Taking the aim of our study into consideration, and because the terms 'Incarnation' and 'Inculturation' do not contradict one another, but rather compliment each other, we have chosen to use both terms interchangeably in this work.

From the brief history of the origin of the idea of inculturation and the examination of the various previous terminologies for it, what can one say, is inculturation? In other words, how can inculturation be defined?

## 5.3 Definition of Inculturation

There are many definitions for inculturation as there are many seroius scholars reflecting on this process of inculturation.[597] The phenomenon of inculturation is better explained than defined. This is because the

---

[594] Richard, L., 'Mission and Inculturation...', 109.
[595] Rayan, S., "Flesh of India's Flesh", Jeevadhara, 6 (1976), 259.
[596] Rayan, 259.
[597] Cf. Nasimiyu-Wasike, A., 'Acceptance of the total human situation as a precondition for authentic inculturation', in: Turkson, P./ Wijsen, F., Inculturation..., 48.

Latin etymological derivation of the English word 'definition' implies delimitation. The Latin verb-root is 'definire', to define, to delimit. But inculturation is all-embracing. For this reason, the fruits of the attempts by some scholars to define it have not been unanimous. According to Chibuko: „Those who attempted a definition ended up with either describing it or explaining it. Whereas others spoke of Inculturation from their pastoral experiences or from the on-going experimentations in their dioceses or region."[598]

For A. R. Crollius, inculturation is: „the integration of the Christian experience of a local Church into the culture of its people, in such a way that this experience not only expresses itself in elements of this culture, but becomes a force that animates, orients and innovates this culture so as to create a new unity and communion, not only within the culture in question but also as an enrichment of the Church universal."[599] Here one observes that for Crollius, only 'the integration of the Christian experience of a local Church into the culture of its people', is not and cannot be inculturation. Rather this integration must be done 'in such a way that this experience not only expresses itself in elements of this particular culture'. It must also become a force which animates, orients and innovates this culture in such a way that a new unity and communion have to be created not only within this particular culture concerned but also as an enrichment of the universal Church. The document of the Vatican Council II explains thus: „The one people of God is accordingly present in all the nations of the earth, since its citizens, who are taken from all nations, are of a kingdom whose nature is not earthly but heavenly."[600] The document goes further to explain:

---

[598] Chibuko, P. C., "Evangelisation as Inculturation", in: Ike, O., et. al. (eds.), Towards an Indigenous African Church (A Post-synodal Theological Review of the African Synod in the Context of Nigeria, Enugu 1996,(50-63), 52.
[599] Waliggo, J. M., (et al.), Inculturation: Its Meaning and Urgency, 43.
[600] *LG* 13.

„This character of universality which adorns the People of God is a gift from the Lord himself whereby the Catholic ceaselessly and efficaciously seeks for the return of all humanity and all its goods under Christ the Head in the unity of his Spirit."[601]

E. E. Uzukwu thinks of inculturation as: „Christ incarnating in a certain culture to bring out a new way of life. That new life emerges from the Good News and culture, it animates and transforms the people into the new People of God in that particular culture."[602] Uzukwu brings in here the christologico-ecclesiological aspect of inculturation. It is Christ incarnating in a certain culture to bring out a new way of life, and this is achieved by the Good News taking root in the particular culture, giving it new life and changing the people into a new people of God still in their culture. Another scholar sees inculturation as: „the dynamic relation between the Christian message and culture or cultures; an insertion of the Christian life into a culture; an on-going process of reciprocal and critical interaction and assimilation between them."[603] Yet another scholar views inculturation from a point emphasizing an important aspect that is to be taken care of –faithfulness to the essentials of the Christian faith. He defines inculturation as: „the process of a deep, sympathetic adaptation to and appropriation of a local cultural setting in which the Church finds itself in a way that does not compromise its basic faith in Christ."[604]

J. Tomko particularising on the operative force of the Gospel message in the use of the cultural potentials of any culture, sees inculturation as: „...the profound insertion of the Gospel in the very heart of the determinate culture, so that the fertile seed of the faith can germinate,

---

[601] *LG* 13.
[602] Uzukwu, E. E., Church and Culture, Obosi 1985, 26.
[603] De Carvalho Azevedo, M., Inculturation and the Challenges of Modernity, 11.
[604] Reiser, W., "Inculturation and Doctrinal Development", Heythrop Journal 22 (1981), 135. See also in Richard, L., 'Mission and Inculturation...', 105.

develop and fructify, according to the potentiality and peculiar character of that culture."[605]

As we clearly stated above, the field of inculturation is so vast that its definition cannot be enveloped into one or two sentences in an effort to define it. The best approach therefore, is to attempt an explanation and description of it. The above attempted definitions only emphasised one aspect of inculturation or the other, which is altogether not out of place. According to the aim of this work, if inculturation must be defined, it sees it as the process through which 'Christ for us' becomes 'Christ in us', for the Igbo say: *Nke anyi bu nke anyi, ma nke m bu nke m* (ours is ours but mine is mine). Christ is both the revelation of God, the Father and the Good News of the Father to mankind and for them. It is the initiative and the will of God the Father to send the Son to mankind in human form and in human culture. However, man has the free will to accept or to reject this Good News. When he accepts it, it becomes his own and its effect touches all aspects of man's life and even his environment to the glory of God. That is why inculturation is indefinable and it is the work of the Holy Spirit. But which areas are to be inculturated? What is the scope of inculturation?

## 5.4 The Scope of Inculturation

We mentioned somewhere earlier that Christianity is supranational. It transcends all cultures and belongs to no particular culture. The Good News is for all humanity and should be carried to all the ends of the earth. This is the command of Christ to the apostles[606] (and to all baptised Christians). And that is bearing witness to Christ.[607]

---

[605] Tomko, J., "Inculturation and African Marriage" in: AFER 28, no. 3/4 (June/August 1986), 155.
[606] Cf. Mk 16: 15; Mtt 28: 19-20.
[607] Cf. Acts 1: 8.

Inculturation is usually mentioned in relation to missionary 'territories' and 'contexts' which gives the impression that it is a concern only for the areas where missionary work still obtains or where the Good News has not yet been announced. This idea is very clear in the provisions made by the Vatican Council II for the adaptation of the Liturgy, where explicit mention and reference were made to the mission lands.[608] Mission lands are known to be areas such as Africa, Asia and Latin America, perhaps where it is believed that the work of evangelisation had been not well done, and that there exists glaring evidence of lack of integration of the faith with the cultural background.

In some areas of the western world, it has been assumed that since they have been already evangelised, and therefore, being regarded as Christian areas, they are thought to have no need for inculturation. But unfortunately, further developments have proved the case, the opposite. After the devastating and corrosive effects and influences, which modernism and secularism with their related tendencies have had on these so-called Christian lands, fresh and very serious questions are being raised. The effect of this ugly and regrettable situation has pushed some concerned persons to think otherwise. For Azevedo: „These cultures cannot be responsibly considered as Christian any more. Most of the meanings, values, and current patterns that underlie their social practice and their symbolic level are certainly not in accordance with the meaning and values of the Gospel."[609] Arrupe, therefore, is not mistaking in any way when he says: „It is clear that the need for inculturation is universal. Until a few years ago one might have thought it was the concern only of countries or continents that were different from those in

---

[608] Cf. *SC* 40, 3. It states: "Because liturgical laws usually involve special difficulties with respect to adaptation, especially in mission lands, men who are experts in the matters in question must be employed to formulate them."

[609] De Carvalho Azevedo, M., Inculturation and the Challenges of Modernity, 29.

which the Gospel was assumed to have been inculturated for centuries. But the galloping pace of change in these latter areas... persuades us that there is need of a new and continuous inculturation of the faith everywhere if we want the gospel message to reach modern man and the new 'subcultural' groups."[610] Arrupe, concluding warns seriously that: „It would be a dangerous error to deny that these areas need a re-inculturation of the faith."[611] H. Carrier also observes that „the culture of modernity is itself in need of evangelisation and this concerns now all countries touched by industrialization and urbanization."[612] For him then „an urgent need is then felt everywhere ..."[613]

It is therefore, no gainsaying that the scope and need of inculturation is the concern only for the so-called mission lands, for to think like that is suicidal. Inculturation is for all people and it is a continuous process. But here we are concerned particularly with the Igbo people of Nigeria.

However, seeing that today so many cultures are fast disappearing into oblivion on account of urbanisation and modernising influences, further perplexing questions emerge: Into what are we inculturating? Inculturation into what? Into a culture that is disappearing, or emerging culture, the forms of which are still only vaguely seen?

In answer to these questions above, and with particular reference to the Igbo people on whom this work is centred, it must be recognised that there is continuity and discontinuity of Igbo traditional beliefs – a continuity that has presented a burden to the authentic Christian inculturation, and a discontinuity that has betrayed our cultural identity and personality. Chupungco here calls attention to the fact that:

---

[610] Arrupe, P., "Letter on Inculturation", Rome 1978, 2.
[611] Arrupe, 2.
[612] Carrier, H., "Inculturation: A Modern Approach to Evangelisation", in: CATHOLIC SECRETARIAT OF NIGERIA, Inculturation in Nigeria: Proceedings of Catholic Bishops' Study Session, November 1988, (4-28), 6.
[613] Carrier, H., "Inculturation: A Modern Approach to Evangelisation", 6.

„Adaptation does not mean returning to primitive or discarded ways. But neither does it mean futuristic approach or assumption of cultural forms that are still in the process of being assimilated."[614] For him, therefore: „Adaptation refers to firmly established values and traditions which have shaped for many generations the religious, family, social and national life of the people. ... it must seek stable cultural elements which the people can identify as their own."[615] So inculturation does not only make for deep faith, it also helps the people to maintain their cultural identity. Here one can as well ask: what are the importance of inculturation? For what reasons is inculturation considered important?

## 5.5 The Importance of Inculturation

From what we have studied so far and for the fact that inculturation should be a universal phenomenon (*de jure*), the importance and the reason become clearly obvious. The following reasons necessitate not only the importance but also the urgency of inculturation:

1. Inculturation (Incarnation) is of Divine origin: This is the most primary and most fundamental reason for inculturation above which there is no other reason whatsoever. „Though he was in the form of God, Jesus did not count equality with God. ... He emptied himself, ... being born in the likeness of men." (Phil 2, 6 ...). Just as Christ incarnated himself within the Jewish cultural background even to the point of anonymity of life, so the Church is expected to incarnate in every people and cultural background without being identified with any culture. This is because the Church is the prolongation in time and space of the same Incarnation of the Word of God.[616] Based on this fact, Chupungco correctly observes that inculturation is „a

---

[614] Chupungco, A. J., Cultural Adaptation of the Liturgy, 77.
[615] Chupungco, A. J., Cultural Adaptation of the Liturgy, 77.
[616] Cf. Onuh,133.

theological imperative arising from incarnational exigency."⁶¹⁷ It is not an option. This fact is clear to the Church, hence the document of the Vatican Council II in very clear and crystal manner states: „If the Church is to be in a position to offer all men the mystery of salvation and life brought by God, then it must implant itself among all these groups in the same way that Christ by incarnation committed himself to the particular social and cultural circumstances of the men among who (sic) he lived."⁶¹⁸ Seeing the indispensability and urgency of inculturation as an exigency of evangelisation, Paul VI in simple and unequivocal words declares: „Evangelisation loses much of its force and effectiveness if it does not take into consideration the actual people to whom it is addressed, if it does not use their language, their signs and symbols, if it does not answer the questions they ask, and if it does not have an impact on their concrete life."⁶¹⁹ So through incarnation, Christ has thought us and has given us example to follow.

2. Another very important reason and need for inculturation is that through it, the Church evanglises the culture through which man achieves true and full humanity.⁶²⁰ The Gospel message addresses the people in the culture proper to their age. This is the centre of the point and Ekwunife makes it clear that the only way to live one's life meaningfully in its manifold relationships is in and through one's particular culture.⁶²¹ The Working Document of Synod of Bishops Special Assembly for Africa, with a skill and perceptiveness states more clearly thus: „Inculturation will additionally relativise the problem of the sects, enabling the African Christian to express his

---

[617] Chupungco, A. J., Cutural Adaptation of the Liturgy, 59.
[618] *AGD* 10.
[619] *EN* 63.
[620] Cf. *GS* 53.
[621] Cf. Ekwunife, A., "African Culture: A Definition", in: CHEA, Vol. 3, no. 3 (Sept. 1987), 14.

faith in his own tongue and in attitudes and gestures natural to him, in catechesis, liturgy and pastoral work as well as in theological reflection."[622]

3. Faith is a free gift of God but it demands a human response. Granted that faith is not culture as such, yet it demands inculturation in order to be expressed. Man responds to this faith by living it within his proper cultural context, and in the forms proper to his culture. If this faith is presented to him outside his cultural framework, it will remain merely at the skin-deep level, only external.

4. Although lack of commitment will be its consequent effect, its complete extinction will not take much time. The synthesis between culture and faith is not only a demand of culture but also of the faith. Faith, which is not a part of culture, is faith, which is not fully accepted, not entirely thought out and not faithfully lived.[623]

5. Inculturation signifies an interior transformation of authentic cultural values through their integration into Christianity and the rooting of Christianity in various human cultures.[624] Inculturation would make Christians feel at home and be permeated to the marrow by Christian values and ideals. This is what the Church teaches when Paul VI in Kampala declares: „We have no other desire than to foster what you already are, Christians and Africans. The process of transforming the authentic values of Africa integrating them into Christianity and thus making African Christians both truly Christian and truly African has been called Inculturation."[625] Crollius highlighting this sense of feeling at home of Christians within their culture, sees „the purpose of inculturation" as „not to salvage a traditional culture, but rather to render present in the galloping process of change which affects all

---

[622] *IL* 53.
[623] Cf. John Paul II, Address to the Zairean Bishops in 1982.
[624] Cf. Chupungco, A. J., Liturgical Inculturation, Sacramentals, Religiousity and Catechesis, Minnesota 1992, 29.
[625] Paul VI, SECAM, kampala 1969.

cultures the light and the life of the Gospel, so that each culture may become a worthy „habitat" of God's pilgrim people –a tent rather than a fortress –and an irradiating light that adds to the splendour of the entire cosmos."[626] This aligns with the Pope's view of inculturation as „the intimate transformation of authentic cultural values through their interaction in Christianity and the insertion of Christianity in the various human cultures."[627]

6. Pope Paul VI, addressing the College of Cardinals enunciates another very strong reason for inculturation. He says: „The conditions of the society in which we live oblige all of us therefore to revise methods, to seek by every means to study how we can bring the Christian message that modern man can find the answer to his questions and the energy for his commitment of human solidarity."[628] The conditions of the society which Paul VI talks about is no other than the modern scientific mentality, which, in the words of Onaikan, „calls for an appropriate theological language, just as the diversity of cultures within the Church requires different formulations if all men are to hear the preaching about the marvels of God each in his own language. Cf. Acts, 2,11."[629]

7. Inculturation will help the African Christian resolve the tension between the two ways of living.[630] In Igboland, it will help to relax the strained tensions created by a lack of dialogue between Christainity and various cultures in various areas in the work of

---

[626] Crollius, A. R., "Inculturation: Newness and Ongoing Process", in: Walliggo, J. M., (*et al.*), Inculturation: Its Meaning and Urgency, 65.
[627] *RM* 52b.
[628] Paul VI, *Evangelii Nuntiandi*, 3.
[629] Onaikan, J., "Why a New Era of Evangelisation", in New Era of Evangelisation, Seminar Proceedings on New Era of Evangelisation (CBCN), 1-3 May 1984, 45. Cf. also *IL* 51.
[630] *IL* 53.

evangelisation.[631]

8. The Conciliar Document, *Gaudium et Spes* had enunciated an inculturation-need about three decades ago, saying: „There are many links between the message of salvation and human culture. In his self-revelation to his people, culminating in the fullness of manifestation in his incarnate Son, God spoke according to the culture proper to each age. Similarly, the Church has existed through the centuries in varying circumstances and has utilized the resources of different cultures in its preaching to spread and explain the message of Christ, ... the Church has been sent to all ages and nations and, therefore, is not tied exclusively and indissolubly to any race or nation, ... ancient or modern. The Church is faithful to its tradition and is at the same time conscious of its universal mission; it can, then, enter into communion with different forms of culture, thereby enriching both itself and the cultures themselves."[632]

Inculturation affirms the human values that are present in each culture. It promotes them and provides a critical analysis that questions some of the existing institutions that do not give life to all its members. Thus, inculturation should lead to shared consciousness, to a determined willingness for the whole community to tackle the difficult task of transforming society for the betterment of all its members. With good faith and enthusiasm the community will take courage and initiative from the shared values and vision.[633]

From the above cogent points one sees why inculturation is looked upon by the great majority of the particular Churches in Africa as a task that is

---

[631] In Igboland, such tensions between Christian values and the traditional cultural values include: polygamy (though not so much practised now), initiation rites, funeral rites, marriage rites, title-taking, oaths, Osu, birth rites, witch-craft and so on. Cf. also New Era of Evangelisation, 83; *IL* 53.

[632] *GS* 58.

[633] Cf. Nasimiyu-Wasike, A., 'Acceptance of the total human situation as a precondition for authentic Inculturation', 55.

urgent, necessary and even a priority.[634] The African Church must feel the need to integrate its faith and its traditional culture in the same movement of dual fidelity. If Inculturation is faithfully and urgently carried out, the African (Igbo) Church will become more mature and relevant. This is true because, Christianity must become African before it can influence Africans.[635] Furthermore, Christianity inculturated in Africa will no longer be considered as an imported (or stranger) religion since Christ has become African and the African has become Christian. If inculturation is not important for no other reason, it is important because as Anne Nasimiyu-Wasike reflects: „As Jesus Christ is the Sacrament of God, so is the Church a Sacrament of Christ. Christ is the love of God personified and the Church should manifest in a tangible way the victorious and superabundant grace of God at work everywhere and at all times. The Church is an instrument of the incarnational mission of Jesus to the World. Just as Christ was at home in Nazareth, the Church should in an authentic way be at home in every culture."[636]

When we are convinced of the importance and the urgent need for inculturation[637], what would be the modality? How is it going to be applied? In other words, what would be the principle for Inculturation?

## 5.6 The Principle for Inculturation

The principal aim of inculturation is neither to form a special sect nor to construct a totally new and different Church.[638] On the contrary, it is to

---

[634] Cf. *IL* 50.
[635] Cf. Sarpong, P. K., Christianity Should Be Africanized Not Africa Christianized, in: AFER 19(1975), 325.
[636] Nasimiyu-Wasike, 49.
[637] *Intrumentum Laboris* treated extensively the issue of Inculturation, see nos. 49-74.
[638] Cf. also *Relatio Post Disceptationen*, 10.

make Christ and his Good News be part and parcel of every person in every culture at all the time, for the greater glory of God and for the salvation of man. This is the message of incarnation- God the Son taking human flesh, and being born in human form and in human culture. Hence the theology of incarnation becomes the basis and justification of inculturation.[639]

Decree on the Church's Missionary Activity, *Ad Gentes*, states clearly and unambiguously that if the Church is to be in a position to give salvation and life brought by God to all men, it must act in the same way that Christ by his incarnation committed himself to the particular social and cultural circumstances of the men among whom he lived.[640] In the same respect the African Bishops in the *Lineamenta* outlined three criteria and two principles[641] for inculturation which include, for the criteria:

i. The capability of contributing to the glory of God the Creator
ii. Putting salvation in Christ in its proper perspective
iii. Being properly ordered to the Christian life.

And the principles include:

i. Compatibility with the Christian message- Christ and his message must have absolute precedence over culture.
ii. Communion with the universal Church.[642]

---

[639] Cf. Wijsen/ Hoeben, 74.
[640] Cf. *AGD* 10.
[641] Cf. *Lineamenta*, 50.
[642] Cf. *Relatio Post Disceptationen*, no. 19. Pope Paul VI points out that the individual Churches... have the task of assimilating the essence of the Gospel and of transposing it without the slightest betrayal of its essential truth.... But on the other hand evangelisation risks losing its power and disappearing altogether if one empties or adulterates its contents under the pretext of translating it.... One sacrifices this reality and destroys the unity without which there is no universality, out of a wish to adapt a universal reality to a local situation (Paul VI, *Evangelii Nuntiandi*,.63).

The above are the 'modus operandi' for a proper inculturation set down by the Church. It therefore implies that any proper inculturation should take into cognizance and operate according to the stipulated program mapped out by the Church. The mission of the Church, basing on the incarnation, is correctly taken to be the evangelisation of all cultures. But then care must be taken for the safeguarding of the essentials of the Christian faith and the necessary relationship between the local Churches and the Universal Church as clearly spelt out by Pope Paul VI, in the principles enunciated in *'Evangelii Nuntiandi'*.[643]

The above two points are of pivotal importance and as such are to be taken special note of in any inculturation. However, inculturation would not be a superficial taking-on of faith (as it seems to be among many people). It will rather be a penetration of the totality of culture. It must not lose the totality of faith, but must be an expression of the essence of the faith in a particular cultural style, thus avoiding secession or helpless isolation, but conscious of the unity it shares with the variety of other cultural manifestations of the faith.[644] It is then no wonder that the Church in 'Sacrosanctum Concilium' carefully stipulates clear norms for adaptation (of the Liturgy) to the temperament and traditions of peoples. The Document plainly states that in the liturgy the Church does not wish to impose a rigid uniformity in matters, which do not involve the faith or the good of the whole community. Rather does she respect and foster the qualities and talents of the various races and nations. Anything in these people's way of life which is not indissolubly bound up with superstition and error she studies with sympathy, and, if possible, preserves intact. She sometimes even admits such things into the liturgy itself, provided they harmonize with its true and authentic spirit.[645] The Church therefore, encourages a thorough study with sympathy of the given

---

[643] Cf. *EN* 63.
[644] Cf. Fitzpatrick, J. P., One Church Many Cultures, Sheed and Ward, 180-181.
[645] Cf. *SC* 37.

culture, by the experts. The competent ecclesiastical authorities would recommend a proposal to the appropriate quarter (the Holy or Apostolic See) for approval. Before it is approved, the Apostolic See grants permission for experimentation of the proposals for a determined period of time. Then comes the approval.[646]

The above procedure that the Church has set out, however contains some cogent points that must be noted. It implies that to carry out inculturation properly, a deep knowledge and understanding of the faith is a *sine qua non*. If the important teachings of the faith would not be meddled with, then one ought to have clear and distinct ideas of the fundamentals of the Christian faith. General or common knowledge is not enough. Expertise knowledge is necessarily demanded.

Sequel to clear and distinct ideas about Christian faith, is a profound and thorough study (and knowledge) of the particular culture in question. Since inculturation implies implanting the Christian message to the very core, the root of culture in order to animate it, it is clear that a haphazard treatment of the culture is bound to remain on the periphery and can only yield a superficial fruit, if any at all. It is equally not easy to penetrate the roots of any culture, culture being as it were, a complex thing. It is in this area that the active participation of 'lettered' men and women, born and brought up in a culture has a great role to play.

In many a culture, an avenue to penetrate into the cultural roots is most often not opened to strangers. Exception is only where there is an intimate participant-observer. But even at that, a stranger is always a stranger. He may never get all the necessary facts from their raw nature, that is, the way the facts are naturally as an indigene may. This is already a great advantage for the indigenous scholars and experts.

However, what is of pivotal importance for whoever may undertake the work of inculturation is the recognition and adequate application of the essential points made out by Arrupe, which among other things include:

---

[646] Cf. *SC* 37-40.

„... careful discernment to penetrate to the deepest meanings of the particular culture; and objectivity and interior humility which seek to transcend the grievances that persons may harbour because of previous mistreatment or injustice; persevering patience in order to avoid sterile polemics or 'easy bargains with error' ..."[647] When these points are neglected, then there is bound to be some error and the inculturation will not last. Already Archbishop L. P. Monsengwo has sounded a not of warning that „it will be erroneous ... to present inculturation in Africa as the search for revindication of the legitimacy of the Africanization of Christianity. It is not the taking away of Westernization and putting Africanization in."[648]

Consequently, the supervisory role of the competent local ecclesiastical authorities becomes very necessary. Without their total involvement but with free hand, open mind and unalloyed support, all efforts towards inculturation would be compared to the Biblical parable of an unwise man who built his house on sand.[649] Chupungco correctly points out that the Church leaders are not only to support the task of inculturation, but they are to take the initiative, lay out the plan, lead and direct it.[650]

On the basis of all these principles, inculturation would no more apply the method of evangelisation „which aimed at building Christianity in a vacuum, having destroyed all that provided the preparatory roots in local cultures."[651] Instead, inculturation would be, according to Azevedo: „... a process of growth for the local Christian community through the critical appraisal of its own culture. They would dig out the age-old 'semina verbi' as improved or perhaps as disfigured by their own

---

[647] Arrupe, 261.
[648] Quoted by Lwaminda, P., "The African Synod's Call To Proclamation and Inculturation of the Gospel", in: Charlton, T., et al., Exploring Our Christian Life in the light of the Africa Synod, Nairobi 1994, 20.
[649] Cf. Mtt 7: 26-27; Lk 6: 49.
[650] Cf. Chupungco, A., Cultural Adaptation of the Liturgy, 53.
[651] Waliggo, J. M., (et al.), Inculturation: Its Meaning and Urgency, 26.

cultural pilgrimage through generations. They would put aside meanings and values, which were really felt to be irreconcilable with the Christian message. In no way, however, would it be demanded of them that they renounce their cultural heritage and adopt foreign cultural patterns. Then, in the light of the Christian message, they would eventually grasp the teleological orientation of their culture, its ultimate meaning."[652]

## 5.7 Conclusion

The above are attempts to establish clearly what inculturation is all about and what the involvement entails. The scope is examined and it is established that inculturation is not a thing only for the so-called mission land but for all. It is also a continuous process.

The result of our study equips one with not only clear concepts, but also the importance and principles for a fruitful and enduring inculturation. After these observations, one has no other reason than be very convinced and concludes with Chupungco that: „inculturation, properly done, is an ideal means of 'Christianising' the entire culture, that is to say, of imbuing culture with the spirit of Christ and his Gospel."[653]

---

[652] De Carvalho Azevedo, M., Inculturation and Challenges of Modernism, 27.

[653] Chupungco, A., Cultural Adaptation of the Liturgy, 85. Archbishop Monsengwo also explains that Inculturation is at the core of the revealed message; born in a given culture, the message of salvation successively borrowed from the diverse cultures which have marked its central history to express itself fully and to speak about its riches which surpass any understanding. Evangelisation implies inculturation; evangelizing without inculturating would be, on one hand, a limitation of the capacity of the conversion to Christ because culture is part of the identity and being of the neophyte. On the other hand, such evangelisation without any inculturation would make our Lord and our Father a God who excludes people. See Lwaminda, P., "The African Synod's Call to Proclamation and Inculturation of the Gospel", 20.

But it must be acknowledged that inculturation is not an easy task. However, it is difficult but not impossible. As E. S. Obot rightly put it: „To promote Inculturation is a difficult business. It demands faith, courage, patience, conviction and loyalty to the Church."[654]

The question: how can the traditional Igbo idea of initiation facilitate pastoral catechesis of Christian initiation especially for the Igbo Christian, forms the area of concentration for our next endeavour.

---

[654] Obot, E.S. "Foreword" to 'Inculturation in Nigeria', CATHOLIC SECRETARIAT OF NIGERIA, 1.

# Chapter Six

# Pastoral Catechesis for Inculturation of Traditional Igbo Initiation Rites: Proposed Models

## 6.1 Introduction

We have gone a long way in the previous study, to expose major aspects of initiation in the traditional religion and culture of the Igbo people, what initiation means for them and the significant role of pivotal importance it plays in Igbo world. Our endeavour here gears towards proposing models and demonstrating how initiation in the traditional religion and culture of the Igbo people could be used for a fruitful and enduring pastoral catechesis of the Christian initiation. But before we get into the main thrust of this section of our work as such, it is considered worthwhile to begin with a very important aspect of the Igbo people's cultural value, as far as good teaching-learning method is concerned. What then is this very important aspect of the Igbo people's cultural value?

## 6.2 Integration of Myth, Stories[655] and Proverbs as effective aid of teaching-learning method in Pastoral Catechesis

Just as Myth played an indispensable role in the Bible especially in the Old Testament times, so it is also very important today in almost all the cultures of the human race including that of the Igbo people. According to Theodor Gaster, „myth, or mythopoeia, is an independent and autonomous faculty of the mind which may operate at any time and in

---

[655] Stories here are taken to include Legend, Folklore and bed-time stories already mentioned somewhere in the Work.

any age, alongside of intellection and speculation. Its characteristic is that it envisages and expresses things in terms of their impart, not of their essence; it is impressionistic, not analytic, and it finds its expression in poetry and art rather than in science."[656] He goes on to explain that: „Its concern is with experience, not with categorization; it articulates a present, existential situation in general, continuous terms, translating the punctual into the durative, the real into the ideal."[657] From this it follows that the individual's relation to myth is necessarily one of involvement. Myth depicts his own situation by means of a particularizing story, but in the final analysis he is a participant, not merely an auditor spectator.[658]

It is then no wonder that in New Testament, parables and stories of life experiences characterise the teaching of Jesus to his disciples (Cf. Mt 13:4-9; Mk 4:1-12; Lk 8:4ff). The Gospel of Matthew bears eloquent testimony to this fact: „In all this Jesus spoke to the crowds in parables; indeed, he would never speak to them except in parables".[659]

Jesus being a Jew (Jn 4:9) and a Nazarene Galilean (Jn 1:45-46; 7:52) assumed and lived the Jewish life of his day, identifying himself completely with his people: he spoke their language, ate their food, wore their clothes and submitted himself to their cultural and religious practices (Lk 2:22-24, 41-42). He mixed freely with them, even with sinners, visiting their homes and bringing salvation to these homes (Lk 19:1-10). „In addition he used their life-experiences, their concepts and their ordinary daily chores, for example, fishing, sowing and baking bread (cf. Mt 13:3-5) as medium for revealing and teaching them about the mysteries of the kingdom. He imported nothing either from imperial Rome or aesthetic Greece to use as the medium for proclaiming the good

---

[656] Gaster, H. T., Myth, Legend, and Custom in the Old Testament, Vol. 1, Mass 1981, XXXIV.
[657] Gaster, XXXIV.
[658] Cf. Gaster, XXXIV.
[659] Mtt 13:34; Mk 4:33-34.

news to his people. Not only that, he used their normal social and religious celebrations as the natural settings for revealing to them his true identity (Jn 2:1-11), or for instituting the sacraments ..."[660]

In all these and similar instances Jesus manifested a deep and profound respect for the values and the way of life of his people. He sanctified them there where they were and taught them to seek and find God in their normal everyday activities and living.[661]

This shows that faith is not incompatible with the culture of peoples. In fact culture that stays on parallel lines, and at times, even in opposition to the faith does not engage in any type of dialogue with the faith.

Our previous presentation of some values and rituals in Igbo culture and tradition so far indicates that the Igbo culture is not incompatible with the Christian faith. This however, does not imply that all the aspects of Igbo culture are in alignment with Christian belief. To say so will make the whole idea look like a child's play. But our concern is based on the beautiful potentials of the Igbo culture, which should glorify and make the Christian faith in Igboland to be deep-rooted and to flourish.

The integration of myth, stories and proverbs which already formed integral part of the Igbo peoples' life, will no doubt make for very effective lively Pastoral catechesis of the Christian faith.[662] Olupona

---

[660] Okure, T., "Inculturation in the New Testament: Its Relevance for the Nigerian Church", in: Inculturation in Nigeria: Proceedings of Catholic Bishops' Study Session, November 1988, (39-62), 44.

[661] Cf. Okure, 44.

[662] Shorter also testifies and succinctly declares that 'proverbs and riddles continue to be part of the basic cultural education of the young'. See Shorter, A., Christianity and the African Imagination: After the African Synod Resources for Inculturation, Kenya 1996, 84. However, they are not only for basic cultural education but also for the fundamental religious and social education for all. Metuh has also a similar opinion and expression. For further details see Metuh, E. I., (ed.), African Inculturation Theology: Africanizing Christianity, Onitsha 1996, 132; Mbiti, J. S., African Religions and Philosophy, 67ff.

expresses the same opinion thus: „Africans utilize their material cultural and environmental objects to convey the secrets and wisdom of the Supreme God."[663]

## 6.3 Traditional Igbo Naming Ceremony and Christian Baptism

One of the most important family celebrations of the Igbo people in connection with the birth of a child is the naming ceremony. The Igbo, like many other Africans love children deeply and have great joy in welcoming them. As Mbiti rightly puts it: „The arrival of a child in the family is one of the greatest blessings of life. African peoples greet this event with great joy and satisfaction."[664] Pope John Paul II in his address to the Zairian families emphasizes the same fact with an irresistible candor and in a very simple but clear and sober way: „They (Africans) love children deeply. They welcome them with great joy."[665]

After the joyful 'arrival' of the child and the joyous reception by the parents and those of the immediate family, the extended families, neighbours, friends, relatives and the entire (larger) community await its hilarious religio-social birth and reception, that is, its epiphany –the naming ceremony[666]. Through the naming ceremony[667], the child is both individualised and incorporated into the society. But what is name among the traditional Igbo? Of what importance or significance is it among the people?

To get into full details of answering the above very important and

---

[663] Olupona, J. K., African Spirituality: Forms, Meanings and Expressions, New York 2000, *xix*.
[664] Mbiti, J. S., Introduction to African Religion, 82.
[665] John Paul II, Address to the Zairian Families, Kinshasa, 3 May 1980. *OR.EE.*, 12 May 1980, nn. 3 and 5.
[666] The Igbo call it "Ikuputa Nwa" or "Iba nwa afa" (lit. bringing out the child or the naming of the child)
[667] See chapter Two on 'Igbo Naming Ritual and Ceremony'.

fundamental questions requires much more space than needed in this particular work[668]

But suffice it to say that in general, „the name is considered in African societies to be very much part of the personality of the person. Therefore, it is taken seriously, and chosen with care and consideration."[669] As Mbiti simply puts it: „Often names of people have a meaning, and it is this meaning which must be given due consideration."[670]

For the Igbo people, however, every Igbo name has an import.[671] We have observed earlier in this work, that for the Igbo people, a name is not just a personal label for the sake of identity. It means much more. Igbo names bear family histories, wishes and prayers. They bear family aspirations and life goals. They point to individual future life assignment (either for the family or for the entire community or both). They are religious and moral norms. They are biblical quotations and maxims. H. A. Wieschoff articulates the points thus: „For the Igbo people, names are records, living personal memories of persons and events. From the natural stand-point, there is more in names –more joy, more sorrow, more pathos and more passion, more tragedy and more comedy, more humanity and inhumanity than possible for civilised people to realised."[672]

If the scale of values reflected in Igbo names are to be placed according to their descending order of importance, Onuh presents it thus: „God, deities, and spiritual beings; virtuous qualities; kinship; natural

---

[668] For more details see Ezeanya, S. N., A Handbook of Igbo Christian Names, Cited before; also Anozie, I. P., The Religious Import of Igbo Names, (Unpub. Ph.D Thesis) Rome 1968.
[669] Mbiti, J. S., Introduction to African Religion, 87.
[670] Mbiti, J. S., Introduction to African Religion, 87.
[671] Cf. Onyeocha, A. E., Family Apostolate in Igboland, Rome 1983, 33.
[672] Wieshoff, H. A., "Social Significance of Names Among the Ibos of Nigeria", American Anthropologist, 43/1941, 212-222.

phenomena; social entities; calendar; titles; non-virtuous qualities; natural physical objects; parts of the body; material assets; occupation."[673]

From the above list of 'scale of values' in Igbo names, the most common name the Igbo parents (and some of their relatives) give to their children are theophoric names. The sprituality attached to such names is provocative. „They express among other things confidence, faith, gratitude, hope, fear, humility, joy, reverence and repentance."[674] As Ezeanya candidly described it: „These are sentiments spontaneously coming from the hearts of the parents and relatives who give the names to their children."[675]

Some of these theophoric names establish the existence of God - *Chukwudi* or *Chidi* (God exists), *Chukwuno* (God is present), and some times to demonstrate their strong faith in God, they answer *Chukwunonso* (God is here very close). There are names that portray God's attributes such as *Chukwudiegwu* (God is wonderful/mysterious), *Onyemauchechukwu* (who knows the mind of God?), *Onyekachukwu* (who is greater than God?). Some names are ejaculatory prayers either in thanksgiving to God for his goodness or invoking for his protection and mercy, for example: *Kenechukwu* (Thank God), *Nnaemeka* (Father or God has done marvels), *Tobechukwu* or *Tobechi-* short form (Praise God), *Chukwuchebem* (May God protect me), *Ebelechukwu* (God's mercy). One sees here that most Igbo names are both names as well as prayers. This also says much about the religiousity of the people.

Other names not only personify virtues but also extol them. Such are: *Ofoegbu* (Truth liberates), *Ifunanyaka* (Love supercedes), *Okwukweamaka* (Faith is good), *Nchekwube* (Hope), *Ndidi* (Patience), *Anuri* (Happiness), *Udoka* (Peace is supreme).

---

[673] Onuh, 191.
[674] Ezeanya, S. N., A Handbook of Igbo Christian Names, 10.
[675] Ezeanya, S. N., A Handbook of Igbo Christian Names, 10.

Some names express the Igbo communal or solidarity spirit such as: *Nwanneamaka* (Brotherhood '*Geschwisterlichkeit*' is paramount), *Ugwunwanne* or *Nwannediugwu* (The prestige of brotherhood or brotherhood is prestigeous), *Igwebuike* (crowd or majority is strength), *Igweamaka* (Great number is better), *Mbabuilo* (Majority show the way). There are however, other names, which in a negative way affirm also the existence, the attributes and the powers of the deities and other spiritual beings especially, the wicked and troublesome ones. But those do not fit in here in the context and interest of our study.

Having considered some of the praise-worthy values in most common Igbo names and the role of pivotal importance they play in our faith as Christians, one could imagine how deep-rooted, solid and firm Christianity could be if it were built on this 'rocky foundation'[676]. If the traditional Igbo naming ceremony, especially those positive aspects that could be considered already fundamentally Christian, were to be taken as the inculturation basis for the Pastoral Catechesis for the Christian initiation- Baptism, no doubt Christianity may not be considered so foreign to the Igbo.

In his Homily of 18th October 1964, the Holy Father declares: „The Church views with great respect the moral and religious values of the African tradition, not only because of their meaning, but also because she sees them as providential, as the basis for spreading the Gospel message and beginning the establishment of the new society in Christ."[677] In another occasion, the same Roman Pontif solemnly instructs: „The teaching of Jesus Christ and His redemption are, in fact, the complement, the renewal, and the bringing to perfection, of all that is good in human tradition. And that is why the African who becomes a christian does not disown himself, but takes up the age-old values of

---

[676] Cf. Mtt 7:25.
[677] Paul VI, Homily of 18 October 1964; *AAS* 56 (1964).

tradition 'in spirit and in truth'."⁶⁷⁸

Apart from the value of the naming ceremony and significance of the Igbo names, there are other factors of great value that can contribute immensely, and as such are considered indispensable for a successful, fruitful and enduring inculturation of the Pastoral Catechesis of Christian initiation. These include: the communal nature of the naming ceremony expressed through the extended family, relatives and friends; the ancestral implication; the key role of the nuclear head of the kin or the lineage (the eldest) of the family; and the festive mode of the ceremony.

The communal aspect of the Igbo life has already been discussed in the earlier part of our study. We can only recapitulate here that for the Igbo, 'to be' is 'to belong'. A principle well formulated by Mbiti: „I am, because we are; and since we are, therefore I am."⁶⁷⁹ The people do not know 'Alone ranger' or absolute individualism. Solidarity „Igwe bu ike" is the key word. Naming ceremony is the first and foremost step towards this 'to belong', the encapsulation into the extended family and into the entire community life. Isiuzo notes that: „… participation in the life of the community, whether in the circle of one's kinsfolk or in public life, is considered a precise duty and the right of all. But exercise of this right is conceded only after progressive preparation through a series of initiations whose aim is to form the character of the young candidates and to instruct them in the traditions, rules and customs of the society."⁶⁸⁰

---

[678] Paul VI, *Africae Terrarum*, *AAS LIX* 1967, 1076-1080, 7-14.
[679] Mbiti, J. S., African Religions and Philosophy, 109.
[680] Isiuzo, C., The Attitude of the Catholic Church towards African Traditional Religion and Culture, 100 Excerpts from the Magisterial and other Important Church Documents, Rome 1998, 25-26. Shorter also explains that "the domestic and social virtues, which constitute the practical teaching of the initiation rituals, all contribute to the promotion of social harmony and the good ordering of interpersonal relationships. This is strictly necessary for the furthrance of life and for the quality of that life,

Such a socio-cultural background of the Igbo communal life provides a solid basis and conducive forum for the Church to meet with the people and thus effect enduring and fruitful Pastoral Catechesis of the Christian initiation. It also offers an ample opportunity for the Church to tap the potentials of the communitarian factor through the recognition of the traditional context, and use this ceremony to construct traditionally oriented preliminary rites of infant baptism. How else can the Church know, „respect and foster the qualities and talents of the various races and nations"?[681] How can she know „anything in these people's way of life, which is not indissolubly bound up with superstition and error"?[682] How can „she study with sympathy, and, if possible, preserve intact and sometimes even admit such things into Liturgy itself"?[683] How can she be certain that „they harmonize with its true and authentic Spirit"[684], if she does not come in closer contact with the facts of life of the people?

It must be notified here that the community-centredness and solidarity, which form the pillar for the traditional Igbo life, have been always conspicuously lacking in the Church's infant baptism. As Okoye rightly observes: „The naming ceremony gathers together kith and kin, a cultural group. The child is acknowledged and received into the kinship, with thanksgiving to God. Our baptism ceremony at the moment does not generate anything like the emotions of the naming ceremony. Besides, we lose a privileged moment for evangelising."[685]

Undoubtedly, the naming ceremony for the Igbo is one of the most

---

which can be said to be one of the goals of human existence on earth." See Shorter, A., Christianity and the African Imagination, 93.

[681] Cf. *SC* 37.
[682] Cf. *SC* 37.
[683] Cf. *SC* 37.
[684] Cf. *SC* 37.
[685] Okoye, J. C., " A New Era of Evangelisation", in: New Era of Evangelisation, Ibadan 1-3 May 1984, 10.

important means of expressing, and consolidating the communal life. Through it, the new baby is not only formerly recognised and accepted into community, where all members, through active physical presence, dancing, eating and drinking together, show their solidarity to the new child, but they renew and consolidate the same themselves. A movement towards the inculturation of the faith within the system would, therefore, be an active physical presence of the Church in this ceremony, which would mean not only a gesture of solidarity with the new baby, but also with her community and the traditional community as well. This also creates for the Church the golden privilege for grass-root and in-depth evangelisation.

Another factor of great importance is the religious implication of the ancestors: the Igbo attitudes towards them expressed in offering and libation, the role value of the traditional shrine and their accompanying cultural and ancestral symbols.

The traditional Igbo, like most other traditional Africans are so much attached to their ancestors, their 'living dead'[686], that often times the great honour and respect given them are misinterpreted as worship by people of other cultures. What the saints meant for the Christians is what the ancestors meant for the Igbo traditional religionists.[687] This is outstandingly clear in striking similarities existing between the Christian notion of sainthood and the traditional Igbo understanding of ancestorship. Perhaps, Rahner's theological concept of the 'Annonymous Christians', -referring to the dead who although never had the opportunity of hearing about Christ in their life time, but lived a decent life and in a God-fearing manner, can also serve as a clue to the

---

[686] Mbiti explains the 'Living Dead' as "a person who is physically dead but alive in the memory of those who know him in his life as well as being alive in the world of the spirit." See Mbiti, J. S., African Religions and Philosophy, 25.

[687] Cf. Oranekwu, N. G., The Christian Saints vis-à-vis Ancestral "worship" in Igbo Traditional Religion (Unpub. BD. Thesis, B.M.S.) Enugu 1995, 44.

fact. One also observes that the traditional Igbo understanding of ancestor is more concrete and vividly expressed in their day-to-day life. Such a background will surely not only yield dividend for Pastoral Catechesis of Christian initiation but also serve as „praeparatio evangelica".

Concerning the place of the ancestors in the Igbo naming ceremony, so long as the living-dead is thus remembered, he is in the state of personal immortality. This personal immortality is externalised in the physical continuation of the individual through procreation, so that the children bear the traits of their parents or progenitors.[688] This highlights the place of pivotal importance the ancestors occupy in the Igbo naming ceremony. They become officially the child's patron-spirit, guiding and protecting the child from possible contingencies which might result much more as the child's parents do.

From the point of view of survivors, personal immortality is expressed or externalised in acts like respecting the departed, giving bits of food to them, pouring out libation and carrying out instructions given by them either while they lived or when they appear.[689] Mbiti, therefore, sees the act of pouring libations as mystical ties that bind the living-dead to their surving relatives.[690] For the Christian notion of sainthood to be deeply meaningful to the traditional Igbo, I would venture to assert that a proper study and the consequent inculturation of Igbo ancestorship as basis for such catechesis is a *sine-qua-non*.

Regarding the ancestral shrines in the traditional Igbo homes, the remarks of Mbiti is very cogent and worthy of particular note. He says: „Within traditional life, the individual is immersed in a religious participation which starts before birth and continues after death. For him, therefore, and for the larger community of which he is part, to live is to

---

[688] Cf. Mbiti, J. S., African Religions and Philosophy, 25.
[689] Cf. Mbiti, J. S., African Religions and Philosophy, 25-26.
[690] Cf. Mbiti, J. S., African Religions and Philosophy, 26.

be caught up in a religious drama. This is fundamental, for it means that man lives in a religious universe. Both that world and practically all his activities in it, are seen and experienced through a religious understanding and meaning."[691] Mbiti goes on: „Names of people have religious meanings in them; rocks and boulders are not just empty objects, but religious objects; the sound of the drum speaks a religious language; the eclipse of the Sun or Moon is not simply a silent phenomenon of nature, but one which speaks to the community that observes it, often warning of an impending catastrophe."[692] Summing up he says: „The point here is that for Africans, the whole existence is a religious phenomenon; man is a deeply religious being living in a religious universe."[693] Mbiti thinks that „failure to realize and appreciate this starting point, has led missionries, anthropologists, colonial administrators and other foreign writers on African religions to misundrstand not only the religions as such but the peoples of Africa. This, among other things, has resulted in the tragedy of establishing since the missionary expansion of the nineteenth century only a very superficial type of Christianity on African soil."[694]

The Ancestral shrine of the traditional Igbo, normally situated in a corner of the house, does not only serve religious purpose. Shelton observes that the ancestral symbols and ritual staffs and spears of authority are housed on the ancestral shrine.[695] These symbols are therefore historical legacies physically handed down (*Überliefert*) from the olden times by the various forefathers in an unbroken chain of succession, to the present generation. They create some aura of awe, reverence and respect for the ancestors whose symbols these things are. They are symbolical legacies of the past, and physical concrete linking objects with the living-dead

---

[691] Mbiti, J. S., African Religions and Philosophy, 15.
[692] Mbiti, J. S., African Religions and Philosophy, 15
[693] Mbiti, J. S., African Religions and Philosophy, 15.
[694] Mbiti, J. S., African Religions and Philosophy, 15.
[695] Cf. Shelton, A. T., The Igbo-Igala Borderland, Albany 1971, 63.

members of the family. To make sure that these traditional, religious and historical treasures are preciously preserved, they are entrusted into the custodianship of the eldest of the clan (family) who is believed to be closest to the ancestors and thus responsible to them.

One can then make more meaning and connection from (St.) Gregory's admonitions to Bishop Augustine of Canterbury among the Anglo-Saxon regarding their shrines. He admonishes Bishop Augustine that: „... the temples of the idols in that country should on no account be destroyed. He is to destroy the idols, but the temples themselves are to be aspersed with holy water, altars set up, and relics enclosed in them. For if these temples are well built, they are to be purified from evil-worship and dedicated to the service of the true God. In this way, we hope that the people, seeing that its temples are not destroyed, may abandon idolartory and resort to these places as before, and may come to know and adore the true God."[696] This was the system used by (St.) Paul in Athen[697], during his missionary journey and he was able to win some converts. If it worked out for (St.) Paul during his missionary days, and even in the early time of the Church,[698] why could it not work in our time? Jesus Christ is the same yesterday, today and tomorrow. Apart from using this wonderful scenario as God's best given opportunity for solid and grassroot pastoral catechesis and inculturation of Christian initiation, could the right attitude to be given to these historical treasures not be like those observed in the places of special honour and respect, where principal personalities must go to pay tribute and honour to the past

---

[696] THE VENERABLE BEDE, A History of the English Church and People, (trans) Sherley-Price, L., Harmondsworth, Middx.I 1955, 30.

[697] Cf. Acts 17:16-34.

[698] See Leuninger, E., *Die Entwicklung der Gemeindeleitung*, St. Ottlien 1996, 87. Here he writes: *Es gab damals schon auf dem Land kleine Tempel oder Räume für die Verehrung der Götter. Diese wurden dann im Prozeß der Christianisierung des Landes (Das ganze Frankenreich) von den Christen als Oratorien übernommen.*

heroes, and even lay wreaths of remembrance to them?

## 6.4 Other Igbo Cultural Basis for Inculturation of Pastoral Catechesis of Christian Initiation

Our study of the Igbo value of marriage[699] and their idea of family exposed a fitting pendant for a formidable stronghold upon which an enduring, meaningful pastoral catechesis of Christian initiation can anchor.
For the traditional Igbo, the role of family cannot be over emphasized. It is a school of values, a natural institution and a sanctuary of life. The parents are the first teachers of their children be it in domestic affairs, in social as well as in religio-cultural or traditional life. One of the concrete expressions of this fact is the family Bed-time story, as we have seen in the earlier part of our work. At this time, especially at the moonlight night, usually after dinner, all the members of the family (and in some places their neighbours) gather together in front of the *Obi* to tell tales. This precious moment is not only for recreational purpose but also for an important, serene and relaxed time when children learn a lot of things from their parents and other elderly ones. What they learn ranges from rudiments of elementary home training and simple courtesy to religio-moral and social life. A description of this family bed-time story could form a work of its own but suffice it to say that what the children learn at this time not only make great impact on them but remain with them through life. Shorter is then very correct in his view: „There is no form of communication as powerful and persuasive as story telling..."[700] To show its significant role of importance, Shorter with powerful candour and sublimity and without equivocation says: „Without stories the

---

[699] See chapter one.
[700] Shorter, A., Evangelization and Culture, London 1994, 97

Church fails as a communicator."[701] Discussions, monologues, hymn-singing, liturgical services are all eclipsed by the story.[702] Above all, story is part of religious language. And „religious language", as Kasper puts it, „is not descriptive but evocative; it aims at opening up particular view of the world, a view which, for the person who accepts it, is authenticated by reality itself."[703] Kasper sees 'language' itself as 'a story in which the mystery of being either conceals itself or addresses us'.[704] Therefore, for him, borrowing the expression of Martin Heidegger, 'language is a house of being'.[705]

The irreplaceable values of story telling and other forms of oral tradition are skillfully and insightfully summed up by Ki-Zerbo thus: „Oral tradition is the great school of life, all aspects of which are covered and effected by it. It may seem chaos to those who do not penetrate its secret., it may baffle the Cartesian mind accustomed to dividing everything up into clear-cut categories. In oral tradition, in fact, spiritual and material are not dissociated."[706]

Most of the traditional stories are awe-inspiring and captivating. „Such forms of communication help to express the ideals and values of a community and to teach them to the younger generation or to candidates for Christian initiation."[707] The Divine Master's didactic method to his followers was always through images built up in stories. These made quick and lasting impression on his disciples and other followers.

---

[701] Shorter, A., Evangelization and Culture, 97.
[702] Cf. Shorter, A., Evangelization and Culture, 97-98.
[703] Kasper, W., The God of Jesus Christ, trans., O'Connel, M. J., New York 2000, 90. Walter Kasper wrote this work originally in German with the title: *Der Gott Jesu Christi*, 3.Aufl. Mainz 1995. We may be making some references to the original work in the future, where necessary.
[704] Kasper, The God of Jesus Christ, 93.
[705] Kasper, The God of Jesus Christ, 93.
[706] Ki-Zerbo, 168.
[707] Shorter, A., Evangelization and Culture, 104.

Kolanut ritual of the traditional Igbo has so many values that can facilitate a sublime, profound and clearer presentation of the Christian Eucharist. Like the Christian 'Eucharistia', its ritual has four parts. It signifies love, unity, and purity of heart and mind among other things. At the kola-nut ritual, the 'present' (the living), the 'past' (the living-dead) and the 'future' (those to be born) meet. At this point the living members of the community and the 'living-dead' together with those to be born commune with one another in a mysterious way. No normal person among the traditional Igbo takes up kola-nut and begins to eat it alone. It is always a communal celebration characterized with prayers of thanksgiving and petitions before the partaking of the kola. Here also the role of the eldest of the community or the priest is transparently made manifest. It is no doubt, a clear fact that the inculturation of the traditional Igbo kola-nut ritual will help tremenduously in the proper pastoral catechesis of the Christian initiation of the Holy Eucharist.

## 6.5 Conclusion

The above section has concerned itself with some serious proposals for models that can faclitate enduring and fruitful pastoral catechesis of Christian initiation especially for the Igbo Christian for a true and deep conversion into the Catholic faith. This is also the concern of the German Catholic Bishops' Conference. They noted with one voice that catechesis is one of the most important Church activities (*Sie ist eine der wichtigsten kirchlichen Tätigkeiten*[708]). Continuing they said: *„Zu betonen ist auch der missionarische Charakter der heutigen Katechese und ihre Fähigkeit, in einer Welt, in der sich das religiöse Empfinden abstumpft, die Glaubenszustimmung der Katechumenen und der Glaubensschüler zu sichern. In dieser Dynamik ist man sich klar*

---

[708] *Allgemeines Direktorium fuer die Katechese*, 15. August 1997, nr. 29. (Hereafter, *ADK*).

*bewusst, dass die Katechese den Charakter einer ganzheitlichen Formung annehmen muss und sich nicht auf bloßes Lehren beschränken darf; sie wird sich bemühen müssen, eine echte Bekehrung hervorzurufen."*[709]

For the realisation of a successful pastoral catechesis of Christian initiation and for a true conversion of the traditional Igbo, the survey of the Igbo traditional cultures and values especially the initiation rites is an area that cannot be neglected. The reason is obvious. In Igbo traditional cultures and values, which are, as it were, revealed in their rites and rituals are the root experiences of their encounter with the sacred. It may be noted with particular emphasis that any catechetical activity of the Church that has its root not anchored in this fundament, its life span is not assured.

However, it must be recognised that nothing good comes so easy. Inculturation can only be difficult but not imposible. With constant and persistent efforts and without fearing so much about errors and mistakes in the process, a true inculturation can be achieved. It is the Spirit of God that inculturates but man's cooperation is needed.

---

[709] *ADK* 29. Cf. also *CT* 19b.

# General Conclusion

Our study has been able to discover and to prove the significant role of initiation in the traditional Igbo culture and religion. It has attempted to excarvating other latent values in the traditional Igbo culture and religion that could facilitate an inculturation basis for pastoral catechesis of Christian initiation. Above all, it suggests practical ways of approach in using initiation in the traditional Igbo culture and religion for a fruitful and enduring pastoral catechesis of Christian initiation. These are the central points, the main aim this work is motivated to achieve and which it has succeeded to put foreword. But this is not all.

A condensed recapitulation of what we have studied so far in this work will refresh our minds here before a final conclusion is drawn.

This study commenced with the presentation of the general sense of the term initiation as 'denoting a body of rites and oral teachings whose purpose is to produce a radical modification of religious and social status of the person to be initiated.'[710] Though initiation, generally, is considered a common phenomenon known to African peoples in one form or another, in the traditional Igbo world, it plays a pivotal and significant role in both family, social, political and religious life of the people. Most cherished is its practical and effective teaching-learning method. The plight of the uninitiated among the traditional Igbo was also stated among other things.

The historicity of the Igbo people who form the focus of this study was attempted- a study that has been a perennial challenge to the anthropologists and historians. The difficulty in this study (Igbo history of origin) has been attributed to the lack of written records. What has been obtained were mostly from oral tradition, usually from elders, and their historical accounts varied from person to person, and from place to place. A situation that has led some 'thinkers' to describe (erroneously)

---

[710] Cf. General Introduction.

the present condition of the history of the Igbo as 'ropes of sand'. But oral tradition has been described as the spoken history, a very frail thread by which to trace 'the Igbo' 'back through the dark twists of the labyrinth of time'.[711]

The Old men, the source of this spoken history are described as hoary-headed old men with cracked voices, memories often dim, and a stickler's insistence on etiquette, as behoves potential ancestors.[712] Whenever one of them dies a fibre of Ariadne's thread is broken, a fragment of the landscope literally disappears underground.[713]

Further, oral tradition has been described as by far the most intimate of historical sources, the most rich, the one which is fullest of the sap of authenticity.[714] Anthropologists and historians who see the history of the Igbo as a problem area and describe its present condition as 'ropes of sand' are called to re-examine their knowledge of the Igbo, their language and their culture.

However, it is noted that the proper history of origin of the Igbo, like every other people could only be traced back to God who is the creator and maker of all things, from whom all things takes its origin[715] and to whom everything shall return. Though history might be confusing, religion is 'clear', and take God away from history, not even the history of man will be understood.

As for the location of the Igbo, it is mentioned that they occupy geographically the south-eastern part of Nigeria, but they could be located in any part of the globe inhabitable. Their total population has been a matter of estimation but they are known to be 'a numerous nation'.

---

[711] Cf. Ki-Zerbo, 7.
[712] Cf. Ki-Zerbo, 7.
[713] Cf. Ki-Zerbo, 7.
[714] Cf. Ki-Zerbo, 7.
[715] Cf. Heb 2:9.

Values and rituals in Igbo culture and religion, the World-view and how they are expressed concretely in their daily life were presented. Our study of them not only bring to the lime-light the dept and richness of their culture and traditional religion, but also revealed and exposed their great influence on the general life pattern of the people, particularly on their belief system.

The next stage was the exposition of initiation in the traditional Igbo culture and religion. Among the Igbo, what counts is the cooperate existence. To live is to be in and with the community. After one is born biologically, he is to be 'born' in the community and this is done through some special rites through which he is incorporated into various stages of life and life's responsibility. The individual does not, and cannot live only for himself, but also for the community and vice versa. And the community involves not only the living but also the living-dead and even those yet to be born. Because of what is involved, one has to be adequately prepared for success to be achieved.

A concentrated attention was given to significant role of initiation in the traditional Igbo culture and religion. It is described as one of the key notions of religion, the gate that leads to the knowledge of the nature and of the will of the gods or the deity. It is the 'gate way' to the new level of reality and religious truth, which is unknown to the uninitiated. Initiation help to define and redefine the communiy's relationship to an individual and the individual's changing place in the community. In some way, initiation rites represent the sum total of the people's understanding of their existence.

Various forms of initiation among the traditional Igbo were mentioned and the significance depends on the particular form of initiation. For the traditional Igbo, initiation rites are not only for educational or socialization process, they represent 'mile-posts' in a person's spiritual pilgrimage. They are ways an individual and his or her community may keep faith with their destinies and through such rites the community acknowledges or reaffirms its belief in the sanctity and sacredness of life.

An honest attempt was made to expose the idea of what Christian initiation is, and what it means. Because Christian initiation comprises of the first three of the seven sacraments of the Church, this section began with a brief historical development of the concept, and other various teachings on sacrament of the Church.

Under the historical development of the concept of sacrament, it was discovered that the idea of sacrament was not originally Christian. There was no concept of sacrament in the early Christian era, as it is understood today.[716] It was rather borrowed from the ancient Roman 'pagan' practice and was introduced into the ecclesiological vocabulary by some outstanding African theologians in the early centuries of the Church. And since its 'inculturation' and inception into the vocabulary of the Church, it has occupied a very important place. It has been identified with the Church.[717]

In 'Other various Teachings on Sacrament', the Teaching Office of the Church, that is, the Second Vatican Ecumenical Council, (1962-65) was mentioned first. The Council states unequivocally the triadic prominent functions of the sacraments in general, which include: „To sanctify men, to build up the Body of Christ, and, finally, to give worship to God." Other details of the Council's teaching on sacraments could be found in 'The Constitution on the Sacred Liturgy': *Sacrosanctum Concilium* 59, 'Dogmatic Constitution on the Church': *Lumen Gentium* 1, and 'Pastoral Constitution on the Church in the Modern World': *Gaudium et Spes* 38.

The Catechism of the Church at various times and from some particular Churches was considered and also some very important teachings of some eminent theologians of the Church. All these various considerations indicate how vast the term of sacrament is. Before the attention was directed to the Christian initiation as such, we looked into the structure elements of the sacrament according to the teaching of the

---

[716] See section 4.2.1.
[717] See section 4.2.

Church, as briefly put by G. Biemer.

In our study of Christian initiation, it is noted that Baptism, Confirmation and the Holy Eucharist are referred to as sacraments of Christian initiation because they „lay the foundations of every Christian life."[718] They combine to bring all the initiated to the full stature of Christ and to enable them to carry out the mission of the entire 'people of God'[719] in the Church and in the world. They commit the initiated to a vocation to live as children of God, brothers and sisters of one another, freed from sin and the power of evil; joined to Christ; empowered by the Spirit; within a community of disciples, a priestly people, all of whom owe allegiance to God in Christ and all of whom are witnesses to these realities before the world.

Our study further reveals that Christian initiation was formerly one single cerebration, and only for the adults, and was only performed by the Bishop. But with the increasing pastoral needs,[720] the cerebration was divided and performed at different times. However, this case is peculiar only in the West. In the East, it is still one single cerebration (Baptism, Confirmation and the Eucharist), and it can be performed by a priest but the oil for the sacred anointing (myron) must be the one consecrated by the Bishop or the Patriach.

Each of the sacraments of Christian initiation was studied and the effects of these sacraments were also tersely presented. Proper attention was also given to the study of the ministers of Christian initiation.

This section of our study generally reveals that Christian initiation has much in common with the traditional Igbo idea of initiation. The question of some differences notwithstanding, both can complement each other. Indeed both has much to enrich the other with. Very

---

[718] See section 4.3.
[719] *LG* 28.
[720] Such needs as increase in number of Christians, infant baptism, growing number of parishes and the distance, so that it becomes impossible for the Bishop to administer the sacrament alone.

revealing also, is the significant role of Christian initiation.

Attempted also are the significant roles of Christian initiation. Without baptism, there is no entrance to the Church, and no access to the other sacraments. Baptism, therefore, opens the door to Christian life and to the other sacraments. It imprints in the recipient the indelible spiritual mark of ownership to Christ. A character, which no sin can erase, even if the sin prevents baptism from bearing the fruits of salvation.[721] Thus making baptism unrepeatable. By baptism, the water symbol (either by immersion or by pouring) signifies not only death and purification, but also regeneration and renewal. Hence the two major effects are purification from sins and new birth in the Holy Spirit.[722]

Baptism not only forgives all sins, original as well as personal, it removes also punishment due to sin.[723] Though it removes all sins and punishment due to sin, it does neither destroy nor remove „the tinder for sin" (*fomes peccati*). Since concupiscence „ is left for us to wrestle with, it cannot harm those who do not consent but manfully resist it by the grace of Jesus Christ."[724]

Baptism makes the newly baptised „a new creature", an adopted child of God, who has become a „partaker of the divine nature,"[725] member of Christ and co-heir with him,[726] and a temple of the Holy Spirit.[727]

Through Baptism, the baptised participate in the life of the divine Trinity.[728] The Holy Trinity gives sanctifying grace to the baptised, the grace of justification which enables them to believe in God, to hope in him and to love him through the theological virtues; he gives them (the

---

[721] Cf. Rom 8: 29; DZ 1609-1619.
[722] Cf. Acts 2: 38; Jn 3:5.
[723] Cf. DZ 1316; (Council of Florence 1439).
[724] Cf. CCC 1264; 2 Tim 2: 5.
[725] 2 Cor 5: 17; 2 Pet 1: 4; cf. Gal 4: 5-7.
[726] Cf. 1 Cor 6: 15; 12: 27; Rom 8:17.
[727] Cf. 1 Cor 6: 19.
[728] Cf. Kasper, The God of Jesus Christ, 198.

baptised) the power to live and act under the prompting of the Holy Spirit through the gifts of the Holy Spirit; allowing them to grow in goodness through the moral virtues.[729]

Baptism makes us share in the priesthood of Christ, in his prophetic and royal mission. It makes the baptised „a chosen race, a royal priesthood, a holy nation, God's own people that declare the wonderful deeds of him who called (them) out of darkness into his marvellous light.[730] It empowers them to profess before men the faith they received from God through the Church and to participate in the apostolic and missionary activity of the people of God.[731]

In the sacrament of Confirmation, the Holy Spirit is poured out on the recipient. The baptised are more perfectly bound to the Church, and are enriched with a special strength of the Holy Spirit. Hence they are, as true witnesses of Christ, more strictly obliged to spread and defend the faith by word and deed.[732]

In the West, Confirmation suggests both the ratification of baptism, thus completing Christian initiation, and the strengthening of baptismal grace and both are fruits of the Holy Spirit.[733]

The sacrament of confirmation is a special seal, which marks our total belonging to Christ, our enrolment in his service forever, as well as the promise of divine protection in the great eschatological trial.[734]

The Out-pouring of the Holy Spirit which brings an increase and deepening of baptismal grace roots more deeply in the divine filiation which enables us cry, „Abba, Father!"[735] Confirmation unites us more firmly with the Church and thus with Christ; increases the gifts of the

---

[729] Cf. CCC 1266.
[730] Cf. 1 Pet 2: 9.
[731] Cf. *LG* 11, 17; *AGD* 7, 23.
[732] Cf. *LG* 11, also CCC1285.
[733] Cf. CCC 1289.
[734] See Rev 7: 2-3; 9: 4; Ezek 9: 4-6.
[735] Rom 8: 15.

Holy Spirit in us; renders our bound with the Church more perfect[736]; gives us a special strength of the Holy Spirit to spread and defend the faith by word and action as true witnesses of Christ, to confess the name of Christ boldly, and never to be ashamed of the cross.[737]

In connection with baptism which it completes, confirmation is received only once, for it too imprints on the soul of the recipient an indelible mark, the „Character", which is the sign that Jesus Christ has marked a Christian with the seal of his spirit by clothing him with power from on high so that he (the Christian) may be his (Christ) witness.[738]

The Eucharist auguments our intrinsic union with Christ, preserves, increases and renews the life of grace received at baptism. It is „an antidote by which we are preserved from grievous sins."[739]. Above all, it gives a pledge of eternal life[740] to those who receive it worthily.

A comparative study of traditional Igbo and Christian initiations reveals common characteristics and dissimilarities between the two, which provides useful materials for a formidable and fundamental inculturation basis for pastoral catechesis of Christian initiation.

Under Inculturation basis for pastoral catechesis of Christian initiation, the attempt to establish clearly what inculturation was all about and what the involvement entails was made. The scope of inculturation was seen as not limited to any particular culture and it was also seen as a continuous process. Its importance was tableted and the principle stated. The result of the study equips one not only with clear concepts, but also the importance and principles for a fruitful and enduring inculturation.

Attempt was also made at proposing some very important and useful features of traditional Igbo initiaton rites for inculturating the pastoral catechesis of Christian intiation. These proposals were considered very

---

[736] Cf. *LG* 11.
[737] DZ 1319; *LG* 11; 12.
[738] Cf. DZ 1609; see Lk 24: 48-49; *STh* 111, 72, 5 *ad* 2.
[739] Cf. DZ 875, *STh* III, 79, 6.
[740] Cf. Jn 6: 54.

essential because they are, as it were, the quintessence, the source of the traditional Igbo belief. They are the root experience of the Igbo encounter with the sacred.

With the help and fundamental background of the Igbo idea of initiation rites, the pastoral catechesis of Christian initiation for the Igbo will no more appear foreign to them. It will no more look abstract but rather concrete, and from everyday experience. In the words of Michel Dujarier: *„Diese kommt –in der Linie von Dtn 6 –innerhalb der Familie, der Gruppe, der Gemeinschaft zustande. Sie ist eine gelebte und geteilte, gefeierte und erklärte Erfahrung."*[741] Through this basic foundation, the pastoral catechesis of Christian initiation is deep-rooted and the Christians have the teachings of their faith at the tips of their fingers and are ready at any moment to give answer to any question concerning the hope that is in them (cf. 1 Pet 3: 15).

The community life aspect of the Igbo idea of initiation awaits the Christian members the opportunity of experiencing the warmth of family and community life and offers the Church a wonderful atmosphere to play and fulfill with great joy, her motherly role. Christian initiation is not an organisation close to the Church. It is also not a specialised service in the Church. It is the Church herself, playing her motherly role. Dujarier presents this point thoughtfully thus: *„Die christlicher Initiation ist keine Organisation neben der Kirche und auch kein spezialisierter Dienst in der Kirche: es ist die Kirche selber, die ihr Muttersein ausübt."*[742]

In the light of the above then, if 'catechesis is an education in the faith of children, young people and adults which includes especially the teaching of Christian doctrine imparted, generally speaking, in an organic and systematic way, with a view to initiating the hearers into the fullness of

---

[741] Dujarier, M., *Erfahrungen von christlicher Initiation in Westafrika*, in: *Concilium, IZT* 15. *Jahrgang*, 2(Februar 1979), 108.
[742] Dujarier, 108-109.

christain life'[743], for the Church in Igboland, the Igbo understanding of initiation rites is inevitable. This is in accord with the mind of the Church who wants that catechesis be adapted to the circumstnces of the people[744], catechesis which is initimately bound up with the whole of the Church's life and not only her Geographical extension and numerical increase, but even more her inner growth, and correspondence with God's plan depend essentially on catechesis.[745]

Finally, since it is the Spirit of God who enlightens all men, gives strength and understanding to all, may He open the eyes of our mind and intellect to discover fully the treasure of Revelation entrusted to the Church for the salvation of her children.

---

[743] Cf. *CT* 18., CCC 5.
[744] Cf. *DV* 25.
[745] Cf. *CT* 10., CCC 7.

# Bibliography

## Sources

### Sacred Scripture

The Jerusalem Bible (Standard Edition), London, 1985.

FLANNERY, A., (ed.), Vatican Council II: The Conciliar and Post Conciliar Documents, U.S.A., 1981.

The Constitution on the Sacred Liturgy, *Sacrosanctum Concilium*, 4 December 1963.

Dogmatic Constitution on the Church, *Lumen Gentium*, 21 November 1964.

Declaration on the Relation of the Church to non-Christian Religions, *Nostra Aetate*, 28 October 1965.

Dogmatic Constitution on Divine Revelation, *Die Verbum*, 18 November 1965.

Decree on the Church's Missionary Activity, *Ad Gentes Divinitus*, 7 December. 1965.

Pastoral Constitution on the Church in the Modern World, *Gaudium et Spes*, 7 December 1965.

Decree on the Pastoral Office of Bishops in the Church, *Christus Dominus*, 28 October 1965.

Decree on the Ministry and Life of Priests, *Presbyterorum ordinis*, 7 December 1965.

### Papal Documents

PAUL VI, Message, *Africae Terrarum*, 29 October 1967, *AAS* 69 (1967): 1076-1080.

Address to the African Bishops in Kampala, Uganda, 31 July 1969, *AAS* 71 (1969): 573-578.

Address to the African and Madagascar Episcopal Conference, Rome 1975, *AAS* (1975): 569-572.

Apostolic Exhortation, *Evangelii Nuntiandi*, 8 December 1975, *AAS* 68 (1975): 5-76.
Address to President Milton Obote of Uganda, Kampala, 31 July 1969.
Homliy of 18 October 1964, *AAS* 56 (1964).
*Divinae Consortium naturae*, 1971.
JOHN PAUL II, Address to the Bishops of Mozambique on '*ad Limina*' visit, Rome 23 September, 1982.
'*Angelus Domini*', Rome 24 September 1995. OR.EE., 27 September, 1995, 1.
Encyclical, *Redemptoris Missio*
Address to the Zairian (now Rep of Congo) Families Kinshasa, 3 May 1980. OO.RR., 12 May 1980, 4
*Dominae Cenae*, February 1980.

## Other Church Documents

SYNOD OF BISHOPS SPECIAL ASSEMBLY FOR AFRICA; *Lineamenta*, Vatican City 1990.
*Instrumentum Laboris*, Vatican City 1993.
*SYNODUS EPISCOPORUM COETUS SPECIALIS PRO AFRICA*; *Relatio Post Disceptationem*; E Civitate Vaticana 1994.
CATHOLIC SECRETARIAT OF NIGERIA, Inculturation in Nigeria, Proceedings of Catholic Bishop's Study Session, November 1988.
New Era of Evangelisation, Seminar Proceedings, 1-3 May 1984.
The Catechism of the Catholic Church, London 1994.
*Katechismus der Katholische Kirche* (German Edition)
*Katholischer Erwachsenen Katechismus*, Köln, 1985.
*Katikiizim nke Okwukwe Nzuko Katolik n'asusu Igbo*, 1996.
Code of Canon Law.
THE EXTRAODINARY SYNOD OF BISHOPS, Message to the People of God, St. Paul's Edition, Boston 1985.

## Dictionary/ Encyclopaedia

Friedrich, G., (ed.), (trans.), Bromiley, G., Theological Dictionary of The New Testament, Vol. 6, Ww. B Eerdmans 1968.

Webster's New Encyclopedic Dictionary, Germany 1996.
BRODERICK, R. C., (et. al.), (ed.), Catholic Concise Dictionary, Franciscan Herald Press, Chicago, Illinois, 1966.
CROSS, F. L., & LIVINGSTONE, E. A., (eds.), The Oxford Dictionary of the Christian Church, 2nd ed., London, 1974.
ELIADE, M., (ed.) The Encyclopedia of Religion, Vol. 7, New York, 1987.
HASTINGS, J., (ed.) Encyclopaedia of Religion and Ethics, Vol. X, Edinburgh 1918.
STRECK, B., (ed.) *Wörterbuch der Ethiologie*, Köln, 1987.
STUHLMUELLER, C., (ed.), The Collegeville Pastoral Dictionary of Biblical Theology, Minnesota, 1996.

## Other Works

ACHEBE, C., Things Fall Apart (Reprinted Edition), University Press, Ibadan, 1998.
AFIGBO, A. E., Ropes of Sand, University Press, Ibadan, 1981.
Towards A History of Igbo-Speaking People of Nigeria, Ibadan, 1975.
AJAYI, J. F. A., Christian Missions in Nigeria, 4th Impression, Ibadan, 1977.
AMPONSAH, K., Topics on West African Traditional Religion, Ghana, 1977.
ANIGBO, O., Commensality and Human Living Among The Igbo, University Press, Nsukka, 1987.
ANOZIE, I. P., The Religious Import of Igbo Names, Rome, 1968.
ARINZE, F., Sacrifice in Ibo Religion, University Press, Ibadan, 1970.
ARNOLD, F., *Handbuch der Pastoraltheologie*, Freiburg, 1964.
ARRUPE, P., Letter on Inculturation, Rome, 1978.
ASANTE, M. K., and ASANTE, K. W., African Culture: The Rhythms of Unity, African World Press, Inc., New Jersey, 3rd Print, 1993.
BALLING, A. L., *Lebensweisheit aus Schwarzafrika*, Herder Freiburg- Basel-Wien, 1985.
BASDEN, G. T., Among The Igbos of Nigeria, Frank Cass & Co., London, 1966.
Niger Ibos, Frank Cass & Co., London, 1966.

BAUR, J., 2000 Years of Christianity in Africa, Pauline Publications Africas, Nairobi, 1994.
BEATTIE, J., Other Cultures, London, 1964.
BIEMER, G., *Symbole Des Glaubens Leben*, Ostfildern, 1999.
BLEEKER, C. J., (ed.), Initiation: Studies in History of Religion, Netherlands, 1965.
CAZENEUVE, J., *Sociologie du Rite*, Paris, 1971.
CHARLTON, T., (*et. al*.,), Exploring Our Christian Life in the Light of the African Synod, Paulines Publications Africa, Nairobi, 1994.
CHUPUNGCO, A. C., Cultural Adaptation of the Liturgy, New York, 1982.
Liturgical Inculturation, Sacraments, Religiousity and Catechesis, Minnesota, 1992.
COSTA, R., (ed.), One Faith, Many Cultures, New York, 1998.
DE CARVALHO, A. M., Inculturation and the Challenges of Modernity, Rome, 1982.
DE HARBE, J., *Katholischer Katechismus*, Mainz-Freiburg, 1863.
DE VAUX, R., Ancient Israel, London, 1961.
EBOH, S. O., *Ozo* Title Institution in Igboland, J. Mainz GmbH, Aachen, 1993.
EDUSEI, K., *Für Uns ist Religion die Erde, auf der wir leben*, Stuttgart, 1985.
EGUDU, R. N., The Calabash of Wisdom and Other Igbo Stories, Nok Publishers (Nigeria) Ltd., 2nd Printing, 1983.
EMBER, C. R., and EMBER, M., Cultural Anthropology, New Jersey, 4th ed., 1985.
EKWUNIFE, A., Consecration in Igbo Traditional Religion, Enugu, 1990.
ESOMONU, L., Respect for Human Life in Igbo Religion and Morality, Rome, 1981.
EZEANYA, S. N., A Handbook Of Igbo Christian Names, C. M. S. Press, Onitsha, 1994
FALOLA, T., (ed.), History of Nigeria 2, Ibadan, 1991.
FITZPATRICK, J. P., One Church Many Cultures, Sheed and Ward, (nd.).
FORDE, D., and JONES, G. I., The Ibo and Ibibio-Speaking Peoples Of South-Eastern Nigeria, International African Instutute, London, 1962.
GASTER, H. T., Myth, Legend and Custom in the Old Testament, Vol. 1, Mass,

1981.
GRADWOHL, R., *Was ist der Talmud? Einführung in der 'Mündliche Tradition' Israels*, Stuttgart, 1999.
GRAINGER, R., The Language of the Rite, London, 1974.
HADDON, A. C., The Lower Niger and Its Tribes, London, 1906.
HAHN-WAANDERS, H., Eze Institution in Igboland, Nimo-Nigeria, 1990.
HEILER, F., Prayer: A Study in the History and Psychology of Religion, (trans.), Mc COMB, S., Oxford University Press, 1958.
HERSHOVITS, M. J., Man and His Works, New York, 1952.
HICKEY, R., (ed.), Modern Missionary Documents and Africa, Dublin, 1982.
HOLST, L. E., Hospital Ministry: The Role Of The Chaplain Today, New York, 1985.
HOPKINS, D., (ed.), Black Faith and Public Talk, New York, 1999.
IKE, O., (et. al.), (ed.), Towards An Indigenous African Church: A Post-synodal Theological Review Of The Africa Synod in the Context of Nigeria, CIDJAP, Enugu, 1996.
ILOGU, E., Christianity and Igbo Culture, Onitsha, 1985.
ISHOLA, S. A., Towards A Contextualized Missiological Approach to the Yomba Religio-Cultural Milieu, Texas, 1992.
ISICHEI, E., A History Of The Igbo People, Macmillan Press, London, 1976.
ISIZO, C. D., The Attitude Of The Catholic Church Towards African Traditional Religion and Culture: 100 Excerpts from the Magisterial and Other Important Church Documents, Rome, 1998.
KALU, O. U., Precarious Vision: African Cultural Development, Enugu, 1982.
KASPER, W., The God of Jesus Christ, (trans.), O'CONNEL, M. J., Crossroad Publishing Company, New York, 2000.
KASPER, W., LEHMANN, K., *Die Heilssendung der Kirche in der Gegenwart Pastorale*, Mainz, 1970.
KAVANAGH, A., Confirmation: Origin and Reform, Collegeville-Pueblo, 1988.
KI-ZERBO, J., (ed.), General History Of Africa, Vol. 1, UNESCO, California, 1981.
KOTTAK, C. P., Cultural Anthropology, Random House Inc., New York, 1975.

LEONARD, A. G., The Niger and Its Tribes, London, 1968.
LEUNINGER, E., *Die Entwicklung der Gemeindeleitung*, St. Ottlien, 1996.
LORD, H., An African Survey, London, 1945.
LUCIEN, R., (et. al.), Vatican II: The Unfinished Agenda, New York, (nd.).
LUZBETAK, J., The Church and Cultures, California, 1970.
MBITI, J. S., African Religions and Philisophy, Heinemann Educational Books Ltd., London, 1975.
Introduction to African Religions, Heinemann Educational Books Ltd., London, 1991.
Love and Marriage in Africa, Longman Group Ltd., London, 1973.
MEEK, K., Law and Authority in a Nigerian Tribe, Oxford University Press, 1937.
METUH, E. I., (ed.), Nigerian Cultural Heritage, Jos, 1990.
(ed.), African Inculturation Theology: Africanizing Christianity, Imico Publishers, Onitsha, 1996.
African Religions in Western Conceptual Schemes: The Problem of Interpretation, Jos, 1991.
Comparative Studies of African Traditional Religions, Imico Publishers, Onitsha, 1987.
God and Man in African Religion, London, 1981.
The God's In Retreat, Fourth Dimension Publishers, Enugu, 1986.
NADEL, S. F., Nupe Religion, London, 1954.
NKWO, M., Igbo Cultural Heritage, University Publishing Co., Onitsha, 1984.
NWAHAGHI, F. N., The Kolanut As A Ritual Symbol Among The Igbo, Jos, 1994.
NWOKOCHA, C. A., Kolanut: Igbo Symbol of Love and Unity, Rome, 1969.
NWOSU, V. A., (ed.), The Catholic Church in Onitsha, People, Places and Events (1885-1985), Etikokwu Press Ltd., Onitsha, 1985.
NZEAKO, J. U. T., *Omenala Ndi Igbo*, Longman Nigeria Ltd., Ibadan, (Reprint Edition) 1986.
OATES, W. E., When Religion Gets Sick, Philadelphia, 1970.
OBI, C. A., (ed.), A Hundred Years of the Catholic Church in Eastern Nigeria (1885-1985), Africana-Fep Publishers Ltd., Onitsha, 1985.

OBIAGWU, M., Healthcare of the Sick Among the Igbos of Nigeria vis-a-vis the Healing Ministry of the Church and the Pastoral Challenges of Today, Rome, 2000.
OBIUKWU, S. C., 'Ala' (Earth Spirit) in Igbo Culture and Traditional Religious Beliefs, Rome, 1978.
OGBALU, F. C. and EMENANJO, E. N., Igbo Language and Culture, Vol. 1, Ibadan, 1975.
Igbo Institutions and Customs, Onitsha, (nd.).
*Ilu Igbo* (The Book of Igbo Proverbs), Onitsha, 1965.
OGUEJIOFOR, J., The Influence of Igbo Traditional Religion on the Socio-Political Character of the Igbo, Fulladu Publishing Company, Nsukka, 1996.
OJI IGBO, Published by the Cultural Division Ministry of Education and Information, Nigeria, 1975.
OKORIE, C. P. A., Priesthood in Igbo Traditional Religion, St. Ottilien, Germany, 1997.
OLUPONA, J. K., African Spirituality: Forms, Meanings and Expressions, New York, 2000.
ONUH, C. O., Christianity and the Igbo Rites of Passage, Peter Lang, Frankfurt, 1992.
ONYEOCHA, A. E., Family Apostolate in Igboland, Rome, 1983.
ORAKWUE, J., Onitsha Custom of Title-taking, (np.) (nd.).
ORANEKWU, G. N., Sacrifice in Igbo Traditional and Christian Religions and Its Significance for Everyday Life: A Comparative Study, PTH., Vallendar, Germany, 1999.
The Christian Saints vis-a-vis Ancestral „Worship" in Igbo Traditional Religion, BMS, Enugu, 1995.
OTT, L., Fundamentals of Catholic Dogma, 4$^{th}$ ed., (trans.) LYNCH, P., Tan Books and Publishers, INC., Illinois, 1960.
PARRINDER, G., Africa's Three Religions, London, 1969.
African Mythology, London, 1975.
West African Religions, London, 1975.
RAHNER, K., *Grundkurs des Glaubens*, Verlag Herder, Germany, 1976.

The Church and the Sacraments, Freiburg, 1963.
RATZINGER, J., *Die Sakramentale Begründung christlicher Existenz*, Meitingen, 1965.
SARPONG, P. K., Girls' Nubility Rites in Ashanti, Ghana, 1977.
SCHELER, M., *Der Formalismus in der Ethik Und die materialle Wertethik*, München, 1966.
SCHILLEBEECKS, E., *Personale Begegung mit Gott*, Mainz, 1964.
SCHINELLER, P. A., A Handbook on Inculturation, New Jersey, 1990.
SCHREIJÄCK, T., (hrsg.), *Menschwerden im Kulturwandel: Kontexte Kultureller Identität als Wegmarken interkultureller Kompetenz*, Fulda, 1999.
SEMPEBWA, J. W., African Traditional Moral Norms and Their Implications For Christianity, Rome, 1983.
SCHELTON, A. T., The Igbo-Igala Borderland, Albany, 1971.
SCHMAUS, M., *Katholischer Dogmatik*, iv/1, München, 1957.
SCHORTER, A., African Christian Theology: Adaptation or Incarnation, Orbis Books, New York, 1975.
African Culture: An Overview, Paulines Publications Africa, Nairobi, 1998.
Christianity and African Imagination, Paulines Publications Africa, Nairobi, 1996.
Evangelization and Culture, Geoffrey Chapman, London, 1994.
SOFOLA, J. A., African Culture and African Personality, Nigeria, 1973.
SOME, M. P., *Vom Geist Africas* (trans.) DIETZFELBINGER, K., München, 1996.
STRECK, B., (Hrsg.), *Wörterbuch der Ethiologie*, Köln, 1987.
TALBOT, P. A., The People of Southern Nigeria, Vol. 1, London, 1926.
TAYLOR, J. B., Primal World Views, Nigeria, 1976.
THE VENERABLE BEDE, A History of the English Church and People, (trans.) SHERLEY-PRICE, I., Harmondsworth-Middx, 1955.
TURNER, V., The Forest of Symbols: Aspects of Ndembu Rituals, Cornell Paperbacks, University Press, Ithaca and London, 1970.
UBESIE, T., *Odinala Igbo*, University Press, Ibadan, 1978.
UCHENDU, V. C., The Igbos of South- Eastern Nigeria, Holt, Rinehard and

Winston, New York, 1965.
UZUKWU, E. E., A Listening Church: Autonomy and Communion in African Churches, Orbis Books, New York, 1996.
Church and Culture, Pacific College Press, Obosi, 1985.
VAN GENNEP, A., The Rites of Passage, The University of Chicago Press, 1960.
VAN RAD, G., Genesis, SCM press Ltd., 1972.
VORGRIMLER, H., Sacramental Theology, trans., MALONEY, L. M., The Liturgical Press Collegeville, Minnasota, 3$^{rd}$ ed., 1992.
WACH, J., Sociology of Religion, Chicago, 1966.
WAINWRIGHT, G., Christian Initiation: Ecumenical Studies in History, London, 1969.
WALIGGO, J. M., (et. al.), Inculturation: Its Meaning and Urgency, St. Pauls Publications Africa, 1986.
WILLIAMS, C., The Destruction of Black Civiliazation, Third World Press, Chicago, Illinois, 1976.
WILSON, M., Ritual of Kinship Among The Nyakusa, Oxford University Press, 1957.
QUAKIN, M-A., *Symbol des Judentums*, Ausburg, 1999.
QUASTEN, J., (ed.), Christian Initiation: Studies in Antiquity, Vol. 17, CUA Washington, 1974.

## Articles

BASU, A., „Disksa", in: BLEEKER, C. J., Initiation: Studies in History of Religions, Netherlands, 1965, 81-86.
CARRIER, H., „Inculturation: A Modern Approach to Evangelisation", in: Inculturation in Nigeria, Proceedings of Catholic Bishops' study Session, November, 1988, 4-28.
CHIBUKO, P. C., „Evangelisation as Inculturation", in IKE; O., (*et al.*), Towards an Indigenous African Church —A Post-synodal Theological Review of the Africa Synod in the Context of Nigeria, CIDJAP, Enugu, 1996, 50-63.

*„Die Liturgische Inkulturation von Initiationsriten, Eine Igbo- Prespektive"*, in: SCHREIJÄCK, T., *(hrsg)*, *Menschwerden im Kulturwandel, Kontexte Kultureller Identität als wegmarken interkultureller Kompetenz*, Fulda, 1999, 301-326.

CULLMAN, O., „Petro, Kephas", in: FRIEDRICH, G., (ed.), trans., BROMILEY, G. W., Theological Dictionary of the New Testament, Vol. 6, Grand Rapids, 1968.

CROLLIUS, A. R., „Inculturation: Newness and On-going Process", in. WALLIGO, J. M., *(et al.)*, Inculturation: Its Meaning and Urgency, St. Paul's Publication, Africa, 1986, 31-45.

DUJARIER, M., *„Erfahrungen von christlichen Initiation in Westafrika"*, in: CONCILIUM, *IZT*, 15. *Jahrgang*, 2(Februar), 1979, 107-111.

ENE, M. O., „Kolanut Communion: Diaspora Dimensions", in: INTERNET; NIGERIAWORLD, May 9 2001, 1-6.

EKWUNIFE, A., „African Culture: A Definition", in: CHIEA, African Christian Studies, Vol. 3, Nr. 3, September 1987, 5-18.

ENYIOHA, B. U., „The Pastoral Significance of Traditional African Concept of Rites of Passage", in: OGBOMOSO JOURNAL OF THEOLOGY, 1992, 18-25.

EZEANYA, S. N., „The Traditional Igbo Family and the Christian Family", in: OKOLO, B. C., (ed.), The Igbo Church and Quest for God, Nigeria, 1985, 53-67.

FINKENZELLER, J., *„Sakrament"*, in: *LThK*, *IX*, 220-225.

GARCIA, S. R., „The Incarnation of the Church in Indigenous Culture", in: Missiology, Vol. 1, nr. 2, April 1973, 21-31.

GESCH, P. H., „The Dynamic Element in Traditional Religion", in: PISKATY, K., and RZEPKOWSKI, H., *SIM*, 56(1993), Germany,

HARRINGTON, W., „Marriage in Scripture", in: MC DONAGH, E., (ed.), The Meaning of Christian Marriage, Dublin, 1963, 14-35.

HILLMAN, E., „Mission Approaches to African Cultures Today", in: AFER, Vol. 23, 1981, 342-356.

ISHOLA, S. A., „The Sociological Significance of the Traditional African Concept of Rites of Passage", in; OGBOMOSO JOURNAL OF

THEOLOGY, 7(Dec. 1992), Ogbomoso, 26-32.

JOHNSON, E. M., „The Role of Worship in the Contemporary Study of Christian Initiation: A Select Review of the Literature", in: Worship, Vol. 75, nr. 1 January 2001, 20-35.

HUGHES, K., „Baptism: Pastoral-Liturgical Tradition", in: STUHLMUELLER, C., (ed.), The Collegeville Pastoral Dictionary of Biblical Theological, Minnesota, 1996, 70-74.

KALU, O. U., „Ancestral Spirituality and Society in Africa", in: OLUPONA, J. K., African Spirituality, New York, 2000, 54-84.

KAVANAGH, A., „Confirmation: A Suggestion from Structure", in: Worship 58 (1984) 386-395.

KATONAH, J., „Hospitalization: A Rite of Passage", in: HOLST, L. E., Hospital Ministry: The Role of the Chaplain Today, New York, 1985, 55-76.

KRESCHMAR, G., „Recent Research on Christian Initiation", in: Studio Liturgica, Vol. 12, 1977, 87-106.

MADUBUKO, L., „Igbo World-View", in: BTS, Vol. 14, 2(July-December 1994), Enugu, 5-32.

MANTOVANI, E., „The Child and Melanesian Values", in: PISKATY, K., and RZEPKOWSKI, H., *SIMSVD*, Styler Verlag, Nettetal, 1993, 309-322.

NASIMIYU-WASIKE, A., „Acceptance of the Total Human Situation as a Precondition for Authentic Inculturation", in: TURKSON, P., and WIJSEN, F., Inculturation: Abide by the Otherness of Africa and Africans, Kampen, 1994, 47-56.

NWAHAGHI, F. N., „The Meaning of Kolanut Ritual Symbol Among the Igbo of Nigeria", in: SEVARTHAN, 21(1996), 93-104.

NZOMIWU, J. P., „The African Church and Indigenisation Question: An Igbo Experince", in: AFER, Vol. 28, No. 5, October 1988, 323-334.

OBENGA, T., „Sources and Specific Techniques used in African History", in: KI-ZERBO, J., (ed.), General History of Africa, Vol. 1, UNESCO-California, 1981, 72-86.

OBI, C. A., „The Christian Village as an Early Missionary Strategy for Evangelisation at Onitsha Lower Niger Mission", in: NWOSU, V. A., (ed.), The Catholic Church in Onitsha, People, Places and Events (1885-1985), Etikokwu Press Ltd., Onitsha, 1985, 18-41.

OBOT, E. S., 'Foreword' to Inculturation in Nigeria, Proceedings of Catholic Bishops' Study Session, November 1988, 1.

OJOADE, J. O., „Pareomiographical Evidences of Ethical Education in Traditional Africa with Christian and Islamic Analogues", in: METUH, E. I., (ed.), Nigerian Cultural Heritage, Jos, 1990, 135-154.

OKOYE, J. C., „A New Era of Evangelisation", Talk delivered at the National Seminar on New Era of Evangelisation, Ibadan, 1-3 May 1984.

OKURE, T., „Inculturation in the New Testament: Its Relevance for the Nigerian Church", in: Inculturation in Nigeria, Proceedings of Catholic Bishops' Study Session, November 1988, 39-64.

ONAIKAN, J., „Why a New Era Of Evangelisation", Talk delivered on The National Seminar on New Era of Evangelisation, Ibadan, 1-3 May 1984.

ONYEABO, O. N., „Kolanut in Igbo Culture", in Sunday Statesman, 25 May 1986.

ONUNWA, U. R., „Christian Missionary Methods And Their Influence On Eastern Nigeria", in: METUH, E. I., (ed.), The God's In Retreat, FDP-Enugu, 1986 (59-84).

ONWURA, E., „The Igbo Social and Ritual Symbol", in: SEVERTHAN 15(1990), 75-83.

RAYAN, S., „Flesh of India's Flesh", in: JEEVADHARA, 6(1976).

REISER, W., „Inculturation and Doctrinal Development", in HEYTHROP Journal, 22(1981).

RICHARDS, P.K., „The Implications of African-American Spirituality", in: ASANTE, M. K., and ASANTE, K. W., African Cultures, New Jersey, 1993, 207-231.

SARPONG, P. K., „The Gospel as Good News for Africa Today", in: *CULTURES ET FOI PONTIFICIUM CONCILIUM DE CULTURA, Citta del Vaticano, Vi*, 2, 1998, 123-133.

„Christianity should be Africanized not African Christianized", in: AFER 6(1975) 322-328.

SCHROEDER, R., „Contextualization of Initiation in a Melanesian

Community", in: PISKATY, K., and RZEPKOWSKI, H., *SIMSVD*, 156, Nettetal, 1993, 294-308.

TOMKO, J., „Inculturation and African Marriage", in: AFER, 28, ¾, June/August 1986, 155-166.

UKPONG, J. S., „Contextualizing Theological Education in West Africa, Focus on Subjects", in CHIEA, African Christian Study, Vol. 3, nr. 3, September 1987, 59-75.

UZUKWU, E. E., „Traditional Initiation Rites: Anthropological and Religious View-points", in: LUCERNA, Vol. 7, 1(December 1986-June 1987), 31-33.

VON BALTHASAR, H-U, „Spirit Creator", in: *Skizzen zur Theologie, Bd.* III, 1967.

WIESHOF, H. A., „Social Significance of Names Among the Ibos of Nigeria", in: American Anthropologist, 43(1941), 212-222.

WIJSEN, F., and HOEBEN, H., „We are not a carbon Copy of Europe", in: TURKSON, P., and WIJSEN, F., Inculturation: Abide by the Otherness of Africa and the Africans, Kampen, 1994, 72-82.

"Fr. George has produced an absolutely indispensable compendium of Igbo resources for charting the course of contemporary Igbology, for exposing epideictically the values of Igbo customs and rituals of initiation in past and present interpretations and their impact on advancing the process of inculturation in Africa; and for discovering a variety of sacral topoi necessary for sound inculturation basis for pastoral catechesis of Christian Initiation in contemporary Igbo Christianity."

Prof. Ukachukwu Chris Manus
Department of Religious Studies, University of Ife, Nigeria


"This Book of Fr. George offers an inspiring view over resemblances and distinctions of Igbo and Christian initiations. It serves as an important contribution n the context of cultural impact of Christianity in Nigeria and expands the field of vision for catechetical and pastoral dimensions in the process of culture building."

Werner Tzscheetzsch
is the Professor of Religious Education and Catechetics at the Albert-Ludwig-University of Freiburg, Germany